Pra[ise for]

Secrets of a [Jewish Mother]

"This is a book a lot about ve[...] importance of maintaining clos[...] very funny and I'm not a Jewish mother." —Mike Huckabee

"All the wisdom, advice, and great good humor you'll ever need are between the covers of this book. It's a delightful read, a great resource, and a lifelong supply of secrets my mother never taught me." —*New York Times* bestselling author Linda Fairstein

"For a read that's spicy and sizzling hot, this book is better than the tastiest matzoh ball soup. It will leave you rolling with laughter and wanting more." —TV host and bestselling author Rita Cosby

"Funny, irreverent, and a must read for every Jewish female on the planet." —M. J. Rose

"A fun-fest of laughs, wit, and homespun wisdom. Throw some cream cheese on your bagel, park your tushes on the couch, and enjoy an unforgettable romp through the pages of *Secrets of a Jewish Mother*. I laughed. I cried. I was entertained. . . . This book is analogous to a giant hug combined with a bowl of chicken soup and a piece of homemade rugelach. Kvell away!" —Judith Marks-White, humor columnist and author of *Seducing Harry* and *Bachelor Degree*

"This book is filled with fun, honest, and heartwarming advice for any woman of any age, even Catholic ones like me." —Heather McDonald

continued . . .

"There are a lot of words of wisdom. It's a fun book to read [and] you can learn a lot."   —Rosanna Scotto, *Good Day, New York*

"Having embraced the advice and received the blessing of my own adopted Jewish mother, I recommend wholeheartedly the wisdom and, indeed, secrets of these three remarkable women. May they become your adopted Jewish mothers . . . or sisters or daughters!"
—Carolina Fernandez, author and founder of
the SheEO Network

"*Secrets of a Jewish Mother* is warm, funny, and full of wisdom; and because it's not coming from my own Jewish mother, I'm a lot more inclined to listen."
—Laurie Sandell, author of *The Impostor's Daughter*

"As a single working (smothering, sometimes hovering helicopter) mom, I am always and forever trying to find some solid advice to help me over the hurdles, humps, challenges, and obstacles of raising a healthy and happy child in today's society. Recently I had to look no further than the fabulous *Secrets Of A Jewish Mother*! Reading through the snippets and tidbits of valuable, practical advice and real-life situations of these three women offered such inspiration that some situations that previously had me screaming, 'Oy!' now can find me intoning, 'Ahhhhh. . . .' This whole book is a fast and delicious read and I enjoyed it thoroughly!"
—Ellen Whitehurst, bestselling author of
Make This Your Lucky Day

"Filled with candid, humorous, and loving advice and personal glimpses into their lives, this trio offers up some tips we should all heed and live by. This is a thoroughly enjoyable read and should be passed around to mothers, daughters, sister, nieces, aunts, girlfriends, and all ladies who might enjoy reading and discovering that in the end we are all basically the same—with the same hopes and desires."   —Hamptons.com

"From friendships to love, marriage to children . . . covers many aspects of life with laugh-out-loud stories and pointed advice."

—SavvyAuntie.com

"You don't have to be Jewish to read this book, but after reading this book, everyone will want to be Jewish. The best practical advice a girl could get from three extraordinary Jewish mothers . . . Jill's, Lisa's, and Gloria's advice will save you a lifetime of aggravation."

—Patti Stanger, Bravo's *Millionaire Matchmaker*

"Gloria epitomizes the Jewish mother! She has a heart of gold and earrings to match!"

—Fran Drescher

"You don't have to be Jewish to need a good Jewish mother. Gloria has sooooooo much good advice. . . . Chicken soup has got nothing on this lady."

—Molly Shannon

"Jewish moms ARE chicken soup for the soul."

—Taylor Dayne

"The gals kvetch on dating, marriage, parenting, family, and money in *Secrets* and do so with humor and insight. Pay close attention and you'll have healthier children, a healthier marriage, and a good relationship with your siblings."

—Courier News

SECRETS

of a

Jewish Mother

Real Advice, Real Stories, Real Love

Gloria Kamen,
Lisa Wexler, *and* Jill Zarin

NEW AMERICAN LIBRARY

NEW AMERICAN LIBRARY
Published by New American Library, a division of Penguin Group (USA) Inc.,
375 Hudson Street, New York, New York 10014, USA
Penguin Group (Canada), 90 Eglinton Avenue East, Suite 700,
Toronto, Ontario M4P 2Y3, Canada (a division of Pearson Penguin Canada Inc.)
Penguin Books Ltd., 80 Strand, London WC2R 0RL, England
Penguin Ireland, 25 St. Stephen's Green, Dublin 2, Ireland
(a division of Penguin Books Ltd.)
Penguin Group (Australia), 250 Camberwell Road,
Camberwell, Victoria 3124, Australia (a division of Pearson Australia Group Pty. Ltd.)
Penguin Books India Pvt. Ltd., 11 Community Centre,
Panchsheel Park, New Delhi - 10 017, India
Penguin Group (NZ), 67 Apollo Drive, Rosedale, North Shore 0632,
New Zealand (a division of Pearson New Zealand Ltd.)
Penguin Books (South Africa) (Pty.) Ltd., 24 Sturdee Avenue,
Rosebank, Johannesburg 2196, South Africa

Penguin Books Ltd., Registered Offices:
80 Strand, London WC2R 0RL, England

Published by New American Library, a division of Penguin Group (USA) Inc. Previously
published in a Dutton edition.

First New American Library Printing, March 2011
10 9 8 7 6 5 4 3 2 1

Copyright © SJM Book, LLC, a Florida LLC, 2010, 2011
All rights reserved

[NAL] REGISTERED TRADEMARK—MARCA REGISTRADA

New American Library Trade Paperback ISBN: 978-0-451-23267-0

The Library of Congress has cataloged the hardcover edition of this title as follows:
Zarin, Jill.
    Secrets of a Jewish mother: real advice, real stories, real love/Jill Zarin, Lisa Wexler, and
Gloria Kamen.
    p. cm.
    ISBN 978-0-525-95179-7
    1. Jewish women. 2. Mothers. 3. Jewish way of life. I. Wexler, Lisa. II. Kamen, Gloria.
III. Title.
    HQ1172.Z37 2010
    306.874'3089924073—dc22   2010001825

Set in Berling
Designed by Jaime Putorti

Printed in the United States of America

*Penguin is committed to publishing works of quality and integrity.
In that spirit, we are proud to offer this book to our readers;
however, the story, the experiences, and the
words are the author's alone.*

To Sol, Bobby and Bill

For Jon, Allyson and Joanna

And their children

Contents

Introduction

*A lot of love and a little matzoh
ball soup never hurt anyone.*

Ah, the Jewish mother. Has there been a more maligned stereotype in American culture? From *Curb Your Enthusiasm* and *Portnoy's Complaint* to the routines of countless comedians, the Jewish mother has most often been portrayed as a domineering, interfering, tactless and loud manipulator of family relationships. To this we say, "And . . . ?" We maintain that it is precisely those stereotypical traits that form the foundation of healthy, stable and accomplished children, marriages that last over time, and meaningful, loving relationships among siblings. A lot of love and a little matzoh ball soup never hurt anyone.

We, Lisa Wexler and Jill Zarin, are the daughters of one very particular Jewish mother, Gloria Kamen. Our family is incredibly close, which translates into communicating with each other every single day, often more than once. We are often asked the secret to our success at maintaining strong family ties and successful careers in an age in which so many people struggle to get along with their closest relatives. When we thought about this, we realized that we were taught these secrets by our mother, Gloria, who made no secret at all of the fact that if a lesson is worth teaching once, it is worth teaching at least two thousand times. We also had lots of help from our grandmothers, Sylvia and Helen, and our incredible loving aunts, Aunt Cooky, Gloria's sister, and Aunt Gloria, our father Sol's sister. Yes, another Gloria. To make it easier on you as you read the "secrets" that follow, Sol's sister Gloria is referred to in the book by her Yiddish name, Nessie.

You'll meet our family as you read these pages, so to help you out, here is a quick note on the cast of characters: Our mother, Gloria, has one husband, Sol, and two daughters, Lisa and Jill. Gloria's parents were our Grandma Syl and Papa Jack. Sol's parents were our Grandma Helen and Papa Benny. Lisa is married to Bill; they have a son, Jonathan, a daughter, Joanna, and a bichon frise, Sugar. Jill's first marriage was to Steven, who is the father of her daughter, Allyson. Jill's second marriage is to Bobby and together they live with Allyson and their Chihuahua, Ginger. Bobby has three children from his first marriage: Jennifer, David and (yes, another) Jonathan. David is married to Jill (yes, another Jill Zarin), and they have two children, Micah and Lila. We Jews keep reusing the same ten names over and over again.

. . . .

We grew up in a time and place in many ways straight out of *The Wonder Years*, complete with suburban cul-de-sacs, bicycle races, homemade go-karts and evening games of tag in the street, with flashlights, not streetlights. Our parents got married and stayed married, fifty-two years and counting. Daddy wore a suit and tie to work and came home by seven thirty. We ate a home-cooked dinner every weeknight, except for Wednesdays, which was "Dad's night out," when we girls had pizza. On Saturdays, our parents went out, and Mommy got really dressed up. She looked like a movie star. Our childhood was America as it used to be.

Every single Sunday afternoon, Papa Benny and Grandma Helen came over to our house in Long Island from Queens in their Pontiac Catalina. You could set your clock by their arrival; we often did. People didn't dress sloppily in those days; Papa always had a hat with a feather in it and we never saw Grandma in slacks. Ten minutes after arriving at our house, they emerged with us, Lisa and Jill, and took us for a Carvel ice cream cone and a comic book. Rain or shine, no matter the season, they showed up on Sundays for a visit with their grandchildren. We were their priority, and we felt it. There was nothing more important on the agenda. Sundays were spent with family.

In most ways the town we grew up in was like America everywhere. However, it also had the distinction of being part of a cluster of small communities called "the Five Towns" on the south shore of Long Island, New York. Don't bother counting them, because you will come up with only four: Woodmere, Cedarhurst, Lawrence and Hewlett. The fifth town, Inwood, never counted for the purposes of the Five Towns stereotype, and nobody ever remembers its name.

So what is the Five Towns stereotype? Jews, fashion and new money. Showy new money. The kind that bought Cadillacs and joined country clubs. First-generation sons of immigrants who were out to prove the American dream. Wives who couldn't wait to climb up the ladder alongside them. Kids who were trained to be either doctors or lawyers, depending upon whether they were good in math or English. You've heard the slang term JAP, short for Jewish American Princess? Invented in the Five Towns, surely. We've spent our lives haunted by that stereotype.

Like so many stereotypes, however, there was a little bit of truth and a lot of exaggeration in the reputation of the Five Towns. Our high school was diverse before it became a politically correct term. Our house size? A grand total of fifteen hundred square feet. There were a couple of very wealthy neighborhoods nearby, but we didn't live in one. Many people we knew were neither rich nor fashionable.

America, circa 2010, is a different place than it was when we grew up. Our family is now geographically fragmented. Our children are not bicycle-riding distance from their cousins, as we were. Mom and Dad now live in Florida—they have traversed what we call the three legs of the Jewish Bermuda Triangle: from Brooklyn, to Long Island, to Boca Raton. As daughters, we currently face the challenges of caring for parents who live a plane ride away. As wives in today's economy, we need to keep up our earning potential because it is neither fair nor realistic to expect only one member of a couple to provide the lifestyle that we want. As mothers, we parent a generation of kids who watch things on television that we didn't even know existed until we were out of college. We are busy. We try to "multitask" and do it all, but what we do instead is drop a couple of the balls we are juggling every day. We don't give our kids dinner every night at five thirty; they are lucky if they get a home-cooked meal twice a week. We look back in awe at our parents' generation and say, "How did they manage?" Maybe one answer is that years ago people did not believe they could do everything well at the same time. For some reason, we think we can.

This is why, more than ever, we need to keep close to the people in life who matter to us, those whose voices resonate with wisdom as well as judgment. We need to connect with those people, if not over a cup of coffee, then through a telephone call or an e-mail. Most days we speak to our own mother at least once. If we have skipped more than one day, we get the infamously cold "Gloria hello" and begin the conversation with "I'm sorry; I meant to call you." We do this not only because we love our mother but also to show our own children how important it is to call their mother. We are not fools.

The women in our family, on both Sol's and Gloria's sides, are women who believe in the power of women. They believe that a good mother could and should strengthen character and influence a child's direction in life. But a Jewish mother's wisdom is not reserved for her children—it is spread around to anyone who will listen. She likes sharing her ideas. To be blunt, she loves telling people what to do. She urges them to listen and she speaks with the voice of true expertise. So many people today are yearning for practical, commonsense wisdom, delivered without apologies, second guesses or excuses—some black and white in a world gone very gray. We always assumed that everyone's mother knew exactly what to do about every single situation in life just like ours did, but apparently that is not the case. Gloria is that mother. She is that person who will tell you the truth, whether you like it or not. She is that person who will give you the answer you know is right, even when you don't want to hear it. There is very little gray for Gloria. What she has passed on to us, we now share with you.

Although the majority of our upbringing came from our family, we were accompanied on our childhood journey by a very special person whom we referred to as our "second mother." Her name was Ethel Hill. Ethel was a black woman from North Carolina who had left her three kids down south with relatives so she could work to support them and send them money, much like today's immigrants. Ethel worked for us as our housekeeper twice a week and slept with Lisa in her bedroom so she wouldn't have to *shlep* to and from Brooklyn as often. We always felt guilty that we had Ethel with us as a mother when her own children did not.

We loved Ethel like family; in fact, she is posed with us in the family photo at Lisa's Bat Mitzvah. At the age of forty-seven, she suffered a fatal, massive cerebral hemorrhage at the train station. We miss her terribly. Life isn't fair, something the Jewish mother knows all too well. Much of who we are today we owe to Ethel, so some of the wisdom you'll find in this book comes from her too.

We need to give a lot of credit to the men in our lives as well. Strong, secure men. Men who would never consider taking hair off in unwanted places, or asking women to do it either. Men who could lift mattresses without working out in a gym. Remember those? Men who considered it a sacred duty to provide for their families; who made sure their mothers and sisters were provided for before they would take on the obligations of a wife and children. Men who believed in sacrifice, who lived what they believed in and who, frankly, didn't talk about it much. We believe that if you search the background of many successful career women, there was a father cheering them on early in life—cheering, guiding, mentoring and believing. That is our father, Sol, in a nutshell. The original *kveller*. Also a *mensch*.

The men in Jewish culture believe that educating their daughters is as important as educating their sons. They love their daughters, they indulge their daughters, but they expect their daughters to have achievements of their own, not to grow up to become a reflection of their husband's accomplishments. Many of our "secrets of a Jewish mother" come from our fathers, who passed them down to their daughters, who became mothers, who told everyone. Naturally.

For example, Daddy always told us never to do anything we wouldn't want to read about on the front page of *The New York Times*. That was when everyone actually read that newspaper, so we knew what he meant. Here was the standard of honor to Daddy: If you were thinking of doing something you would be ashamed for anyone else to know about, then don't do it! Stay away. Another pearl from Daddy? Never be less than who you are. Don't feel bad about doing the right thing even if it is not reciprocated, even if it goes into the "no good deed goes unpunished" file. Keep being the best you can be; that is what you are supposed to do in life. You'll see a lot of Sol in these pages too.

....

The Jewish mother lives to analyze and worry, the two being inextricably entwined. It's no coincidence Freud was Jewish; there is no question in our minds that the first psychoanalyst was probably Freud's mother, but he got all the credit. Moreover, the Jewish mother is actually quite happy worrying; it's the default setting in her computer. Over what does she worry, incite and instigate? Family relationships. Money, health—yes, these are important too. But what keeps her up at night is the fight with her sister, her mother and her daughter. Once in a while, a fight with a husband can intrude on her mental tranquility, but it would have to be a really big fight. Over time, Jewish mothers build up an immunity to everyday bickering; they stop thinking of it as arguing and view it as a normal means of communication. (You don't want to miss it when one partner stops hearing—that's when the fun really begins.)

Do you have to be Jewish to embrace the secrets of a Jewish mother? Of course not. We share much with Italian mamas and African American women, as well as Greek, Russian and Latina ones—in fact, mothers everywhere. Most of the things we discuss in this book are universal truths about the need for respect, the sanctity of family, the importance of love. This book just has a dose of our particular culture added to the lessons. We hope that you will find our traditions interesting if you are not Jewish. And if you are Jewish, we'd be happy to compare notes.

You should know that our family is not particularly religious. Although we celebrate many traditions and Jewish milestones, our level of observance tends toward the Conservative branch of Judaism, which is in between the Reform movement and the Orthodox branch. The Conservative movement tries to reconcile modern thought with traditional worship. It is a very tough road it tries to straddle, but it suits us; it is how we were raised. Moderate, in all things. We are proud to be modern American women with our heads held high who dress as we please. Yet we are also very proud to be Jewish; extremely proud of our heritage, our culture and our faith. We were raised to believe that Judaism is not just a religion; it is a way of life. Even though we do not observe a lot of the religious tenets, we strive to incorporate a lot of Judaism's values and teachings in our lives.

One thing we do want to stress is that we have made lots of mistakes in life and continue to do so. Perfect we are not, whatever that is. Not even close. One of the subtitles we thought of for this book was *Advice by Three Women Who Know They Don't Know It All.* Nevertheless, we try our best. We each have these voices in our head, and they penetrate. They advise us what to make for dinner. They whisper to us to make the phone call or send the card. They command us to attend the funeral. They tell us to persevere, to stick together and not to take life too seriously. They make us laugh and urge us to "pay it forward." Above all, they remind us to love each other. This is the voice of the Jewish mother.

We have divided this book into chapters that each contain three main parts. The first is context, in which we explain a particular "secret" or life lesson. Then we relate the lesson to our lives by telling a story. We love stories. Telling them allows us to learn and teach at the same time. Afterward, we urge you to ask yourself the questions that we think are the important ones raised by the lesson and illustration. We are hoping that at the end of this book you will have accomplished several things:

1. You will know more about the Jewish family.

2. You will know more about our Jewish family, presuming you care.

3. You will laugh.

4. You will have taken some nuggets of wisdom to apply in your own life.

We believe the secret to life is to learn how to love each other. Not only is it the secret to life, it is the purpose of life. Our spirituality, such as it is or is not, comes from this essential truth. To the extent we learn the lessons we are meant to learn, we grow as human beings. To learn these lessons, we have to ask ourselves the hard questions and answer them truthfully, even if only to ourselves. Difficult as it is, sometimes we need to change our behavior, if not our character. If we make excuses, continuing to rationalize what we do despite the fact that we bemoan the outcome, we get stuck. We are doomed to keep repeating our mistakes, to keep whining and complaining about the same problems in our lives. Aren't you bored? Don't you want different problems to complain about? Change up your behavior, your attitude, your responses. Find the funny in life, and begin with laughing at yourself. See what happens.

Writing this book has been a blessing for our family. We view it as our legacy for our children and their children. Maybe we haven't repeated these values loudly or often enough; if not, the words are right here, on the page (where we can throw them at you kids, if necessary). As Mommy said, life is short. It goes from Rosh Hashanah to Passover and back again, in the blink of an eye. At the end, people judge their success by the quality of their relationships: who has stood by you, who will take care of you, who loves you, no matter what you have done or what you are going through. These are the people who matter. Love them. Accept them. Forgive them. And get a pet. Although people may disappoint, dogs and cats never will.

Love, Lisa and Jill

SECRETS

of a

Jewish Mother

1

Friendship

Finding a friend is finding the best part of yourself and setting it free.

Do you remember that "falling in love" feeling when you discover a kindred spirit? It's heaven—the endless phone conversations, the excitement of discovering the things you have in common. Like romantic love, friendship can bring joy, but it can also wound to the core. As much as we cherish the friends we do have, we all carry scars from friendships that did not last.

Our philosophy? Once you've loved someone, particularly a good friend, a part of you never stops loving that person, even if you can no longer tolerate her in your life. The key is being able to judge who is worthy of your loyalty and devotion. At times, we've all had to figure out when we needed to fight for a friendship and, sadly, when it was time to let go. We hate to let go of anything, whether it be that great bag on sale or the pantsuit that used to fit us twenty years ago. Jewish mothers believe in second, third and fourth chances.

Our friend Amelia once shared with us that she thinks of friends in terms of theater seats. There are front-row friends and those who sit in the orchestra section. Occasionally, a friend shifts; a close friend may move to the balcony, or someone who was sitting in the orchestra all along can suddenly move up to the front row. The idea is that at any time in your life you may have many friends, but the closeness you feel with them may change.

We agree with Amelia's analogy. However, it also begs the question—what makes a close friend? A Jewish mother values her friends and does all she can to be there for them. But she'd like her friends to be there for her too. So when she calls her best friend to ask her to drive her to get a colonoscopy, she expects her friend to wait till she finishes, even if it takes three hours, because hey, that's what she would do.

Who Are Your Real Friends?

We've all heard the saying "You can pick your friends but not your family." Well, not necessarily. You can't pick your schoolmates or your coworkers. Yet you need to make friends with those people to survive and thrive. What you need to do in life is figure out how to get along with as many people as possible, while at the same time discerning among them who can be truly called a friend.

One thing we've learned is not to mistake business relationships for friendships. If you go into your work relationships understanding the difference between friends and colleagues, you will save yourself a lot of grief. Of course, we ourselves are guilty of blurring these lines more than once, causing ourselves much disappointment. Jill is more adept at keeping these boundaries than is Lisa; Lisa is trying to grow a second, thicker skin and hoping it won't add weight.

Let's talk about character. Who is a real friend? The easy answer would be the person who helps you when you are out of a job, have just lost your biggest client or are going through an ugly divorce. Everyone appreciates a consoling phone call, a sympathy card and someone who takes time to listen. We love these qualities in a friend. However, for the Jewish mother, these traits alone would not make a front-row friend.

You know you have a front-row friend if she will *kvell* from your *nachas*. In other words, a true friend is someone who is sincerely happy for you when good things happen.

You hear the word *kvell* a lot around Jewish grandparents, as in "I could just *kvell*; my youngest grandson just won that big genius award—you know the one, named after the general." *Kvell*ing is expressing your own feelings of pride and joy about someone else's accomplishments. A real friend will *kvell* when you receive that promotion you've been working for, your kid has gotten into Harvard (it should only happen!) or you finally manage to lose those last ten pounds. The good fortune itself, that we call the *nachas*.

By sharing your *nachas* with others, even your closest friend, you do risk the dreaded evil eye. But if you can pick up the phone and brag, and know that the person who answers that phone will be truly happy for you and not send the evil eye your way, then you can call that someone a real friend.

Based on that test, how many front-row friends do you have? We consider ourselves very lucky—between the three of us, we do have quite a few. Each friend is a gem; each relationship is truly cherished. Lisa has a particularly unlikely friendship that has lasted more than thirty years.

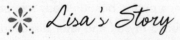

Lisa's Story

On the first day of college, in the fall of 1977, I spied a long-haired, beautiful, hippie-looking girl living right next door to me in one of the only all-girls dorms left on campus. Sandy was a missionary kid, an American who grew up in Mexico while her Baptist parents established churches wherever they settled. Missionary kid? Wasn't that something out of a nineteenth-century novel or *The African Queen*? I was enthralled. Sandy was not only my first non-Jewish friend; she was actually exotically foreign, from a completely different culture than my own. Our philosophical meanderings often lasted until dawn. My new best friend had arrived.

Our friendship has lasted through everything that life has thrown at us, including overwhelming joy, real tragedy and the everyday life that comprises true friendship. Sandy has changed my perspective on political issues and given me insight into cultures vastly different than mine. Have we argued? Yes. Have we gotten on each other's nerves? Once in a while. Is there anything in the world I wouldn't do for Sandy? I can't think of a single thing.

On the same day I met Sandy I also sat next to the man who would become my husband three years later. How is that for a lucky day? ■

Mommy has an example of a friendship that not only changed her life but significantly affected Jill's as well.

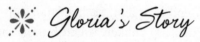

Gloria's Story

Twenty years after my college years, I was back at NYU to pursue my master's degree in business education. One night in the ladies' room, a petite, beautiful lady stepped out of the stall. I introduced myself and later discovered that Karen Gillespie was the dean of retailing at NYU, a revered professor who had published more than forty books. We started to talk, and each week after class I would spend some time with her. I wasn't taking her class, but we found time to get to know each other outside of the classroom.

Jill was working after school and at age sixteen already showed signs of business acumen. I made the *shiddoch* between Karen and Jill, and they clicked. Karen is the one who recommended Simmons College for Jill; had we never met, we never would have known about Simmons's fabulous retailing internship program. There is no question in my mind that this education set Jill on a successful career path. Jill and I both have my friend Karen to thank for it, may she rest in peace. We all miss her. ■

Even though Jill has a wide circle of people around her, she has historically had difficulty discerning good friends and good character among a sea of casual acquaintances. This is probably because Jill has very inclusive instincts. She gives people the benefit of the doubt, but her antenna is occasionally a little faulty. When Jill was cast in *The Real Housewives of New York City*, she was thrown in with a varied group of people who were expected to become her friends in real life, as well as on-screen. This has led to some awkward predicaments and surreal situations, as she explains:

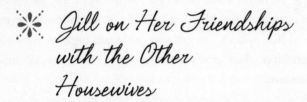

Jill on Her Friendships with the Other Housewives

BETHENNY

People think that Bethenny and I were very close friends because of our relationship as shown on the first two seasons of the show. However, I really had known Bethenny casually for only a couple of years before the show began. I met Bethenny through a mutual friend when she was on the Martha Stewart *Apprentice* show.

She was pretty and smart. I liked her. As it happened, I had been approached and auditioned to become part of a reality TV show that was originally entitled *Manhattan Moms* but we all now know as *The Real Housewives of New York City*. The producers asked me to help cast the show with more people who were in my circle of acquaintances and who fit their profile. Bobby and I saw Bethenny at a Hamptons polo event during the summer, and Bobby said to me, "What about Bethenny?" Because of her *Apprentice* experience, it seemed Bethenny wanted to be famous and on TV. We approached her and she was immediately interested. Even though Bethenny was not a mom, she was a mom "wannabe," in a committed relationship at the time and living in Manhattan. Bobby and I thought she would be a great addition to the cast.

Once Bethenny was cast on the show, we got close very quickly, becoming very involved in each other's lives and calling each other many times every day. Our bond of course was the show itself, but I believed we had developed a real friendship. We helped each other and we were there for each other. As I write this I get very sad, because our friendship has recently hit some tough times. As of this writing, I'm not sure what will happen with our friendship. But no matter what, I will always love Bethenny.

LuAnn

Ah, the countess. I met Countess LuAnn de Lesseps at a party the summer before we filmed the first season of the show. We became casual friends. After I was cast as the first Housewife and the producers asked me to find more potential cast members, I found LuAnn's pink business card in my closet and said, "Oh my God!" I knew she would be perfect. LuAnn had been on Italian TV and was already a local TV personality. Obviously, she, too, wanted to be famous. LuAnn loves to sing, and I thought she would add class to the show. I have to say that I got lucky when the producers chose LuAnn, because I found a true friend. I can always count on her for good advice, even though I am stubborn and usually don't take it. I also think she is an outstanding parent. We will be lifelong friends, and I am grateful she is in my life.

RAMONA

My relationship with Ramona is at times both awkward and surreal. I met Ramona through my social circle ten years ago. I tried to become her friend and was rejected. I even remember her having holiday parties and not being invited. I felt a little hurt but not surprised. When Ramona's mother passed, I sent her a card. I called. I made the effort and tried to do the right thing. I knew that Ramona had been kind to her husband Mario's mother, and that showed me a side of Ramona that I liked and could admire. I always try to look for the good in people. Since she was friends with my good friends, there had to be good, right? But we have a very weird friendship. I don't know why. I think we push each other's buttons sometimes, and perhaps there is some underlying competition between us. It is probably unlikely that we would have become friends had we not been cast together on the *Housewives*. Yet we have to see each other often because of the show.

One thing we will always have is our shared experience on the *Housewives*. All the drama, the publicity, the red carpets. A hit show can be a once-in-a-lifetime experience, if you are lucky. In reflecting on my friendship with

Ramona, I have read this chapter twenty times to help me decide whether Ramona is a real friend, and I still can't figure us out. Maybe that's the best answer I can give right now.

ALEX

I met Alex and her husband, Simon, on the set of the show. I never knew them before. We are very, very different people with different values. I respect Alex as an intelligent woman who loves her family. I still don't know what makes them tick. I have tried to include them in my life for the show, but in reality that is all it is. A show friendship.

KELLY

I have to admit to myself that Kelly and I would never have met or become friends if not for the show. We simply traveled in different social circles. However, I can already see that Kelly is generous, thoughtful and an extremely good mother. I don't know how our friendship will develop over time, whether we will become close friends or ultimately drift apart. We will just have to see.

NEW CAST MEMBERS

As of this writing, the producers have added two new members to the cast whom I did not know beforehand. Obviously, it's premature to discuss true friendship with either of them, but I am always open to the possibility of finding another front-row friend in my life. You never know where that person will come from. ■

ask yourself

1. Among the people you know, how many friends are "front-row friends"? What makes them so?

2. Are you a friend who is truly happy for your friends?

3. Do you mistake business relationships for true friendships?

4. Have you ever been disappointed in those whom you thought were your friends but turned out not to be? What could you do differently next time to avoid the same result?

Our Golden Rules of Friendship

We can't ask people to be our friends unless we are willing to act as real friends. We believe there are four basic rules of friendship. Of course, each of us has ignored these rules more than once (in fact, many times; who are we kidding?), but in an ideal world, we would:

1. Be there.

2. Apologize when wrong.

3. Forgive. Let it go.

4. Not cross the line. There are a few no-nos even a close friend can't forgive.

GOLDEN RULE 1: BE THERE

When we say "Be there," we do not mean standing still like Peter Sellers did in the movie *Being There*, watching the world swish around him. For Jewish mothers, "being there" is active, as in

"Move yourself," "Go out of your way for that person," or sometimes "Get out of our way," because we need to help that person. Jewish mothers recognize that friendships require active participation. You can't expect your friendship to last if you are always the one who receives the phone call; eventually the person on the other end will stop calling. You have to pick up the phone too.

For Jill, being there means entertaining her friends at home and elsewhere. Ever since Jill founded her own party-planning company in college, JSK Productions, she has always gone out of her way to share fun times and good memories with the people she loves. For Lisa, being there means hosting the family for the Jewish holidays and cooking everything from scratch—start to finish—from the chicken soup to the chocolate chip cookies. For Mommy, it means calling her friends often just to see how they are, not for any special reason, just to let them know she cares. If you want to be there for your friends, here are some of our suggestions:

1. Call after an affair to tell the hostess how great the party was, even if the party was just so-so. Participate in the dissection.

2. Call after surgery—always. Even when people say, "It's no big deal," it's always a bigger deal than they anticipated. Your call counts.

3. Try very hard to go to the funeral of your friend's loved one. If you can't make the funeral, do your best to pay a *shiva* call (a condolence call), or send a thoughtful letter by actual snail mail.

4. Congratulate as well as commiserate. Share the *kvell*. Even if you are feeling the tiniest bit envious, do it anyway. If you are feeling more than the tiniest bit envious, then maybe you need to evaluate whether or not that friendship works for you and why you are jealous.

5. Call once in a while just to check in. E-mail counts a little bit, but it can't substitute for an actual catch-up between friends. Besides, don't you forget what is said in e-mails? We can't remember a thing unless we've had an actual conversation, and even then . . .

6. Send a gift or at least a card for the appropriate occasions—big birthdays, Bar/Bat Mitzvahs, weddings, graduations and engagements of your friends' children. Thoughtfulness is greatly appreciated, and even small gestures can mean a lot. Our Aunt Cooky is queen of the greeting cards; she never misses an occasion. We love her for that.

A Few of Our Recommended Gifts for Every Occasion

BIRTHDAY: A gift card from the recipient's favorite store or restaurant.

COCKTAIL PARTY OR DINNER PARTY: A good bottle of champagne; a great candle*; dessert.

FUNERAL: For Jews, send food to the house for *shiva*. Call a local deli near the person's home. For non-Jews, we hear flowers are appreciated. Personally, we prefer plants—they don't die.

BAR OR BAT MITZVAH: A check is the usual custom, but if you know the child well, a personal gift is a nice gesture.

WEDDING: The wedding custom among Jews in the Northeast is to give money. Jill thinks about how much money the hosts spent on the party as a guide.

BABY: A selection of children's books, preferably inscribed by you to the new baby.

Important: Always have custom stationery for each adult in the home. A small gift card with your name is a classy calling card.

*A note on candles and perfumes: Gloria, Cooky and Lisa are, in varying degrees, actually quite sensitive to smells. Therefore, and quite selfishly, we have decided that it is simply good manners not to inflict a heavy scent on anyone else. In other words, if you are going to wear perfume, please excuse us. We'll need to leave the room. Seriously.

Lisa's Story on Being There

My best friend Sandy's husband had been diagnosed with an inoperable form of cancer. The initial prognosis of three to six months had been reduced to three to six weeks. Sandy lived in Arizona and at the time I was representing a client in a full-blown divorce trial in court in Connecticut. Trial dates are planned months in advance and they simply are not something you can cancel. I was sick at heart, and I knew my friend needed me. So, I walked into the courtroom, explained the situation and asked the judge for a postponement of a few days so I could fly to see my friend. To my surprise, the judge granted it and wished me well. I got on the earliest flight I could, which was the following day. Sandy's husband died while I was en route to Arizona. I never got a chance to say good-bye, but at least I was able to be there for a while with Sandy. Remember that old musical title, *Stop the World—I Want to Get Off*? Sometimes you need to stop your world when someone else's world is falling apart. ◼

✳ *Gloria's Friends Who Were There for Her*

I needed to pass the bookkeeping final to get my lousy two credits to graduate NYU. The problem was that I was flunking the course and didn't understand a thing. My friends came to my rescue. Three of my male friends, who had grown up with me in Brooklyn, stayed up with me all night before the final to literally cram the material into my head. Were it not for their help, I would have failed. With their help, I managed to pass and graduate NYU on schedule. I always had more luck in friendship with men than with women. ◼

ask yourself

1. Who in your life needs you now?

2. What can you do to help?

3. What kind of a friend are you?

4. How do you keep in touch with your friends?

5. In what ways do you expect your friends to be there for you?

GOLDEN RULE 2: APOLOGIZE WHEN YOU ARE WRONG

Jews make a big deal of apologizing. In fact, it is such a big deal to us that our holiest holiday is named after the act—Yom Kippur, translated in English as the Day of Atonement. We even fast on that day, which, as you may imagine, is a huge sacrifice for us. Of course, we make up for the fast by gorging ourselves at sunset as if we have never seen food before and never will again.

On Yom Kippur, our rabbis tell us that in order to be forgiven for our own sins and to be written into the Book of Life for the following year, we must first ask forgiveness from those people we know we have hurt during the year. Before asking forgiveness from God, we must ask forgiveness from our fellow men and women. We even have to do it three times, just to make sure. If we are not forgiven after the third time, then the sin is on them—because what else can you do?

Do you remember a specific thing you did to a friend that you know was wrong? Did you admit it or hide from it? Our father, Sol, believes that people always know when they are doing something wrong, but they do it anyway (unless they are complete psychos who can't discern what is wrong). Daddy believes that we should still forgive people, but we shouldn't fool ourselves into thinking that a person didn't know exactly what he was doing.

Incidentally, not all apologies are created equal. All too often people say things like "I'm sorry if I hurt your feelings" or "I'm sorry if you feel that way." These are not real apologies. No one is actually saying he or she is sorry for doing anything. They are merely apologizing that you took offense. That kind of "apology" dismisses the judgment of the person being apologized to and essentially faults that person for being overly sensitive and having her feelings hurt. This is unacceptable. If "I'm sorry if I hurt your feelings" is the best this friend can muster, the friendship will never feel the same.

A good apology is sincere, without excuses. A few of our favorites include "I screwed up," "I'm sorry," "I shouldn't have done it. I didn't think about it beforehand" and "I'm really sorry that I did hurt your feelings. I feel awful about it. Please forgive me."

As you can see, we are well practiced in the art of apologizing, having screwed up many, many times.

Jill's Apology

I always take stock around Yom Kippur and think about the people I need to apologize to. A few years ago, I invited my friend James on my boat for the July Fourth weekend. James came and had a great time. A few weeks later, I invited my friend Ethan on my boat for Labor Day. James called up and asked if he could come back for Labor Day too, so I impulsively said sure. I had introduced James and Ethan to each other and knew they had become friends, but I also vaguely remembered that they had had some kind of falling-out. When Ethan found out that James was coming for Labor Day, he told me very nicely that if James was going to be there, he didn't want to come. How did I react? I called James and shared Ethan's honest feelings, hoping James would back out since I had just said yes to him a few days before. I figured that since James had already spent one weekend on the boat that summer, it was fairer to give Ethan his turn. I did not expect James's reaction. James was very offended that he had been "disinvited," even though he had just invited himself only three days before. He told me he would never talk to me again. The whole episode upset me so much that when Yom Kippur came that fall, I called James to apologize. James told me he forgave me, and the conversation was polite. He even said, "Let's move on." But the truth is I don't think he really meant it. Our friendship has never been the same. ∎

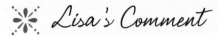

Lisa's Comment

I think this episode should be in Jill's "No Good Deed Goes Unpunished" file. This is the thanks you get for inviting someone on your yacht for a summer weekend and for introducing him to a new friend. ■

Sometimes, your life unfolds like a movie. As you are living it, you are also watching it. Many years ago, Lisa was part of a scene straight out of a B movie, and Aunt Cooky was there as a witness. Actually, Lisa has never gotten over this incident. It taught her a great lesson about being there and what happens when you are not the friend you should be.

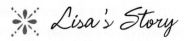

Lisa's Story

There are some friends you choose and some that are chosen for you. Mommy always wanted me to be friendly with a particular girl named Sarah who was the daughter of her close friend. But every conversation with this girl was an effort. I tried to be kind, but the friendship, from my point of view, was more of a *mitzvah* than anything else. When college began, we saw each other once or twice, then lost touch completely. It was nobody's fault; neither one of us had called the other.

When I was twenty-nine, my mother called to tell me that Sarah had a brain tumor and was in the hospital. Coincidentally, I had a friend who was working at that hospital, and I asked her to check up on Sarah. My friend reported back to me that she seemed to be doing fine. After I heard that Sarah was doing fine, I did nothing. I made no visit to the hospital, no phone call, nothing. I put Sarah out of my mind, assuming she would heal.

Aunt Cooky got the phone call that Sarah had died. I knew I needed to go to the funeral. Even though I hadn't seen the family in years, I wanted to pay my respects.

Imagine the scene: the funeral chapel, filled to capacity. The funeral ends and the family is ushered into a room where they stand in a receiving line, greeting all the guests. I get in line. Aunt Cooky is right behind me. I make eye contact with Sarah's mother, a woman whom I had known since I was ten years old. I even called her "Aunt Rita." She sees me and starts shouting at me, in front of the whole group of people. "How dare you show up today? Sarah loved you like a sister! What kind of friend were you? You knew she was sick and you never even called . . . ," and on and on. I felt sick. My heart was pumping out of my chest. Aunt Cooky grabbed my wrist like a vise and pulled me outside. Talk about guilt. I was a mess. What could I do to make it up to this mother? How could I make the guilt go away? Sarah was already gone. I did the only thing I could think of—I wrote a beautiful, heartfelt note of apology. I hoped to hear from her, but I never did. After Sarah's funeral, I made a promise to myself to be there for my friends and their families. Since then, I have never ignored a phone call telling me someone I know is in the hospital. ■

ask yourself

1. To whom do you need to apologize? Fess up.

2. How much does it bother you that you are not on good terms with this person?

3. How difficult is it for you to apologize in general? If it is difficult for you, ask yourself why. Are you afraid you won't be forgiven?

4. Did someone apologize to you in a way that you felt was insincere? How did you handle it?

GOLDEN RULE 3: FORGIVE. LET IT GO.

This is the really hard one for all of us, isn't it? We always expect that others will forgive us, but notice how much time and energy we spend thinking about whether or not we should forgive somebody else. Nonetheless, if you want to be forgiven, you must forgive. The Jewish mother will always accept a sincere apology. She may not forget, but she will usually forgive.

If you value your friendship, then you will occasionally need to let go of a thoughtless remark, a plan that went awry, a forgotten birthday (admit it, you forgot hers too) or a friend who sometimes drops out of touch. You may also need to ignore that you don't care for her significant other, that she still smokes (or drinks, or whatever) or that she keeps complaining about those same problems without changing a thing. If you care about this person and want to keep this friendship, *lezem gayne*—let it go.

Is everything forgivable? Of course not; we get to that a little later in this chapter. The scale is sliding too—some people are simply much more relaxed about flaws than others. However, we think some transgressions are clearly forgivable. For example, it's okay if a friend stands you up—it happens to everyone. Friends also forget to respond to invitations. Don't stand on ceremony— make a phone call yourself and find out why you didn't get the RSVP. You'll probably get either an apology or an excuse. Either way, move on. We mentioned birthdays already. Don't be so thin-skinned. People are busy. And don't be spiteful, either, and pur-posely forget hers because she forgot yours.

 ## Gloria's Struggle

One day a few years ago, I looked up and realized an entire circle of my friends in Florida was no longer return-ing my phone calls or inviting me out. It was like I had been cut out of their lives entirely. These were people whom I had known for years and whom I had utterly respected for what they had accomplished in their lives. Months went by, and finally a mutual friend told me that I had been excom-municated because I had not attended a luncheon given by one of the women and had not called to say why. I was shocked to hear this from my friend. Obviously I had com-pletely forgotten. These women knew me for years and knew that I would never intentionally forget their party. If they cared about me at all, they would have phoned me to find out why I wasn't there, and I could have jumped in the car to join them. Instead, they acted as if I had committed an unforgivable sin and needed to be punished. I learned that day that these friends were not my friends. Real friends would have forgiven and let it go. ■

What else is forgivable? Believe it or not, we think that some gossip is forgivable, depending upon what was said. If the alleged gossip about you wasn't so terrible, even if it was said behind your back, let it go. Haven't you gossiped yourself every single day of your life? Jill was both the victim and the perpetrator of some gossip herself, as seen by all of us who watched season two of *The Real Housewives of New York City.*

Jill's Story

Who would have thought a few words in *New York* magazine would be the opening scene of season two? After season one the show was deemed a big success, and many media outlets approached all of us for interviews. In the *New York* magazine summer issue for 2008, this quote appeared in an article about Simon and Alex McCord, two costars of the show:

"I've always loved to study people. I mean, for example, Jill's from Long Island, and boy that shows."

I read that quote, which was from Simon, and I didn't like it. It hurt my feelings; I wasn't sure what he meant by that remark. But if you hurt me, I will react. So after I read this article, I gave an interview to Cindy Adams in the *New York Post* in June 2008:

"I do not speak to those two. First of all, he drinks too much. And is very insulting. She and I will keep doing the show, of course, but I will have nothing to do with her otherwise."

Uh-oh; I had overreacted. I had started a war. Cindy Adams is a famous New York gossip columnist. Everybody reads her. Bobby was not happy with what I said about Simon and thought I overreacted. Bobby is always right. This incident, the tit for tat in the press, became content for the first episode of season two. Eventually, the Jewish mother wisdom that I got from Mommy kicked in, and I knew I needed to apologize. I still think Simon was wrong and should have apologized. He never did.

> But I can only control my own behavior. So I did. On camera, I called Simon to apologize. ■

Sometimes forgiving means consideration of the whole *megillah*—the full story—of the friendship, the fact that you have been friends for so long with this person. Your shared memories are not only irreplaceable, they are indispensable. After all, if you lose that friend, then who will remember that time you lost all your luggage on your once-in-a-lifetime European vacation?

The *Avlas*

Some people love their grudges. They love holding on to them. They nourish them with bitter commentary, and they nurse their grievances like they would feed a bottle to a starving infant. We all know people like that. Eventually, those people end up with lives that are like very small rooms. There is no space for anyone else to fit in.

ask yourself

1. How good are you at forgiving your friends?

2. Do you have "rules" and stick to them, or are you flexible?

3. Who have you not forgiven? Why not?

4. Admit it: What grudges are you still holding? Don't you know it's not healthy for you?

5. When was the last time you apologized for your behavior? Was it sincere?

6. What was the reaction to your apology?

7. Are there times when you know you should apologize and you don't? Why not?

8. Do you recall an incident in which you sincerely apologized but you were not forgiven? How did you feel?

GOLDEN RULE 4: DO NOT CROSS THE LINE

Jewish mothers know friendships require being there, apologizing and forgiving. But we also know that some actions will not be forgiven, no matter how much one apologizes. Certain acts are irrevocable; some words cannot be put back inside your mouth after you've uttered them.

We have a few examples of these absolute no-nos, the unforgivables that can kill a friendship. These behaviors can destroy trust and intimacy to such a degree that even if you are forced to kiss each other on both cheeks once in a while, you will never, ever, consider that person a true friend again.

No-No 1: Criticizing the Kinder

You can criticize your own kids, obviously. Three Jewish mothers are writing this book—criticism of our kids comes to us as naturally as overeating. Your own mother can criticize your kids, but she better be careful what she says and she ought not say it in front of your husband. Occasionally even your mother-in-law can get away with criticism, provided she, too, is extremely careful to balance it with effusive praise. But that's about it.

Nobody else has the right to criticize your kids. Nobody else gets to discipline your kids either, unless you expressly give them your permission. This may seem obvious, but this behavior can kill even the closest of long-standing friendships.

Every mom is sensitive when it comes to her children. If you are the mother of the local terror, you know that this is the one area of your psyche that is the rawest. When your friend criticizes your child, it hurts you. Let's face it—your child isn't going to change based on what your friend says; instead, her criticism will only make you feel like a lousy mother. One jab may not extinguish the friendship, but over time your enthusiasm for your friend will diminish. A friend who is not sensitive to your emotions about your child does not deserve to remain a friend. A friend who actually takes on your kid and decides to substitute her mothering skills for yours inevitably forces you to choose between your kid and her. Guess who wins?

This lesson cuts both ways. If you do not want your friend insulting your child, you must treat her with the same respect. Even if your friend's kid strikes you as hateful, be very careful. If you volunteer a criticism, you will very likely lose your friend. If you are asked your opinion, tread lightly when answering. Don't evade the subject, but be tactful and answer it with a question back, like "Why are you concerned? Have you considered getting some professional help?" If you are never consulted at all about negative behavior and you simply cannot stand the brat, then you know what to do. See your friend when she has a babysitter.

An unfortunate habit of the Jewish mother is the reflexive tendency to focus on the negative. We know that we do this, and still we do it. Is it genetic? Nature or nurture? Whatever . . . it's there. The best thing to do about it is to laugh about it when you recognize it. Trust us; you are not going to stop yourself or the Jewish mother in your life, no matter how hard you try.

✳ *Lisa's Story*

I tend to have very intense and close female friendships. I had one very dear friend named Annette. Annette had a caustic wit and a temper, but our families were close. Jon was eleven at the time, and he also had a sharp tongue. I wonder where that comes from. One day Annette did me a favor and drove Jon and his two friends to my house. Driving three rowdy boys can be tough. I wasn't there, but I know that Annette and Jon got into an argument about something. Later, Jon's friends told me that Annette had, in their words, "gone crazy," raising her voice and hurling false accusations at Jon. Annette had her side too, of course. I was put squarely in the middle between my good friend and my son. But regardless of who was at fault, I felt that Jon needed to respect my friend as an adult. So I instructed Jon to apologize, in writing, for the comments he had made. He did so. I read the apology and deemed it acceptable. Would you believe Annette rejected Jon's apology? She told me it wasn't good enough and she wouldn't accept it. Right then and there, she forced me to choose between my son and her and caused enormous friction in my home. My son comes first. ■

ask yourself

1. Have you ever criticized a friend's child? What did you hope to accomplish?

2. Has a friend ever criticized your kid? How did you react?

No-No 2: Neither a Borrower nor a Lender Be

Lending money can irrevocably change a friendship. You no longer have a friend. Instead the relationship becomes one of debtor and creditor.

Our Jewish mother motto is simple: Do not lend anything you cannot afford to give. If a friend asks to borrow money from you, the answer is yes, if you can afford to never see that money again. The answer is no if you need the money for yourself. What do you tell your friend? You say, "Here is the money you need. It is a gift. The minute I give it to you, I will forget I ever gave it to you. Now let's eat."

If the friend wants to pay it back, then you can decide whether or not to accept it when the friend has the money in hand. In the meantime, the money is a non-issue because you have made a gift, not a loan.

Here is an experience Jill should have learned from at a young age:

❋ *Jill's Story*

> Years ago, right after college, a friend of mine asked me to loan her $500 to help her start a T-shirt company. After I gave her the money, she never returned a phone call. She couldn't face me. Of course, she had spent the money on something other than her business, but she didn't want to tell me that. I lost a friendship because of this incident. It taught me to be prepared to lose the money the next time I was asked to lend any and not to lend any money I can't afford to lose. Unfortunately, this lesson didn't stick. Bobby and I were burned recently when we lent money to a friend—we never got the money back and we lost the friendship anyway. ∎

ask yourself

1. Aren't we totally right on this one? Have you ever had a *good* experience when you lent money to a friend?

2. Did you ever borrow money from a friend and not pay it back? Shame on you. It's not too late.

No-No 3: Don't Be Cruel to a Heart That's True

You would not expect a friend to be mean, but occasionally someone reveals a side that is just plain cruel. If you see that side, run, and don't look back.

All of us have experienced varying degrees of cruelty when it comes to peer relationships, particularly as kids. Jill and Gloria were scarred by certain experiences, and Lisa, observing some of this, developed a spine of steel, preventing her from some, but not all, of the hurt of being rejected by friends.

Daddy bought us a book on self-esteem when we were young, and he insisted we read passages of it out loud. One phrase stayed, a quote by Eleanor Roosevelt: "No one can make you feel inferior without your consent." That is a mantra in our homes. We tell it to ourselves when other people try to put us down. You'd be surprised at how often that does happen in life. Hasn't it happened to you?

Jill and Mommy have a lot in common in that both suffered early rejection from their peers. But their reactions differed dramatically. While Mommy chose to confront people's hypocrisies and criticize their faults, even testing them with her hostility, Jill chose to avoid discussion of negative traits altogether, in an effort to please everyone and be liked by all. Jill's favorite saying is "It's all good." She sums it up in these words:

 Jill's Take

I've said on the show that I am the girl who always wanted to be popular in high school and never was. At least I thought I wasn't. Since then, I have reconnected with high school friends who saw me differently than I saw myself. Sometimes I think the most popular girl in high school wouldn't even remember herself as being popular.

A lot of my insecurity comes from feeling rejected by my peers when I was younger. Lisa can tell this particular story better than I can because she was there and I blocked out a lot of it. ■

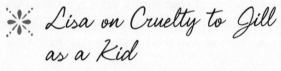 Lisa on Cruelty to Jill as a Kid

I remember one day very clearly. I was in sixth grade and Jill was in second grade. Jill and I were walking across a great expanse of empty field where our school intersected the highway. We had just gotten lunch at the local luncheonette and had to cross the field to get back inside school. We were more than halfway there when some of the kids in Jill's class started to throw rocks at us, saying mean things to Jill. I grabbed Jill's hand, tight, and told her to hold her head up and pretend nothing was happening and not to run. We just walked right through it as if in a trance. We didn't get hurt on the outside, but I'll never forget that day. I'm glad Jill doesn't remember it. ■

ask yourself

1. Have you ever been knowingly cruel to someone? Why?

2. Have you been cruelly rejected by peers? How did you react?

3. How has your personality been shaped by your relationship with your peers?

No-No 4: Other People's Messes . . .

Friends are supposed to keep confidences, right? After all, that's why you have good friends—to keep your secrets. But sometimes, a friend can take advantage of your loyalty. Years ago, Gloria was unwittingly made the minor player in a neighbor's extramarital affair, and it didn't make her feel very good at all. She recalls it this way:

☀ *Gloria's Mess*

Talk about secrets! I was very sick when I was thirty-four years old. I had a large benign tumor that necessitated the removal of a large part of my colon. I almost died, and I lay in the hospital for approximately six weeks. It was Yom Kippur, Sol had left for a few hours, and I was all alone. My friend Caroline came to visit me with a man who was not her husband. I had suspected that my friend was cheating a few weeks prior to this, but this was the first time I really knew. Would you believe at that exact same time she was there with her lover, Caroline's husband came to visit me too? I didn't know what to do; I panicked. I thought I would faint and broke out in a sweat. I could see that Caroline wanted me to make up a story about who her paramour was, so I introduced him to Caroline's husband as my cousin. Now I was made part of her affair.

After I got out of the hospital, I got a hysterical phone call from a woman who was apparently this paramour's wife, accusing me of having an affair with her husband! She said she was going to sue me for alienation of affection, which of course she never did, because I had nothing to do with anything! But the worst was when Caroline's husband, who had been my friend too, came into our home and accused me of covering up for Caroline. He was so enraged, I thought he was going to kill me. His fist was clenched, and I was afraid he was ready to hit me when he saw my mother in the den. He had just learned of the affair and he blamed me for not telling him. I said that I was put in an untenable position and couldn't help myself. I was very scared. To this day, I think there might have been violence, but after he saw my mother, this poor man left our home, utterly lost.

In retrospect, I guess I should not have covered up for Caroline. I suppose I could just have let the room go silent, which might have forced Caroline to figure out a way to introduce her lover to her husband. But at the time, I responded in the only way I could.

I was used that day. My friend Caroline was disloyal to me, encouraging me to perpetrate a lie on her behalf. And I was in turn disloyal to Caroline's husband, who has not spoken to me since his divorce. Years later, Sol and I befriended a couple who knew Caroline and her paramour, now her new husband. She told me I was the only one who hadn't known about the affair. Everyone else in town had known exactly what was going on. Caroline had sworn me to secrecy, so I kept the secret. Obviously, no one else did! So much for keeping secrets. . . . ■

ask yourself

1. **What secrets are you willing to keep in a friendship?**

2. **Did you ever break a confidence? Why? Did you feel guilty about it?**

No-No 5: Getting Too Close for Comfort

There is one more unforgivable that we ought to mention. Sometimes adults behave like immature adolescents out of their own need for love or drama. If so, they may do the unforgivable and make eyes at a friend's husband. If you cross that line, there is no going back.

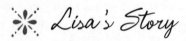

Lisa's Story

When Bill and I were first married, we lived across the way from an attractive couple with whom we became friends. One day, and one day only, I spotted this "friend" getting a little too cozy with Bill. Something about the way she looked at him made me wary. Who knows if anything would have happened? The point is—you take no chances. We never, ever socialized again with this couple, even though they were hard to avoid in our tight-knit condo community. Bill protested that I was making a big deal out of nothing, but I think he was flattered by the whole episode because this girl was very attractive and I gave up our friendship with this couple because of the threat. You just never can be too careful—and when it comes to my husband, my claws come out. ∎

ask yourself

1. Have you ever committed one of these no-nos?

2. What sins can't you forgive in a friend?

3. How willing are you to overlook flaws or sins in order to keep a friendship going?

The Gray Areas . . .

Even if you follow our four basic rules that are intended to help you keep your friendships solid, in life you still encounter a multitude of situations in the gray area. These are the moments where you might be forced to turn the other cheek if you feel wronged, or on the other hand decide whether your efforts in this friendship are worth your time. We cite just a couple of examples here—the drama of parties and the reality of keeping in touch.

GRAY AREA 1:
IT'S HER PARTY AND I'LL CRY IF I WANT TO. . . .

What happens when you are not invited to a party your friend is throwing? Ah, that classic gray area. Here is the judgment call: Is the party an intimate gathering or something to which many people are invited? If it is a big affair, then of course your feelings will be hurt if you are excluded. On the other hand, be fair—if you've ever thrown a wedding or Bar Mitzvah, you might even have had your own "A list" stamped and your "B list" ready for those who returned their response cards early with a no. You can't always invite everyone, even if you want to. Neither can your friends.

GRAY AREA 2: KEEPING IN TOUCH

We all know the hallmark of a good friendship is communication, but we have many good friends with whom we simply do not keep in touch on a regular basis. Let's face it—your dynamic, interesting friends are busy. If you haven't heard from someone in months, and you miss her, pick up the phone and start the conversation as if you just spoke with her yesterday. She probably has a really good reason for why she hasn't been in touch—why not find out what it is?

We hate when friends make us feel guilty that we haven't spoken to them in a while. Here's how it's done: Your friend whom you haven't spoken with in three months calls you up and instead of saying "Hello—I miss you, how are you?" the first thing she says is "Hi—how come I haven't heard from you in so long?" These types of conversations immediately make you defensive and also remind you why this particular friendship is such a pain in your *tuchas.* If this happens to you, you could respond with "Why haven't I heard from you? Couldn't you pick up a phone also?" But what you will do instead is sputter some sort of speech about just how busy you've been. Who needs that? Real friends pick up where they left off with no need to make each other explain or apologize.

When to Say When

Friendships are some of the most difficult relationships in life to maneuver. Although we do pick our friends, sometimes we make the wrong choices. Then what? What is the kind way to back away from a friendship once you discover there are things about this person that you no longer like? Close friendships, in particular, are just like love affairs. Endings can be very painful. We are reluctant to let go of people whom we once loved. The Jewish mother's answer? When a door closes, a window opens. Eventually, another friend will come along. So, then, how do you end a friendship?

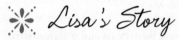 *Lisa's Story*

With Annette, I agonized over ending our friendship. There had been so many slights, insults and confrontations that I knew it had to end, but it was difficult nonetheless. How did I end the friendship? First, Annette herself knew she had crossed the line, so the ending came as no surprise to her. My phone calls to her ceased. I told all our mutual friends that our friendship was over and asked them to please not put me in awkward situations. I would always act civilly, but others were not to expect us to be the pals we once were.

Ironically, Annette's husband had warned me years beforehand that our friendship would eventually end this way; he had told me that Annette had a pattern of doing this to people. Of course, when he told me this, I said it would never happen to us.

About a year after we had called it quits, Annette walked up to me in a parking lot and told me that she had heard I was starting a radio show and wanted to help out. She clearly was making an overture to restart the friendship. But with me, there is no going back. Once you have crossed the line, it really is over. The offer to help was politely refused.

Years later, I still think about her and miss our fun conversations. That's why I believe that once you've loved someone, a part of you will always still love that person, even if you believe that you are better off not having that person in your life. ■

ask yourself

1. When is a friendship really over for you?

2. How do you end your friendships?

3. Do you think there is a graceful way to end a friendship? How?

4. Have you ever been dumped by a good friend? Why?

5. Do you still think about close friendships that have ended? Do you have regrets?

It's Never Too Late. . . .

On the other hand, friendships do come in cycles. Sometimes we simply drift out of each other's lives and then reconnect. In today's Internet world, it's easier than ever to find someone. Mommy used to pine for a college roommate with whom she had lost touch years ago. One day, Lisa finally decided to do something about it.

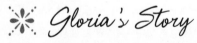 *Gloria's Story*

My roommate at college in Vermont was a girl named Betty who was three credits shy of graduation when she quit school to marry a guy who was a certified genius and as crazy as a three-dollar bill. This girl came from a poor family that had struggled to keep her in college, and here she was, throwing it away to get married! But I was really fond of Betty, and we had a great friendship. After college, she moved back to New York, and Sol and I started seeing them as a couple once in a while. Her husband developed severe mental as well as physical illnesses, and they shut themselves off from social contact. Eventually, we lost touch and I couldn't find her anymore. I missed her.

One day, Lisa decided to surprise me and work her magic on the computer. She couldn't find Betty, but she did track down her son after calling a few people who had the same name. I was so happy to find my long-lost friend! We see each other now as often as we can and she visits me in Florida. You cannot duplicate your shared history with old friends; it is irreplaceable. Since her husband died several years ago, she has made herself a busy and satisfying life, and her only son is very successful. Some friendships don't die, they just go on hold for a bit. ■

ask yourself

1. Whom do you miss?

2. Have you tried reconnecting?

3. What are you waiting for? Life is short. Pick up the phone.

In Conclusion

How important are our friends? How important is oxygen? Without both, we can't breathe in this world. The Jewish mother judges the success of a person's life by the quality of her relationships with others. You don't have to like everybody, and believe us, not everybody has to like you. But when you do find those special connections with people, you need to appreciate them, nourish them and sustain them.

In the end, does it matter how much money you have if no-body wants to take a trip with you anyway? Does it matter how beautiful your home is if you never entertain, never fill it with great conversation and hearty laughter? What difference does it make if your daughter becomes a doctor if there is no one in your life who can *kvell* over your *nachas*? Friends do all of that for us.

Great friendship is of paramount importance for Jewish people. The famous prayer we say in *shul*, the Shehecheyanu, which is as hard to pronounce as it looks, goes: "Blessed are you, O Lord our God, King of the Universe, Who has granted us life, sustained us, and enabled us to reach this occasion." Jews say this prayer on the first day of every holiday and at major celebrations and occasions. This prayer is also said upon seeing a friend whom we haven't seen in thirty days or more. That's how much we Jews value friends; we say a prayer of thanks to God when we reunite.

Speaking of prayers, do you know the ending to one of our favorite movies of all time, Frank Capra's *It's a Wonderful Life*? The hero, George Bailey, is reading the inscription on the Bible that the angel Clarence has given him, after George realizes that his own life was worth saving. What is inscribed on that Bible? *"Remember, George: No man is a failure who has friends."* Our sentiments exactly.

2

Dating

*Just because he isn't perfect
doesn't mean he won't be
perfectly right for you.*

O ur kids are growing into a generation of young adults that forgot how to date. What happened? Dating as a courtship ritual seems to have disappeared. Where did it go? More important, what replaced it? Random, anonymous conversations on social networking sites? Hook-ups? Or is that yesterday's word? We can't keep up. Even the word "partying" has morphed into a pejorative term, implying drug use rather than enjoying yourself at a party without drugs. Many of our young people are lonely. They don't have "socials" the way we used to or safe places to meet other young adults. For some reason their own friends don't "set them up" the way we did. If they are not in college and cannot afford an apartment of their own, their social world is tiny. So many kids today are content to sit home at their computers, watching life from a screen in their comfortable bedroom, rather than getting out there and participating in life. Joanna tells her mother, Lisa, all the time: The computer is both a blessing and a curse.

Despite the lack of what we used to call "dating," meeting people and seeking a life partner is still an important part of life.

The rules may change daily, but that just makes socializing more confusing, not less essential. Twenty- and thirty-somethings are still out there looking for their perfect mate. We have also noticed that the issues of dating resurface frequently in middle age, because so many people are either divorced or widowed. There may be a lot more baggage at that stage, and many more complexities, but whether we are twenty-four or fifty-four, we still have the same feelings of anxiety and rejection: Is he or she out there? Why didn't this one work? Why didn't he like me? The key is to maintain hope: I'll check in tonight on JDate; maybe Mr. Right is waiting on my desktop.

In this chapter we explain how we found our Mr. Rights. More important, we tell you how to identify the definitely Mr. Wrongs.

What are the sexual expectations of today's youth? Of course, it depends on whom you ask. But there is no doubt that we have saturated this latest generation with an abundance of sexuality. Did you put a condom on a banana in ninth grade? Joanna did. Did you learn about the nuances of hetero- and homosexual intercourse before you were sixteen? Our kids know more than we did then, or now. In our quest to ensure that our kids know every possible bad thing that could happen to them as a result of being sexually active, we have taken some of the mystery and romance out of life. We have created a jaded generation.

The *Shiddoch*

If you are serious about getting serious, then you have come to the right place. For casual dating, move to another book—the

Jewish mother is not interested. Dating is serious business to the Jewish mother; she knows that few things in life are more important than finding the right mate. Did you know that all Jewish mothers are born matchmakers? It is true. Lisa and Jill pride themselves on their matchmaking abilities. Plus it's a huge *mitzvah*, and we need as many of those as we can get.

How do you find the right person for you? We think the *best* way to meet someone is through a match, the traditional *shiddoch*. Our parents, Sol and Gloria, met that way. Jill met her first husband, Steven, that way too. If you are single, get the word out. Tell your friends you are looking. You can't expect them to read your mind; everybody has his own life to worry about. If you do not know anyone who is willing to set you up, there are professional matchmaking services in every region and on every desktop. Do not expect your white knight to magically appear one day when you are waiting in line for coffee, on the elevator or at the airport terminal. If you want to find love, you have to think of it as a second job (provided you have a first job). That means you have to be open to a *shiddoch*. Have a little trust—and carry pepper spray, just in case.

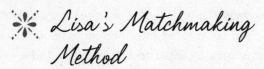

✳ *Lisa's Matchmaking Method*

I do matchmaking all the time. If I find out that you are single, I begin the interrogation: What are you looking for—kids, no kids, city, country, age, religion, interests? Then I begin the match in my head. Whom do I know who might be suitable for you? I can't help it—I assume everyone wants to be in love. Everyone needs love, so I assume everyone also wants to meet that perfect match. If I know someone who might be right, I ask only one thing of each person in the match—they have to agree to go out on a second date. I read that someplace in a magazine and I thought it was a great rule; it takes all the pressure off the first date. I have at least one marriage I can take credit for, and right now two friends of mine whom I fixed up are dating steadily. Of course, my kids would never let me fix them up—they're still too young to be desperate enough to have their mother set them up on a blind date. But not to worry . . . I'm out there looking anyway. Who said I needed their permission? ■

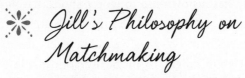

Jill's Philosophy on Matchmaking

I take matchmaking very seriously. It is not a sport for me. I truly believe that God will give me credit for this one day, and I love to get credit! I matched up a nice Jewish girl and a widowed dentist, and they got married. I am keeping my fingers crossed on some other matches I have made.

If I were dating today, I would definitely go on JDate .com, which is an Internet matchmaking site for Jews. There is no stigma attached to online dating today like there was just a few years ago. In fact, Bobby's son, David, met his wife, Jill, on JDate.com. So did our cousin Rebecca, Aunt Cooky's daughter, who married Mark. Simon and Alex McCord, my costars on *Housewives*, met on an international dating site. They say they were looking for a one-night stand and not a relationship but ended up falling in love instead. Cast the net as wide as you possibly can—listen to your friends, go on blind dates and go online. You have to work to find love! ■

Of course, you can't create chemistry. It's either there, or it's not. The matchmaking Jewish mother puts the pieces in place as best she can and then leaves the rest up to God and Cupid.

By the way, the savvy Jewish mother does not believe that there is only one perfect match for someone. She is way too practical for that. What happens if, God forbid, bite your tongue three times, something happens to that person? Does that mean you should be alone the rest of your life? Absolutely not. What about divorce? Maybe he was perfect for you for a while, but you weren't so perfect for him. What are you supposed to do—just sit there and feel sorry for yourself? Jewish mothers are not only resilient, they are flexible. Many shoes can fit the same feet. Now, will you please call the number we gave you? We hear he is a nice boy from a very good family.

On Dating Men You Meet Online

Look up your date on Google before you go out with him. If you really like him, but want to know more, you can even have an online search service check him out. You can never be too safe.

ask yourself

1. Are you looking for a serious relationship?

2. Have you told everyone you know that you are looking and asked them to set you up?

3. What are you waiting for? Perhaps more precisely, what are you afraid of?

4. Have you signed up on an Internet dating site yet? What did you like or dislike about it?

The Jewish Husband: Myth and Reality

Let's face it: Everyone is looking for a good Jewish husband. Jewish girls for sure are looking, but so are Irish lasses and southern belles. They've heard that Jewish men make the best husbands too. We have a few things to say on that subject:

1. Not all Jewish men make the best husbands. Trust us on this one.

2. Why is a Jewish husband better than others? He has been trained, from birth, to respect women. He may not like his wife, he may not even love his wife, but he definitely respects his wife.

3. Jewish men usually are great fathers. Even if they are lousy husbands, they are usually devoted daddies.

4. Traditionally, Jewish men didn't drink and didn't fool around. But today, we wouldn't swear for either virtue. . . .

5. If you do find a good Jewish man who makes a decent husband, give us Jewish mothers some credit for this. God knows we get the blame. And for the record, Jewish wives can be pretty terrific too, thank you very much.

The Courtship: A Good Man Is Hard to Find, but So Is a Good Woman—Don't Settle for Less Than You Deserve

After you have figured out how you are going to meet someone eligible, with good potential, then the selection begins. Contrary to the popular assumption that a good man is harder to find than a good woman, we believe that a good woman is just as rare, if not rarer. So, ladies, value yourselves. Do not settle for less than you deserve! How do you know which traits in a man are the most important? Pay attention to our mother, Gloria.

 *Gloria*:

It is more important to like a man than to love him, because you can love someone and not get along with him. If you like and respect that person, the relationship can grow and mature. Love often comes as a result of a caring and strong relationship. Physical attractions are of paramount importance when one is young, but as you age you find that intelligence and character play a much greater role. It is wonderful to have both, but if you must choose, it is wise to choose the latter. ■

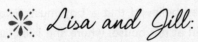 *Lisa and Jill*:

What are you saying here, Mommy? Are you saying that Daddy wasn't the most handsome guy you ever saw? Actually, we know—we've seen those early pictures. No offense, Daddy, but you are a lot more handsome today than you were then. ■

Jill's Take

I have my own philosophy about choosing a mate. I believe that when two people are attracted to each other, endorphins are released, a "love potion" if you will. The truth is the potion lasts for no more than three months. Then it disappears. That is why I firmly believe that sex and love are very different things. Did you ever go out with someone for a few months and have lots of hot sex and passion, only to wake up one day, look at each other and wonder why you were ever attracted in the first place? I dated my share of men early on and I remember those feelings. You need to cycle through at least four seasons with the same guy to know if you are really compatible. ■

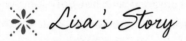

Lisa's Story

I dated Bill for three years before we got married. During one summer, he lived in Manhattan and I lived in Woodmere at home with my parents. Instead of having him come out to the Island to pick me up for a date, it was more convenient to meet him in the city, so I started doing that. Bill got used to that routine. My parents didn't like it one bit. "You live in Woodmere—the boy comes to you!" they said. They believed that a boy must always come pick up the girl at her house, where she lives, and deposit her home safely. No exceptions, no excuses. When I raised the issue with Bill, I could hear in his voice his protest and just a little bit of taking me for granted. I didn't like that one bit. We had a huge fight about this issue and almost broke up that summer because of it. Needless to say, guess who started getting picked up again in Woodmere? My parents were right; you must demand respect to receive it.

By the way, Bill remembers this story differently. He does not even remember our fight—all he remembers is *shlepping* to and from Woodmere all summer long to take me out on dates. ∎

GLORIA'S MUST-HAVE QUALITIES IN A HUSBAND

The Jewish mother leaves as little to chance as possible when evaluating a potential husband. Our mother, Gloria, very consciously told us the characteristics that were essential in a good husband and those that we had to avoid at any cost. Here they are:

1. *Generosity*: *Never* marry a stingy person. It will ruin your life.

2. *Dedication*: Better if he loves you a little more than you love him. It lasts longer that way.

3. *Kindness*: Above all, kindness. Giving your spouse "five minutes of understanding" has saved many a marriage and ended many an argument.

4. *Fidelity*: Always be on your toes; always make sure your husband is on his toes as well. Never take this for granted.

5. *Ambition*: Money is round; it comes and goes in life. Money itself is not important; character and ambition are what is important. It's not where you come from that matters, it's where you are going.

6. *Fatherhood Capabilities*: How can you tell a good husband will be a good father? Often you can't, and you hope for the best. Our own opinion is that most decent men make excellent fathers, if given the chance. We hit the jackpot with our father, Sol.

7. *Brains*: The sine qua non of keeping life interesting and giving your children a good chance of being smart too. For a Jewish mother, this is the one that goes without saying, and it is the first trait evaluated upon meeting a prospective mate. An Ivy League education may give you bragging rights, but the Jewish mother knows it is no guarantee of success.

8. *Sense of Humor*: Without which life is simply not worth living, especially to a Jew. If we don't laugh, we cry.

9. *Age Compatibility*: Try not to marry a man much older than yourself: It lasts longer that way. To this Jill says, "I do know that I won't be with Bobby as long as I want, that being forever, and that I might have many lonely years in front of me. This is all the more reason to try to cherish the moments as much as I can."

10. *If You Are Jewish, He Has to Be Jewish Too*: You may not like this one, but we are being honest here—it is one of Gloria's essentials. If he wasn't born Jewish, he needs to convert. The kids must be raised Jewish. If you aren't Jewish but have a strong faith or cultural identity, keep this in mind as you make your choices. No matter what your faith, two conflicting belief systems are confusing for children, especially as they begin to ask questions. We think you should pick a team.

GLORIA'S MUST-AVOIDS

1. *Possessive Jealousy*: Use your antenna on this one; a little jealousy is normal, even healthy. But creepy, threatening jealousy is just a big red flag. Get out of this relationship quickly.

2. *Dishonesty*: This behavior does not go away over time, it becomes worse. The lying could be about money, his family, his past—anything. Make sure you have dated long enough and spoken to enough other people to confirm the basic facts about his life.

An article was published about our cousin Ella some years ago. Ella had become engaged to a man we'll call Harold, because we can no longer remember his real name, having purposely blotted it out from our memory. Harold told Ella that he had been an Olympic skier and was also a successful businessman. Ella and Harold were all set to be married at the Pierre. The wedding was to cost $25,000, in those days a huge amount of money. Ella was an only daughter. Her parents were thrilled and proud. The wedding announcement had been submitted to the newspaper and was all set to be published. Two days prior to the wedding, Ella got a call from the fact-checker. Nothing Harold had said about himself was true. Olympic skier? No. Businessman? Not that either. It turned out Harold was a pathological liar; every single thing he had said about himself was completely false. Poor Ella. What did she do? She canceled the wedding. Today the bride might go on with the party; in those days, it was unthinkable. Ella never married.

3. *Stinginess*: Beware the man who needs to know how much money you spent today and exactly where that ATM withdrawal went. We cannot stress this enough; a guy who insists on controlling every aspect of your purse strings will absolutely ruin your chances of happiness.

4. *Violence of Any Kind*: Not tolerated. Not negotiable.

5. *Addiction to Drugs, Gambling, Alcohol*: If you discover this issue, know that whatever you do, you will not cure him. You will suffer if you stay together. Don't be a martyr or an armchair psychologist. Find someone else.

6. *Stubbornness and Stupidity*: Together, a lethal combination.

THERE IS ONLY ONE PEACOCK TO A COUPLE— GLORIA'S CAVEAT

Excessive attention to one's outward appearance reveals much about a person's inner character, especially when it comes to men. Have you ever seen a couple that competes with each other to see who looks better in the mirror? They cannot last. It is a rule of nature: only one peacock to a couple. We believe that it is optimal for the woman to be the strutter, but if the woman is comfortable wearing the gray feathers instead of the purple ones, so be it. Only be careful not to suppress your own inner peacock just so your man can show off his shinier feathers; in the end, it will only cause you heartbreak.

Gloria's Take on Vanity

    Men whose egos are too large are usually quite vain. A woman who is tied to such a man will often end up being submissive to the needs, wants and desires of this man. I tried to teach my girls that a woman is equal to and never less than her mate. I knew a couple where the husband's clothes took up three closets (!), leaving his wife with only one. Her small closet was a sign of how unimportant her opinion was in that household. I knew another couple who eventually got divorced because there was such obvious competition between the two as to who was the more glamorous half of the couple. There is only one peacock to a family. ■

Jill has thrust herself into the limelight, a place where anyone who is not a peacock should fear to tread. Luckily, Bobby is a strong and confident man, happy to let his peacock shine.

 *As Jill Puts It:*

I know very well that I am the peacock in my family. I was the peacock in my first marriage too, so I knew how to get that part right! Last June, we arrived for a huge red carpet for the Gracie Awards show in New York City. The red carpet was more than two hundred feet long, with hundreds of photographers and cameramen. I walked on first, alone, to the sound of "Jill, look here!" I heard them also call out Bobby's name. I turned around to grab Bobby's hand; he reluctantly came onto the carpet, and as soon as I let go . . . he disappeared. I was blinded by the flashbulbs, and as I continued walking down the carpet I could see Bobby's head over the shoulder of a cameraperson. He was quietly walking in tandem with me, making sure I looked OK, never looking away. At the end of the seemingly endless red carpet, Bobby met me, handed me my scarf and held my hand again. In contrast, another couple was posturing and posing, and it was clear to me that the man was trying to steal the spotlight. It does not matter, though, who is the peacock. The rule to remember is that there can only be one. ■

Lisa thinks Gloria may be a bit sexist here because she does not ascribe the same negative traits to vain men as to vain women. Nevertheless, Lisa agrees with the conclusion.

As Lisa Says:

I distrust vain men. I got that from my mother. There is nothing that turns me off a man faster than an aftershave that smells stronger than my perfume, and I don't even wear perfume. I think I equate vanity in men with selfishness. If a man is thinking about how good he looks, he is not thinking about how I look. Not a good sign. ■

However, all of us like our hubbies to look as handsome as they can for those special occasions. Nobody likes a slob.

MEETING OUR MATES

When it came time for us to choose our mates, how did each of us apply these wise precepts? Let's start with Gloria herself.

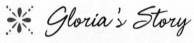

Gloria's Story

When I think of it now, I am really ashamed of myself. I was practically engaged to two men at the same time! I began dating Leon in my late teens, and we had been seeing each other steadily for about two years. I'm sure he thought we would eventually get married. Nevertheless, I used to date other guys in between, because until you have a ring on your finger, you are not committed to one person. One day I had a blind date with Sol. The date was totally forgettable, but Sol was rather persistent, and I remember he had a wonderful telephone voice. So I started seeing Sol too. I would see Sol at a luncheonette and then around the corner Leon would be waiting to take me home. I was crazy! That phase did not last long, thank God. But I never told Leon that I was engaged to Sol until the night before we were to be married. I have always regretted the way I behaved. It was disgraceful! Sometimes I think I never told Leon because I was uncertain of my feelings for Sol, so I had a backup plan to get back with Leon in case I broke off my engagement with Sol. Why did I choose Sol over Leon? I always tell the girls that if I had married Leon, they would have had green eyes but they would have been dumb. Leon was better-looking than Sol, certainly. But Sol had something else: He was really smart. No question, I chose brains over looks. Thank goodness, I made the right choice. I was the lucky one and so were my children. ■

Gloria and Sol celebrated their fiftieth wedding anniversary on December 25, 2007.

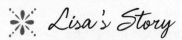 ## Lisa's Story

I systematically ran through what I thought were the eligible Jewish men at Johns Hopkins during my freshman year of college by dating a new one almost every Saturday night. By dating, I mean dinner or a movie. In those days of yesteryear, men and women actually accompanied each other socially without expecting any sexual favors. Shocking, right? Anyway, none of those guys made a real impression on me. Right before sophomore year, I got a new haircut. Plus I had bought some snazzy Calvin Klein jeans and an electric-blue shiny shirt with a gold shiny vest to wear on the disco floor. It was 1979—what can I say? The Bee Gees' "Night Fever" was practically our "Star-Spangled Banner." Bill Wexler, Andover preppie, the sole Republican Jew on campus, must have been struck by lightning caused by the electric blue of my shiny shirt. He took one look at my new haircut and decided we were meant for each other.

I had known Bill only slightly, having dated both of his freshman roommates the prior year (only one of whom was Jewish, but that's another story . . .). When my Grandma Syl first laid eyes on Bill as he was standing across the quad, she literally said, "What a hunk." I'll never forget that. Picture a woman who never had a good word to say about anybody for most of her life and you can see just how funny that was. But it was true. Bill was six feet four inches tall, Rock Hudson in person, complete with that gorgeous black curly hair. I fell for his pink monogrammed shirt. Two weeks after our first date, Bill wrote a letter to his parents saying he had found the girl he was going to marry, but there was one problem: She was Orthodox Jewish. (Bill was wrong, but compared to his Bostonian Jewish upbringing, he might have had a point.) Every day I still wear the first gift Bill gave me, for our first Hanukkah together, a necklace that says YMETM (You Mean Everything to Me). I ran down the list of essentials Mommy had given me, and Bill passed every single one. He was funny, generous and kind. He was Jewish and smart. And he was absolutely drop-dead gorgeous. Chemistry was not an issue. But what did I know? Was there any guarantee it would last? Of course not. If you ask me now, I think the whole thing is a bit of a crapshoot. You increase your odds if you follow Mommy's must-have and must-avoid rules, but you cannot know ahead of time what life is going to throw at you. You just have to pray you get your share of good luck. ■

Lisa and Bill are coming up on their twenty-eighth wedding anniversary; Lisa was a child bride compared to the ages her peers married. First love; sometimes it sticks.

Jill Says:

My love life has always been a bit more complicated. Before Bobby, there was Steven, my first husband. I was in my twenties and living in Boston. I had decided that I had dated enough and was ready to get married. I always set goals for myself, and I had no doubt I would get what I wanted. But looking back, I attribute that to hard work and a little luck. I wanted to go to college, open my own business and become a buyer for a clothing store, and I did all of those things. Now I wanted to get married. So I literally told everyone I knew that I was looking for a husband. I left no stone unturned; every person was a potential connection to my unknown groom. Soon after, I was having dinner with my dear friends Jill and Robert and their friend Sue. I got right to it. I told Sue my life story and asked her if she knew any "nice Jewish boys" for me. She said she did know someone, and the descri[p]tion sounded pretty good. I gave her my number [and] asked her to make the match. Then I never heard [from] her. Like any well-trained salesperson, I let no le[ad go] cold. After not hearing from this guy, I called Sue[.] A day or two later Steven Shapiro called me. I [was] cited. We talked for about an hour, and he asked me if I was coming to New York City anytime soon. Actually I wasn't, but I didn't tell him that.

After our first "blind" date, when I flew to New York and met him in person, we fell in what I thought was love. It was a whirlwind courtship. Steven proposed just eight weeks after we met. I had just been promoted, but I didn't feel guilty resigning that Monday morning. I was too excited about my own future. Looking back, at twenty-three years old, did I really even know what love was supposed to be? We seemed compatible. We had the same goals and values. Some said we even looked like brother and sister. Unfortunately, my marriage with Steven did not last. We were married ten years when I realized Steven was not the love of my life. Steven was my best friend, but it wasn't enough. I was torn because of my daughter, Ally, and the effect the divorce would have on her, but I believed that separating before her teenage years would be better in the long run. I was also thinking of myself. I thought I had a better chance of finding what I was missing while I was still in my early thirties, with a very young and well-behaved child.

Steven and I had a most civilized divorce, although I hate that word, "divorce." Divorce sounds final, and when you have a child together, there is nothing final about it. We are still raising a child together. We speak often about and attend important occasions together on her on, we agreed that all decisions would be is best for Ally, and I am happy to say that we are both sticking to it. ■

✳ Jill's Story of How She Met Bobby

Bobby is the great love of my life. Some people may call it lucky, but I believe that meeting Bobby was *b'shert*—in Yiddish, "meant to be." I have these little miracles and co-incidences that happen in my life all the time. In my mind, God clearly wanted us to be together. I first met Bobby in his fabric store shopping with my in-laws, Steven's parents. They took me there to buy vertical blinds (very popular in the eighties) for our newly built weekend house in Pennsyl-vania. A few years later, my cousin Sharon's son Michael was a counselor at Camp Nashopa, also in Pennsylvania. Sharon asked me to go to see Michael on "visiting day" at camp since she lived in Florida and wasn't able to come. I went. Guess who Michael's bunkmate was? Bobby's son, Jonathan. I met Bobby again at camp that day.

During that same summer, I invited Michael to my house and he brought Jonathan along. At dinner that night, I told Michael that I was getting divorced from Steven. Michael was extremely upset, but Jonathan consoled him by shar-ing that his parents were getting divorced too. A few weeks later, I was bowling with Ally at Chelsea Piers, and Bobby was there with Jonathan. We literally ran into each other walking on the docks outside. Jonathan suggested we all have lunch together. Soon after, we were madly in love.

Of course, I ran down all of Mom's criteria, and Bobby passed with flying colors. Plus Bobby was very successful, which was a big bonus for me. I have to admit that. I re-ally admired the way he earned his own money and thought about business and investments. I learned a lot from him about business and still do. This aspect of his personality was a big attraction for me. One of Mommy's critical rules is to marry smart!

When people ask me about my ex-husband, Steven, I always say he reminded me of my father. So does Bobby. My philosophy on this issue is you should marry someone from whom you would want to be divorced. I did not go into either marriage planning to get divorced, but I can say I married two wonderful men. Steven, Allyson's dad, was my best friend, and I still know if I needed him now, he would be there for me. Bobby . . . well . . . we all know my Bobby. He never has a bad word to say about anyone and wishes I didn't either. ■

After all the dos and don'ts and must-haves and should-avoids, it comes down to this: the Jewish mother's secret to a good match—"Don't settle, but be realistic." Don't compromise on the essentials, but be willing to compromise on the things that are not that important to you. Just make sure you know the difference.

Playing Second Fiddle

Some women feel they must drop everything and change their whole life for the man they love. The Jewish mother says: "Wait just a second. I didn't pay for you to go to four years of college just to watch you move to rural Montana, wait tables and see if your relationship will 'work out.' He wants you, he knows where you are. He comes to you. You don't go anywhere until you have that ring on your finger. Then, and only then, you decide what is best for both of you." A woman should never play second fiddle; she should always think of herself as first string.

ask yourself

1. Take a look at Gloria's checklist and be honest. Does your guy fall short? If so, move on. The right guy is out there.

2. Not dating anyone yet? Why not? Have you asked everyone you know to set you up with someone? Have you gone online? What are you waiting for?

3. Are you settling? Don't give up the important things. If you want kids and he doesn't, don't assume that will change once you get married. If he isn't working now, what makes you think he'll be able to support you later? Better you should be alone than end up with someone who makes you miserable.

4. Are you in a terrible relationship, married or otherwise? Life is too short to stay sad forever. Gather your courage, cry on your best friend's shoulder and get a divorce. Marriage is not supposed to be a jail sentence.

Breaking Up

Breaking up may be hard to do, but it is much worse being the one dumped than the one dumping. Much as it may pain you to do the rejecting, inside yourself you know you get to walk away. The only thing we can advise? Be kind. "Kind" does not translate into "doormat." "Kind" does not mean stay with him because you are afraid you will not find anyone else. "Kind" does not mean stay with him because he guilts you into it. "Kind" means deciding what is right for you and letting him know.

Nobody's Perfect; Don't Expect Him to Be

The Jewish mother wants everyone to be happy in a mature, loving, committed relationship. She yearns for that state of contentment for everyone she loves. But she is no fool, and she doesn't want you suffering any illusions either.

Just because he isn't perfect doesn't mean he won't be perfectly right for you. You're not perfect either. If you want unconditional love, go buy a puppy. In the world of human relationships, you need to earn it. You need to find someone who isn't perfect and love him anyway, even *because* he is not perfect. That's the way you want to be loved, isn't it? You want to be loved when you're cranky because you are about to get your period or you're cranky because you've just gotten your period. You want to be loved both when you've just gotten that promotion and when your boss has passed you over and given the job to someone else.

We are not saying you should settle for someone you don't love; we are saying that a mature person recognizes that all people have faults and loves anyway. And if you want to get love, you've got to give love.

Aunt Cooky makes a list when she evaluates any relationship. She lists the pros and cons. If the good still outweighs the bad, she stays in. There is a huge difference between settling in choosing a mate and understanding that nobody is perfect. The key is whether or not you can live with the particular faults of this particular person. If you can stand the fact that he will never ask for directions, wonderful. If you cannot live with his tendency to forget to call you for an entire day, or that nose-hair problem, or his speech impediment, then this is not the right guy for you. Don't settle for the faults with which you know you cannot live. But remember, you are not so perfect yourself.

⚹ *Gloria Says*:

When I first married Sol, I didn't expect him to be perfect; if I had, we would have gotten divorced a long time ago. Even before we got married, I already knew he was not going to get along with my parents, particularly my mother. I knew Sol wasn't terribly articulate either; even though he was a lawyer, he had a very quiet demeanor and didn't express himself verbally as well as I would have liked. But I had issues too. Even though looking back I can see that I was beautiful, I didn't feel all that desirable. Being overweight when I was younger had made me a little brittle. I didn't get along well with a lot of people. I was twenty-three when we became engaged, already considered a little old for marriage in those days. Even though Sol was very poor, I could see that he had a lot of potential. I felt I could live with the faults I knew about and hoped our love and some luck would take care of the rest. ■

⚹ *Jill's Story*

I do think Bobby is perfect, but I knew our situation itself wasn't perfect, even though I did a good job telling myself it was. After you are divorced, everything is more complicated. Bobby came with three almost-grown children, an ex-wife, two sisters and a close family of nieces and nephews. I wanted everyone to love me because I loved Bobby. I went out of my way to include his family in everything—to host holidays, vacations and weekends where all of us would be together. I hoped they would like me, even love me, but you can only control what you do, not the way someone else feels. My priority was making sure that Bobby and Allyson would get along, since we were going to be living together. As you could see in the first season of *The Real Housewives of New York City*, I am always trying to bring them closer together. Entering into a second marriage, I was no longer looking for perfection; I was so happy to be in love with Bobby that I was determined to make everything else work out as well as I could. ■

ask yourself

1. What are the faults you know you cannot accept in any man?

2. What are your faults? Come clean.

3. What are his faults that you can live with? (For example, that he doesn't cook, clean or know how to fix the smoke alarm that keeps beeping? Wait a second, that's Sol, Bobby *and* Bill!)

4. Even if the situation is not perfect, what can you do to improve it?

5. How much effort is this relationship worth—and are you willing to sustain your efforts in the long run?

Look for the Signs That Your Chosen Will Be a Good Parent

Even while dating, you should have an eye out for a person who will be a good parent to your kids, whether or not you already have them. Even if you are sure you do not want kids, sometimes they come anyway. Perhaps you already have kids from a previous relationship, in which case you need to navigate a host of emotions and motivations. Or perhaps he has kids already, in which case you get to fight against hundreds of years of negative stereotypes of the "wicked stepmother."

We cannot stress this principle enough, even though it seems like such a no-brainer. A good prospect for you as a spouse needs to be a good prospect for you as a co-parent of your child. So many women, in particular, foul up this part. They go for the "bad boy," the one who is still rebelling at age twenty-eight for no good reason. They go for the one who can't seem to get his act together, who hasn't held a job in a year, who thinks it's OK to live like a teenager in a dorm after age twenty-five. You want one of those? Good luck to you. The Jewish mother knows better.

What are the signs of a good father? Let's not skip the basics, like the ability to make a living. We are not saying he has to be tomorrow's Warren Buffett, but the unemployment line is no picnic. Is it sexist to expect a man to be able to provide for his family? No more than it is sexist to expect a woman to do the same, and we do. So make sure that if you have to go on bed rest for nine months, you are with someone who can afford to keep the refrigerator lights on. Pregnancy makes you very hungry.

What else should you look for? Patience is good. A quick temper is bad. Parenting exposes all the fault lines in the relationship anyway, so try to increase your odds by finding a man who is essentially gentle at heart.

❋ Jill and Lisa Put It This Way:

We think gentle men make the best dads, but we are prejudiced. We have an exceptionally patient father. Neither one of us can really remember Daddy ever raising his voice to us, but to be fair, in our house rising above the decibel level of the females was a doomed effort from the start.

We do not think that if a man is not interested in kids he won't make a good father. Why should he be interested in anybody's kids except his own anyway? Don't take the fact that he won't go with your nieces to see the latest animated movie as a sign he will not be a good father. Men's paternal instincts kick in when the cub belongs to their cave and nobody else's. Conversely, if he adores your nephews, will he make a good father? Maybe. It's as good an indication as any. But make sure you've read the first part of this chapter—be certain he can earn a living. ■

Even though Jill did not think she and Bobby would be starting a family of their own, it was extremely important that Jill consider the kind of father Bobby would be because he would be Ally's stepfather, a role that requires enormous patience and understanding.

✳ *Jill Explains How She Evaluated Bobby*

When I decided to get divorced, I had to think about who would be the best substitute father possible. Allyson was only five years old. Steven, Allyson's dad, would always be in her life, but who would be the right man to see her off to school every day and treat her as if she were his own, including giving financial support if necessary? When I met Bobby, I had already met one of his three children, Jonathan, who was very kind and thoughtful. Jonathan adored his father and I thought this was a very good sign. Over time I met Bobby's other children, David and Jennifer, as well as his sisters and nieces and nephews. Bobby is truly the patriarch of his family. Everyone looks up to him as a generous and caring man, and he has earned their love and respect. I truly think Bobby treats Ally no differently than he treated his own children when they were young, which means that he loves Ally and is here for her, but he does not micromanage her life. That's my job. ■

ask yourself

1. Have you observed this guy with kids? And?

2. Can you imagine him in the caretaker role, supporting both you and someone else?

3. Does he have a quick temper, or is he patient?

Sex Before Marriage: Double Talk and Double Standards

When it comes to sex, the double standard is alive and well. For women, our advice is to take your time and let him do the chasing. On the other hand, don't be afraid to be aggressive when you really want to be. Men love that too. Our bottom line: If you are looking for a long-term relationship, you need to build up the sexual tension.

Gloria's Recollection

On the issue of premarital sex, there was only one rule when I was dating. It was not done! If you did engage in premarital sex you did it at your own peril. Those were the days when the morals of life were clearly black or white, never gray. ◼

Gloria grew up in the 1940s. Lisa and Jill grew up in the sixties and seventies. Were the sexual standards of those eras different? You bet—but you wouldn't have known it if you had been sitting in the Woodmere kitchen of Gloria and Sol. Funny how Lisa and Jill remember it differently, though . . .

Lisa on What She Learned Growing Up

Actually, Daddy was much more hung up on making sure I understood the rules about sex than Mom was. He was determined that I "get it"—that I understand that real men did not respect women who slept with other men before they got married. I should understand that sex for a woman was bound up in love and long-term commitment. My mother clearly felt the same way, but it was my father who insisted on having these conversations with me. Naturally, as soon as he started talking about anything to do with sex, I ran out of the room. You would think from all the running I did that I would never have gotten the message. But Dad was clever; there was always the car, in which I was a captive audience. ■

The message came through a little differently to Jill.

 ## Jill Recalls:

Premarital sex? Did Lisa and I live in the same house? It was the seventies—free love! I won't say we didn't talk about sex, but I swear I don't remember! Lisa always listened to Daddy and I never heard him. I had undiagnosed ADD and rarely focused on anything for a long period of time. Maybe that's why I had so many boyfriends. I was boy-crazy at an early age and do remember a fourth-grade assembly trying to teach us about sex education and going slow, but it didn't help. I had my first kissing boyfriend at fourteen, and we practiced for hours on the sofa in the attic. ■

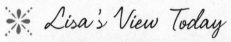 ## Lisa's View Today

I am old-fashioned. I believe young women should keep their legs closed as long as possible, preferably until marriage, or at least until they find themselves in a loving, committed relationship. I tell my daughter that she does not have to have sex, or other acts of great intimacy, in order to know if the chemistry is there, and that if he loves you, he will never pressure you into doing something that is uncomfortable for you. Of course, I have no illusions. My daughter will either take my advice or not. I fully recognize that for some people, this advice is not only hopelessly outdated, it is also sexist. Some might even think this advice could be dangerous, in that it does not cover birth control before marriage or could lead my daughter to an unsatisfying sex life. But I can't be a phony, espousing the virtues of promiscuity when I don't believe they are good for anybody. Double standards may be sexist and outdated, but the last time I checked it's still the girl who gets pregnant. And a baby needs a mother and a father, both of whom are fully capable of and committed to raising a child. My children know they can come to me with any issue and I will be there for them. But they also know that I believe that if you want to live a moral life, then you cannot separate the act of sex from love. ■

ask yourself

1. How comfortable are you with your sexual boundaries?

2. Have you ever slept with a guy just because he wanted to, even if you didn't want to?

3. How long do you make a guy chase you before you sleep with him, if you do?

4. Have you ever tried not sleeping with a guy until you were sure you were in love?

5. Have you ever accidentally gotten pregnant? What did you learn from that experience?

Living Together Before Marriage: Why?

A Jewish mother does not advise you to live together before marriage if your goal is to get married to that same guy one day. Why? Use your *kepele* (your head). Why would a guy choose to get married if he gets all the benefits of marriage by living together, without the burdens? Why offer up all the fun stuff without requiring some of the hard stuff? Why should he get to see you in your pretty underwear without having to accompany you to your parents' on the holidays or help pay for all those pretty negligees?

The research on this bolsters our premise: If you live with a guy for a long period of time before marriage (as opposed to just a short time with the intention of becoming married), your chances of long-term survival as a couple do not increase. Moreover, economically, you are often worse off. This is because when people just live together, they see themselves as single, parallel engines of finance, not a joint unit. They figure they can walk out at any time, so why combine the bank accounts? When they break up, often the woman is left worse off economically with no legal recourse, even if she has been the equivalent of a wife. In the vast majority of situations only legal marriage protects the right of each spouse to an equitable share of what the couple has accumulated over time.

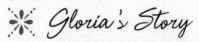 *Gloria's Story*

    In my day, people simply did not live together before they got married. We never saw the need for long engagements either, unless men were going to war. If you are very young, why are you engaged in the first place, unless you want to get married right away? If you are older, why wait? I view engagement as a waiting period, but if you require more than a year to decide if you are doing the right thing, you might as well keep dating. ■

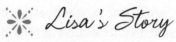

Lisa's Story

I got the message to Bill that after three years together at Johns Hopkins, we were either getting married or breaking up. Either I was going to New York to attend law school with a ring on my finger, or I was going as a single girl. I figured he might propose that summer. But Bill surprised me and proposed in March of my senior year. Bill is a traditional guy. He actually flew to New York to ask my father for my hand in marriage, before coming to propose to me in Baltimore, having already bought me a beautiful diamond ring. He got down on one knee.

I didn't live with Bill until after we got married. Our first apartment was at 300 Mercer Street in Manhattan. Everything was fresh and new. Aunt Cooky threw me a surprise bridal shower at her house. I don't understand couples who would rather live together before getting married just because they want to save up for a ring. To me, the ring itself is not important—it's just a token—and you can trade up to a nicer ring if you want when your fortunes improve. What's important is getting it in the right order: first the dating, then the commitment vows, then the living together. ■

Jill's Story

One of the rules I learned from my mother is to never move to a city for a man without a ring and obviously never move in with a man without a ring. Doing either goes against reason if your goal is to get married. From his point of view, why get married when you can live together? What's in it for the girl?

The old-fashioned saying "Why marry the cow when you can get the milk for free?" is true. It is exactly why someone who wants to get married and close the deal holds out. I probably told my first husband, Steven, this wisdom by our third date. He got the message and knew I would not move back from Boston to New York for him unless we became engaged. We commuted to see each other almost every weekend that summer until he asked me to marry him.

Much later, when I was dating Bobby, I made a rule that even if Bobby came over to my apartment, Allyson could never wake up and see him there. Of course when Ally went to her dad for weekends, Bobby would stay over, but we both viewed it as temporary. We were passionately in love and knew we would get married. It was very important for me to set a good example for Ally. ■

All Things Being Equal, It's a Lot Easier to Have a Relationship with Someone of the Same Faith

You knew this was coming, right? Yes, we know plenty of people, Jewish and non-Jewish, who do not care about this issue. The idea of being with someone of an entirely different culture or faith might even intrigue them. We also know people who are offended by this idea; they think it is prejudiced to marry only people of your own faith or heritage.

There is still a large group of very observant Jews who would banish a child from the clan for marrying out of the faith, just like in *Fiddler on the Roof.* We are not from this group; we would never do such a thing, even though Mommy may have threatened it from time to time.

But we strongly believe that Jews should marry Jews, Christians should wed Christians and so on. Why? For one thing, it is a lot easier. You don't have to fight about every Bris, baptism or Bar Mitzvah. Marriage is hard anyway; why pile on more difficulty?

In addition to the pragmatic, for Jews there is also the principle. We have a duty to our ancestors to keep the faith. The faith of Judaism is what keeps us together as a people. Statistics show that fewer interfaith couples practice Judaism than those in which both members are Jewish. If we want the values of the Jewish people to be passed down, we need to marry Jews, or people who are willing to convert to Judaism. In general, we think it is a lot easier for people of the same faith to marry each other, because it's so much easier on yourselves and your parents. But if you are of different faiths and decide to marry, at least make sure you agree beforehand as to what religion you will raise your children. Don't leave that biggie to decide after the ceremony.

Notice that we put this particular piece of advice in the dating section, not the marriage section. Why? The Jewish mother believes in avoiding heartache. Therefore, if you are looking for a commitment, we strongly advise you to date only those whom you would consider eligible to marry—and in our opinion, that should be someone who shares your faith. Why fall in love only to have to break it off? Romeo and Juliet you are not, God forbid.

Ever think of becoming a Jew? If you watched Charlotte convert in the *Sex and the City* series, you'll know it's no easy feat. Much studying and many ritual observances are required. Plus the rabbis insist that an individual not convert merely for the sake of marrying another Jew. They realize the commitment to the faith must come from one's own belief system; it will not last if it is imposed by another or done impulsively as a way to get permission to marry. If you are serious about converting, you should know that the only kind of conversion recognized in Israel is one handled by an Orthodox rabbi. We think this is grossly unfair, but the Israelis didn't ask us, and that is their rule. From a Jew's point of view, we say this: If you'd like to become a member of our tribe, by all means, we'd love to have you. But have you really thought about it? Mull it over—you may change your mind. It's not so easy being a Jew.

Despite the fact that our mothers drilled this rule into us, none of us—Gloria, Lisa or Jill—obeyed this rule all of the time. And in each case, we indeed courted heartache. "Do as I say, not as I do"—isn't that the saying?

Jill's Story

When I was a teenager, I dated a lot of guys who drove white Corvettes. At fourteen, I fell in love with a guy named Michael who was twenty-one and in college. Can you imagine? Eventually, I introduced him to my family as Michael Sniderman, a nice Jewish boy. Only his name wasn't Michael Sniderman, it was Michael Baladucci, and he was Italian and Catholic, not Jewish. Even then I knew what the rules were; I just didn't obey them. But when it came time for me to get serious, I only dated Jewish guys. I didn't want any more heartache and I definitely wanted a big, beautiful wedding. Mommy was really clear on that one—"If you don't marry a Jew . . . not only am I not making the wedding, I am not coming either." ∎

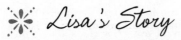 ## *Lisa's Story*

I was always the good girl. It would never have occurred to me to lie to my parents. So when I started dating a minister's son named Ian my freshman year, I reported that fact in my weekly telephone call from college. One weekend, two weekends, three weekends. On the fourth weekend, when the weekly report still included a date with Ian, my dad got on the phone and told me that if I did not break up with Ian that exact same night, I was to consider myself an ex-student of Johns Hopkins. I would be coming home that Thanksgiving to stay, permanently.

My first reaction was laughter. I thought he was kidding. Then it turned into hysteria. The truth is I was really shocked. I never expected my parents to threaten me like this. I always knew they wanted me to date Jewish guys and marry one; they were very clear on this issue. But I also thought they trusted my judgment, and now they had overreacted about a very casual dating relationship. What did I do? I broke up with Ian. I'll never forget what Ian said that night: "The only reason I'll accept for you breaking up with me is because I'm not Jewish." Um, yes. Yeah, that was the reason. Ian's roommate, Bill, later told me that Ian had been in love with me. That is the same Bill I have been married to for twenty-eight years. ∎

ask yourself

1. How important is your faith to you?

2. How important is your faith to your family?

3. Do you want to raise your children with the same faith you were raised with?

4. Is this an issue you are willing to compromise on, or is this a deal breaker?

5. Would either of you consider converting?

In Conclusion

Dating may be gut-wrenching and heartbreaking, but it is also the stuff of every great romantic comedy. "'Tis better to have loved and lost than never to have loved at all" may not have been written by a Jew (thank you, Alfred, Lord Tennyson), but it surely could have been written by the Jewish mother. We want you to plunge into life, and feel all the joy of love, despite the risk of heartbreak. Use both your head and heart to find the one who is right for you. Just remember, if you've made a mistake, your life is not over. As Grandma Helen always used to say, "There's another bus coming." Hop on. We might have a nice guy for you to sit next to.

3

Beauty and Health

*Let's face it; it's hard to undo
a first impression, and if a first
impression is really lousy, you won't
have the chance to make a second.*

We are discussing health and beauty together in one chapter because we see beauty as a reflection of good health and because good health radiates its own kind of beauty. But if there is one thing the Jewish mother never takes for granted, it is the health of herself and her loved ones. We mean never. Never. Lisa wakes up every morning and says a gratefulness prayer that her arms and legs move and that she is free of pain. Recent health scares that affected Bobby and their Jonathan have made Jill more aware than ever of the fragility of life. And we won't begin to recite the litany of bridge partners Mommy has lost in the last few years. Living in Florida means instant immersion into the details of every single thing that can possibly go wrong in your body. *Oy vey!*

Nonetheless, here is Mommy's philosophy of life:

Rich is better than poor

Smart is better than dumb

Young is better than old

Thin is better than fat

Tall is better than short

Pretty is better than ugly

We all know these statements aren't necessarily true—there are lots of wonderful poor, dumb, old, fat people out there. (We're kidding. . . . Where's your sense of humor?) But let's face it; it's hard to undo a first impression, and if a first impression is really lousy, you won't have the chance to make a second. Maybe you aren't tall, thin and twenty-five, but taking pride in your appearance no matter what your age or stature tells people that you value yourself. Jewish women are all about self-respect. Plus, do you really think all those anchorwomen get on television strictly because of their brains and experience? Get real.

Everyone has a different perception of beauty. Some cultures value a rounder figure, others a certain skin tone or hair color. Rarely do people see themselves as others do. If you ask people what they would like to fix about themselves, you'd be surprised at their answers—teeth, feet, eyes, features you might not consider flaws at all.

Jewish women have a cultural obsession with physical beauty, which is not always the healthiest thing for ourselves or our families. We inflict and have been subject to countless admonitions to stand up straight, avoid desserts, and change our hairstyles. How many girls did we know who got nose jobs at sixteen? It was almost a rite of passage. Mommy always said (we kid you not) that she chose Daddy for his nose. Our family is both shallow and deep.

Grandma Syl used to say, "Beauty is as beauty does," but what she really meant was "You need to be beautiful on the outside, but beauty alone is not enough." She would say this as we were picking at the divine Ebinger's blackout cake that always sat on her yellow kitchen table. Of course Grandma Syl was right. If you are not beautiful on the inside, you eventually appear ugly to people as they get to know you. Think about your best friend's eye color. Do you even remember it? Yet we're sure if you were to describe her, you'd say she was lovely. We do not mistake superficial good looks for inner beauty, the true and lasting kind. But what's wrong with having both? The Jewish mother wants it all.

Since Looks Count, Our Beauty Secrets

We believe the three most important variables that affect your appearance are hair, weight and skin. All are a reflection of good health, and we realize that disease and medications can affect these aspects of your appearance at times. In general, however, a good figure, lovely hair and clear skin guarantee that you are a pretty person to the rest of us, even if you may worry that your nose is crooked or your eyes are small. Don't worry too much about your features—that's why we have makeup. If you possess two out of three of these aspects, you are probably still attractive but not the knockout you are capable of being. If you have only one of these beauty assets right now, then our advice is to begin working on one of the others. When we talk about hair, weight and skin, what we mean is this:

Hair: A flattering cut and color are essential. We are not snobs when it comes to the process—all we care about is the result. Our Aunt Nessie has the most gorgeous hair, and she colored it herself for years. The great thing about changing your hairstyle is that it is the quickest and easiest way to dramatically improve your appearance. Plus it's fun to experiment; sometimes we go to the flea market in Florida just to try on wigs.

Skin: If you have acne, get rid of it, preferably without resorting to potentially dangerous medicines. If you have acne scars, consult a good dermatologist or plastic surgeon. Many are now recommending "blue light" or other laser treatments. If you do not want a laser treatment, then find excellent cover-up/fill-in makeup. Do not neglect this aspect of your appearance, as your skin quality reflects your overall health and energy aura. (And by the way, make sure you get a "mole patrol" checkup regularly for skin cancers.)

Weight: We have a lot of sympathy for this issue; if there is one thing we identify with, it is being overweight. However, if you want to be at your most attractive, you must be more thin than fat. You know the cliché: "Which is it— if you look better, you'll feel better, or if you feel better, you'll look better?" It's irrelevant. Obesity is a health issue. If you are too heavy, please change your diet. If necessary, have gastric bypass surgery. Being of healthy weight is the single most important thing you can do for your appearance and your health.

Shall we write an entire book on our own weight neuroses? We could—we are Jewish, after all. Most of us were born with body types that do not resemble Heidi Klum's, and yet we beat ourselves up about our bodies anyway. Nature or nurture? Who the hell knows? How many dollars have been paid to how many shrinks to discuss how many body-image issues? Here are a few stories:

Body Image

How do we keep our figures? Gloria never eats sitting down, only standing up. (Didn't you know there are no calories when you eat standing up?). Jill picks at food, throws water on it, and throws in a few chocolate squares instead of a meal. Plus Jill drinks a lot of diet soda—she is never without her diet soda, which Gloria and Lisa constantly nag her to stop drinking, because they believe diet soda to be an incredibly unhealthy substance. Lisa eats whatever she wants and then moans and complains about it. That's why she is still fighting those last ten pounds.

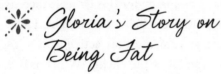

Gloria's Story on Being Fat

I never remember a time in my early years when I wasn't chubby. From "chubby" I went to heavy. By the time I started high school I weighed about 140. When I graduated I was 150 and when I entered college I was 160 pounds, a lot for my five-foot-four-inch frame. At a time when most girls look their best, I was at my worst and would stay that way for a few months into my freshman year. Toward the end of that year, I began to lose the weight. By the time I left college in Vermont a year and a half later, I weighed 128.

The following Christmas I was invited to a party in New York. While I was there I met a guy from the college that I had left six months before. He didn't recognize me. He was making a play for me when I told him who I was. He was shocked and asked me up to Vermont for the big dance. I refused to go, but I felt really, really good about myself. I also realized a very important thing. Your first impression is the most important. People don't really see you after that. Even though I had lost the weight gradually while I was still at that school, no one really took notice until I left. Then they "resaw" me with new eyes. ■

Jill's View

I have a lot of food noise in my head and always have. Was I born with it, or was it maybe that Mom sang the chorus every time I put on a "few"? I have always been within 12 pounds of what I weigh now, except when I was pregnant with Ally. After eighteen months, I was in the 140 range I started at before pregnancy, and sixteen years later I got down to 130, which is a great weight for me. Why did I take so long to go down to my best weight? I have no idea. I am so much happier now. I admit my breast reduction helped me lose the last few pounds. Every day I negotiate my meals in my head. For example, if I have an ice cream, I won't eat a big dinner. If I know I am going out for dinner, I won't eat a big lunch. I tell Ally that no particular food is forbidden, but portions count. Sharing is the best—you save money and eat everything you want in proper portions. Restaurant portions are way too big for anyone to eat regularly if you want to sustain a normal weight.

You need to eat breakfast to start the engine and eat five small meals a day for fuel. If you starve your body, your body will literally hold on to your fat in order to reserve the fuel. Tell the waiter to wrap up half the meal before serving it. Now you have dinner for two nights. For me, eating offers diminishing returns. Aren't the first few bites of something decadent the most satisfying? I have been "killing" food for a long time, as I talked about in an episode of the show when I killed some French fries by pouring water on them. ■

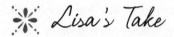 *Lisa's Take*

I hardly ever go clothes shopping because my figure always looks awful to me in the dressing room mirror. I know that my clothes size is normal; I even think I look good naked. Yet somehow, trying on clothes always makes me feel fat and ugly. Recently I got the news that my thyroid is probably failing, which is as good an excuse as any on which to blame my weight issues. Not that I'll do anything about it. As far as my actual diet goes, I graze on a lot of dark chocolate. ■

Our Beauty Basics

Here are our views about specific beauty techniques. You will see we don't always agree.

1. *Facials*: Jill and Gloria are big fans of facials—but no more than one per month. Go to a salon with a good reputation. Make sure you get a referral before having someone touch your face.

2. *Manicures*: Jill likes manis and pedis and believes nails should be kept short. Lisa likes French pedicures but thinks regular manicures are a waste of money because she always chips within two days. Gloria doesn't like either manis or pedis because she is afraid of infections.

None of us are fans of fake acrylics. Remember that the salon you attend must follow the strictest hygienic standards and be immaculately clean—look for sterilized equipment, stored separately for each client, and examine the soaking basins yourself.

3. *Botox*: Gloria, Lisa and Jill all admit to using Botox, but in varying amounts. Lisa goes once a year, Jill once every six months and Gloria once a week . . . just kidding. Jill advises that Botox works best if it is reinjected before the last shot wears off.

4. *Breasts*: Breast implants are a nonissue in our group, as each of us is plentifully endowed, and then some. Jill recently had her breasts reduced and is thrilled with the results. She believes it has changed her life, enhanced her body image and given her freedom to wear all the clothes that were off-limits for the past thirty years. She has been trying to persuade Lisa to do the procedure; so far, no dice.

5. *Plastic Surgery*: Gloria believes in fixing all of it—ears, eyes, face, whatever you can, whatever you want to do. She thinks plastic surgery is like orthodontics on the face—both are intended to achieve the same end result, which is a nicer appearance. Of course, we've all seen botched jobs, and we've seen people who keep going long after they should have stopped. We feel sorry for those who cannot stop trying to make themselves "beautiful" and end up looking terribly distorted. The key? If you want to get plastic surgery, go to a great doctor. And know when enough is enough.

6. *Liposuction*: We pause. Have you heard the story of Olivia Goldsmith, the author who died having liposuction?

For what? Thighs that were a little too fat? Lisa is skeptical of the whole thing. Jill thinks lipo should be used as a last resort to reshape a figure only if you can't lose any more weight. Jill's advice: Don't use lipo to take out what you wouldn't want to see elsewhere. Don't lipo your stomach to get thin, because when you put on a few pounds you will most likely gain it in your arms and breasts.

7. *Tanning Salons*: We don't have to recite the latest medical data to warn you to stay away from those fake rays. Why expose your skin to anything harmful when you can get a great spray tan in a bottle? Jill is a huge fan of spraying it on. Spray-tan side effect? You look and feel thinner.

8. *Going Too Far*: We know there are now surgeries out there that advertise changing the way the most private parts of our bodies look. It's a *shanda*—a disgrace—that otherwise capable surgeons would prey on women's insecurities. Unless there is a genetic deformity, there is no discussion.

9. *Hygiene and Grooming*: Must we elaborate here? Beauty begins with a shower. Also it's best to be hairless where you should be. We'll leave it at that.

❋ Gloria's View on Plastic Surgery

I do believe that because I felt so unattractive for many of my formative years, I am more concerned about looks than are many of my contemporaries. I make no apologies for this. If you do want cosmetic surgery, the most important factor is finding the best doctor. A doctor can help you understand the procedure and its limitations. If you have an unrealistic view of yourself or if the surgeries are too frequent, then you need to seek counseling. ■

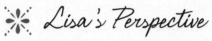

Lisa's Perspective

My mother did look like a real-life movie star when we were kids, but only on Saturday nights. During the week, it was jeans and no makeup, but on Saturday night, Mommy was a glamour girl, complete with the "fall" hairpiece and gobs of fabulous makeup and accessories. I used to watch in awe as she got dressed. I didn't think Mom needed a facelift when she got one. But she did think so and it's her face.

Intellectually, I hate the idea that we women have to maintain a youthful appearance to keep our social standing. But emotionally, I don't like looking sad, angry or ugly. Lines can do that to you. Therefore, I make no rules. If the turkey-gobble neck appears, I'm running to the best doctor I can find. Even Grandma Syl had that done, and she was seventy when she did it! ■

Jill's Ideas

I think you need to constantly maintain your appearance and make subtle adjustments. I am horrified by some of the faces I see. I know people who have had so much work done that they look like freaks at forty-five. One woman I know got such high cheek implants that she looked Asian—and she wasn't. Of course, when I asked her for advice after I tried some saline in my lips, she told me she never did anything to her face. Did she think I was blind? I don't think you should lie about plastic surgery. If you do it, own it. ∎

Note: If you are thinking of doing anything that requires a doctor, make sure you read the section in this chapter called "Finding the Best Doctor." If there is one thing Jewish women know, it's how to find the best plastic surgeon. And by the way, we would think nothing of going to Brazil, if that's where the best doctor just happens to be located. Call it a "working vacation."

ask yourself

1. Are you self-conscious about aspects of your appearance?

2. If so, can you change those aspects yourself? What will it take?

3. Is there something about your appearance that you cannot change on your own that significantly affects your self-image? Have you done research into your options about changing your appearance?

4. Is your confidence affected by what other people think of you and not by what you think of yourself?

5. How much do you judge other people by their appearance? (Be honest; no one's looking.) Do you live up to the standards that you judge others by?

A Word on Fashion

Gloria and Jill are the fashion plates in the family. Gloria should have been a fashion designer, but since that never happened she has spent her life critiquing other people's clothing and surreptitiously designing better looks for them. Now she buys material for herself and designs it with "the boys" in Florida, her close friends who can sew as well as design. Gloria and Jill take clothing very seriously. Lisa does not, but she is affected by the Jewish mother voice in her head that tells her it is important to present a great appearance, even if you hate shopping and would rather stay in your pajamas all day.

Actually, Gloria has a particular theory on the origin of today's super-skinny fashion model. If you look back at the models of the 1950s, they were a good three inches shorter and at least twenty pounds heavier. Have you ever wondered why? Why do today's runway models look like clothes hangers? Flat chests, no hips, all legs? Gloria thinks it is because a majority of the designers of women's clothing are gay men. Whom do gay men usually find attractive? It isn't women with curves, that's for sure. The men designing women's clothing today (with some exceptions, of course) are subconsciously designing for a young male frame. Think about it.

We've been to those runway shows. If you think the models look tall and thin on the television set, imagine them without the extra ten pounds that the camera adds. Lisa had to literally look away while watching the Project Runway show live in Bryant Park—it was that painful to see. No wonder those models never smile; they are clearly starving to death. (We know we get particularly cranky when we are hungry.) The three of us think it's about time that we women create a reasonable standard of beauty for ourselves. We should insist on being able to buy clothes for actual women with bodies that have hips, busts and legs that do not resemble a giraffe's. Do you think those clothes are easy to find? Have you gone shopping lately?

JILL'S FASHION AND MAKEUP TIPS

1.   You are what you wear. If in doubt, do not wear it. If you don't feel good in your clothing, you will radiate insecurity and others will notice.

2.   For skirt length, remember the "hand test": If you place your hands down by your sides, your skirt length must be longer than your fingertips.

3.   Always have double-sided fashion tape and scissors on hand, to cut out tags, repair falling hems and fix your bustline.

4.   For a fancy event, a watch should be a piece of jewelry. If you don't have a dress watch, just wear a bracelet.

5.   Shoes should be comfortable first, look good second. I like platform shoes because the arch isn't that steep and it gives you the height you need.

6.   Buy good basics—they last. Then add accessories to change the look every season.

7.   Always use a good tailor. The fit makes all the difference.

8.   Clothes are made to fit four general body types: apple, hourglass, ruler and pear. Know your type and dress accordingly.

9.   Nails should be trimmed and light-colored.

10. Fake eyelashes do open your eyes. Try them.

11. Moisturize your face and hands as often as possible.

12. Do not buy a piece of clothing just because it is cheap or on sale. There are tons of stores that have fabulous clothes for less, so make sure that you love something before you buy it. I still have tags on clothes that were a "great deal."

13. If you know you are being photographed, photograph yourself first before you leave. Often, you will look great in an outfit in person but not as great on camera. Take the photo just to make sure.

14. If you wear lip liner, keep checking it.

15. Don't fidget, play with your hair or bite your nails. Also, don't slouch. This is where I start to hear my mother's voice come out of my mouth.

16. Always bring a sweater. The Jewish mother is never without a sweater.

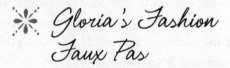

❋ Gloria's Fashion Faux Pas

When I was around thirteen, Mother had given me money to buy some clothes. It was the first time she allowed me to go shopping alone. I went to the city and found myself in a little shop. I bought summer clothes and a bathing suit. The suit had a black back and a white front with a huge peacock on it. Looking back, it really was dreadful, but I came home so happy and proud of my purchases. Mother took one look at me in the bathing suit and went berserk. She hated it, which sent my ego down below the basement floor. My father was much nicer and a lot more supportive, as dads are of their little girls. When Mother insisted that I return everything, I asked her to go back to the store with me. She refused. I dreaded going back there, but I managed. After that episode, I had zero confidence in my own judgment about clothes. I never went shopping alone again until many years later. ■

Jill's Story

It takes a lot of work and many details and decisions to put together a red-carpet look. I actually become my mother and obsess over what to wear. I might try on fifty dresses before deciding what I will wear and hate forty-nine of them on me. Here is an example of one event: I was asked to present at the LOGO awards in 2009. I called up my friend and designer Marc Bauwer because he has the sexiest clothes. Before my then-recent boob reduction, I had always had to wear a bra, but now I was excited to see what I could fit into. A week before the event I went to his showroom, and after trying on twenty dresses, I found the perfect one, a solid red gown. What next? Hair and makeup. Marc said long straight hair and big red lips. He hired his GLAM squad to meet me in a hotel room where the event was being held. We got started at three in the afternoon for a six p.m. event.

It took three hours to do the hair extensions and makeup. At six, Marc walked me down the red carpet and I felt like a queen. It was worth every second. ■

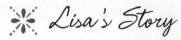

Lisa's Story

Hey, I know what I wear is important, but there is another part of me that just doesn't care. The night I met Bill, remember I told you I wore my new fancy jeans and gold shiny vest over an electric-blue shirt? I know I looked sexy and that looking that way made me feel more attractive. No doubt wearing that outfit on that night changed my life. If I had dressed dumpy, I might never have caught Bill's eye or been in the mood to flirt. For me, fashion is fun to look at and occasionally fun to play with. When I have an important occasion, I pay attention. When I do not have that occasion, I wear blue jeans and a sweater. Hopefully the jeans fit and the sweater isn't too baggy. If my outfit doesn't fit, Mom will surely let me know. ■

If It's Right for You, It's Not Right for Me: Fashion Competition

There shall be no fashion competition between mother and daughter. Gloria and the aunts are adamant on this issue. When shopping together, we often heard, "If it's right for you, it's not right for me," and because Jewish mothers are nothing if not repetitive, "If it's right for me, it's not right for you." Do you see the subtle difference there? Neither do we.

The principle is very simple: If an outfit looks good on the daughter and is appropriate for the daughter, then the daughter should wear it. If the daughter wears it, the mother should not, because the outfit would be too youthful and stylish and maybe a little too revealing for the mom. Conversely, an outfit that would be appropriate for the mother to wear would not be appropriate for the daughter, as it would presumably be a little too matronly for her. And if your sixteen-year-old is wearing a bikini, for goodness sakes, wear a one-piece suit.

Fashion competition between mother and daughter is dangerous territory. Of course, today fashion trends do overlap more than they did in the past. The rigid generation gap that existed when we were growing up seems to have gone away, which makes the line more fuzzy regarding what is age-appropriate. Everyone wears blue jeans and T-shirts. But even with jeans, there are some styles that work for teenagers and others that work for moms. You know it when you see it—the sixty-year-old trying to look like a babe, or a mother trying to dress like her teenage daughter. It's embarrassing. But more than that, it sends dangerous messages to the daughter: "Mommy is afraid to grow old"; "Mommy is trying to look sexy"; or worst of all, "Mommy thinks she is prettier, or sexier, than I am." These are terrible, terrible messages. The answer is simple. Women should go through life looking as elegant as they can for the age they are.

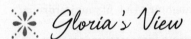

Gloria's View

I think sixty-year-old women who try to look thirty end up looking ninety. Dressing like a Barbie doll at fifty makes you look like an idiot. ■

Jill's Story

I take great care to dress appropriately, and I try not to outshine my daughter or create a competitive atmosphere. Ally and I communicate through shopping and it is a great sharing experience. She values my opinion and I value hers. We don't always agree, but since I am paying . . . you know how it usually ends up, right? ■

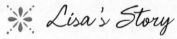

Lisa's Story

Thank God my sixteen-year-old daughter actually has a healthy body image. This is somewhat of a miracle in our group, for which I take no credit whatsoever. We have a very outspoken relationship—if something is too old for her or too sexy, I tell her, "Take it off, now," and she does. If I wear a style that she thinks is inappropriate, she tells me the same, and I always listen, even if I don't agree. If it's right for her, it's not right for me, and vice versa. ■

ask yourself

1. Did your mother compete with you in the fashion realm?

2. If so, how did it make you feel?

3. Do you steal your twelve-year-old's clothes? (What, you can't afford new ones for yourself?)

4. Are you sensitive to your daughter's view of your wardrobe?

5. What clothes are inappropriate for you to wear at your age? Do you wear them anyway? Why?

The Dreaded E-Word: Exercise

There is a generation gap on this one for the Jewish mother. The older Jewish moms—for example, Mommy and her mother—rarely exercised. Bending was about it, and even bending was to be avoided if someone else was around to pick it up. Maybe this is because people used to get more exercise during the day. Mothers didn't need to run on a treadmill going nowhere for hours to prove they could sweat. If they wanted to sweat, they could

squeeze into the back room of Loehmann's and try on special designer clothes on sale from the middle of the rack.

We of the somewhat younger generation power sweat. We've got
it all covered; call the young Jewish mom for the latest in Pilates,
yoga, bikram yoga, the Reformer, Bodypump, Jump and Pump, Pump
Your Eyeballs Out, whatever. Our preoccupation with our less-than-
perfect bodies has many of us living in the gym. Personally, we don't
like running on treadmills. We run and run and don't get anywhere.
On the other hand, we love to Zumba. Put on a little Latin music and
the Jewish mother is singing, "*Cuando, cuando, cuando,*" all day long.

✳ *Gloria's Point of View*

I don't do any formal exercise. I should. Lisa tells me
every day to start a yoga class. But I'm afraid at my age to
start—I could end up hurting myself and be worse off
than I am now. I just try to stay active. I get up very early
to do my errands. I usually take an afternoon nap and go
out to dinner or to play cards with Sol. ■

✳ *Lisa's View*

If only talking burned more calories—I would be so
thin! For me, the best part about any exercise class is at
the end when you are lying on the floor. I know exercise is
good for me. I have much more energy on the days I do
exercise, and it gives me the best chance of preventing
Alzheimer's disease. (*Kaynahorah* knock wood.) But if I
don't make it to the gym for the eight thirty a.m. class,
the day is gone because my schedule is so packed. I love
New York City because I get my exercise just by walking
around. Dancing, walking and talking with my friends are
my favorite forms of exercise. Plus lying on the floor. ■

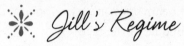

Jill's Regime

Exercise? I remember playing tennis as a child. Daddy told me to stop playing as soon as I started to sweat. I think even now I subconsciously stop working out when I start to sweat. Thanks, Daddy!

I did Pilates regularly for two years and recommend it highly. It improved my posture and flattened my stomach with minimal sweating.

I started to work out again before the third season of *The Real Housewives*. All the ladies have stepped it up, and I decided to do the same. The only way I get through exercise on the machines is by watching TV at the same time. I also have a music playlist specifically for the gym—all my favorites from the disco era. I strongly suggest bringing an iPod to the gym loaded with movies and music. If you can watch an entire episode of any hour-long show, you just had a great cardio workout! ■

ask yourself

1. How often do you exercise? (Using the remote control doesn't count.)

2. Is exercise a priority for you? Why not?

3. Do you consider bending an exercise?

4. Can you figure out something you actually enjoy doing that would require you to move your body more, like walking with a friend, taking dance lessons, or moving your refrigerator farther away from your bedroom?

Finding the Best Doctor

So far we've discussed beauty, fashion and exercise, all things related to appearance. But health is integral to everything. Looking for a doctor? You've bought the right book.

Just how important is finding the *best* doctor, as opposed to merely a *good* doctor? Do you really want us to recite all the stories of botched procedures and misdiagnoses? Obviously, if you'd used the *best* doctor, you would have saved yourself pain and aggravation. The Jewish mother has an instinctive radar for the best doctor for every single specialty on earth. Endocrinology? No problem—just name the zip code. Best plastic surgeon? Depends on whether you want to stay in the States or fly to Brazil; you tell us. The real Jewish mother is a card-carrying DWD—Doctor Without a Diploma. (Who needs four years of medical school anyway? The point is to *find* the right doctor, not *become* one.)

How do you find the best doctor? The most important principle here is "Do not be shy." It isn't a matter of privacy, yours or theirs, when it comes to these issues. After all, do you really think anyone else is as concerned about your health as you are? They've got their own problems. If you or someone you love is seriously ill, do all of these things simultaneously and as quickly as possible:

1. Ask everyone you know who had that particular disease: Who treated them? How happy were they? Where did the doctor go to school? Was he or she a *mensch*? How quickly can you get an appointment?

2. Do research on the Internet. But take your findings in stride. Every person's case is unique, and until your doctor tells you your particular set of facts, do not go into panic mode. We've been in panic mode, and it usually isn't necessary.

3. Call the doctors you know and ask them for the best doctor they *personally* know.

4. Call your nearest high-prestige hospital and ask for the chairman of the department of the particular specialty you are seeking. Insist on seeing that doctor personally and as soon as possible.

5. When we need a surgeon, we look for someone with good hands. We assume he has a good head and we don't especially care if he has a good heart. Ask about the hands. Don't forget. The other doctors and the nurses will know exactly what you mean. If you get a weird, funny smile when you ask about the hands, you haven't found the best doctor yet. Keep searching.

Once you find the doctor you want to see, it is fine to beg and plead for the next appointment. You can even show up without an appointment. Being nice to the receptionist and the nurses will help too.

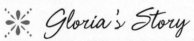 *Gloria's Story*

Years ago, my good friend Lucia recommended a very fine gynecologist on Park Avenue. He was still practicing in his eighties; I like to say that he forgot more than the average doctor will ever know. One day Lucia's daughter, a young woman in her twenties, was distraught because a famous hospital had told her they needed to remove her uterus to prevent her from getting cancer. I asked Lucia if she had taken her daughter to our Park Avenue doctor and she said no, she had not thought of it. Dumb, very dumb. Our doctor promptly reviewed the slides himself, then sent them to California for analysis. Guess what? Lucia's daughter never did have cancer and she still has her uterus, as well as two healthy children. The lesson is simple: Find the best doctors, and when you've found them, remember to go to them! ■

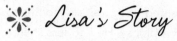 *Lisa's Story*

For Mom and Dad's twenty-fifth wedding anniversary, we threw a surprise party at our home in Woodmere. Every invitation came as a large page of a book, which had to be completed and brought to the party. I drew my page as a medical diploma, officially crowning my mother as a DWD, a Doctor Without a Diploma. Long may she reign. I, too, have earned a DWD.

I love what my rabbi, Israel Stein, says: "When you are sick, pray to God—and go to a doctor." I often devote my radio shows to exploring medical innovations. I admit I have an ulterior motive—not only do I educate my audience, but I also stay informed. You never know when the knowledge will be useful. When my father had lung cancer last year, I contacted one of the finest pulmonary cancer surgeons in the world. However, before moving forward with this particular surgeon, I corroborated his credentials by speaking with a surgeon at my alma mater, Johns Hopkins. I also did research on the Internet and asked every doctor I knew whom they would recommend. When we found the right surgeon, I asked the surgeon's staff about his hands. After that, I was satisfied. We were very, very lucky, thank God, *kaynahorah*. Dad needed no follow-up treatment of any kind and is, thank God, all better. ■

Jill's Story

Bobby was diagnosed with prostate cancer about eight years ago. How? He had a PSA test that was a little elevated and the doctor wanted us to wait six months to retest. I said no. I wanted a biopsy. He had less than a 15 percent chance of cancer, but guess what? He had it. Bobby's first reaction was to keep it a secret. That lasted about three hours. Then I decided to tell everyone so we could find the best doctor. My father's partner had been recently diagnosed, and I worked with his two sons, who were both doctors (of course). We sent their father and Bobby to the best surgeon in New York. Bobby recovered beautifully and, thank God, that cancer has not reappeared. The moral of the story is to ask everyone for help and the answer will present itself. ■

ask yourself

1. Are you completely satisfied with your medical care? If so, congratulations. You win a prize for being the only person in the world who can say that.

2. Do you need to find a good doctor? Take the advice above. If you do and you still don't have the right doctor, contact us and we'll give you a referral. We're sure we can find you the *best* doctor.

"Alternative" Health— We'll Try Anything

Jewish mothers embrace the best of Western and Eastern philosophies of healing, even though we have no idea why some of them work. What do we care why they work? All we know is that we feel better. Acupuncture, reiki, chiropractic care, therapeutic massage—if it can make the pain go away, we want the number, immediately.

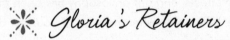

Gloria's Retainers

I do admit to having regular acupuncture, massage and chiropractic treatment for various aches and pains and ailments. Sol calls these practitioners my "retainers." I believe they work. Sometimes they are much more effective and less harmful than taking medicines. ■

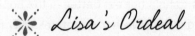

Lisa's Ordeal

My cycle has always been irregular—it took me eleven years to conceive two kids. In my thirties, my body changed, and instead of too few periods, I had too many. Occasionally the bleeding wouldn't stop; once I had to leave a cruise ship to seek medical attention. I was living on eggshells all the time. There was nothing wrong with my organs; my problem was "hormonal bleeding." I was definitely headed for an early hysterectomy, and for no good reason. A friend told me about an acupuncturist who had cured her endometriosis. I made an appointment for myself, thinking, What the hell? Since then, I have not missed a single period for more than ten years. I even recommended this acupuncturist to Ally for her arthritis. Thank God for Dr. Ho, may he live forever. ∎

Jill Seeks Help for Ally

Allyson has a rare form of arthritis called spondyloarthropathy. We have had her seen by the finest specialists and even took her to the National Institutes of Health to confirm the diagnosis, since it is so rare. But lots of medicines have side effects, and our philosophy has been that they should be taken only when needed. If you saw the early episodes of *Housewives*, you might recall when I sent Ally to a "detox" center to rid her body of impurities. Do you know the stuff they drained out of her feet was actually black? Who knows how many chemicals she had absorbed between her diet, her medicines and our environment? Anyway, that approach was an attempt to teach Ally some tools to help her eat better, in the hopes that a better diet might improve her symptoms. We are always trying to find alternative ways to treat Ally's arthritis. We never give up. ∎

ask yourself

1. Do you have a condition for which the usual medical treatment has failed you?

2. Are you open to other kinds of healing?

3. Do you know anyone who has received alternative treatments? Don't they swear by them?

In Conclusion

Would you believe that our Grandma Helen was preoccupied with her appearance until the day she died, at age 106 and a half? Completely deaf by then, even at that age she wanted to know if her hairstyle looked pretty. She would tell us how we looked as well, whether we were too fat or too thin, and of course give us her opinion of our hairstyle. (What is it with the hair in our group? It's an obsession.) People don't change. Everyone wants to look pretty; everyone feels better when they know they look good. Doesn't the Bible say "Vanity of vanities, all is vanity"? But in real life, a little vanity is usually enough. Don't endanger your health in pursuit of your vanished youth. Good health is incredibly attractive. Vitality, energy and a wide smile make all of us look beautiful, even if we don't have perfect teeth. Don't be as hard on yourself as we are on ourselves—we *know* that's not healthy. On the other hand, we must admit we look pretty good . . . don't you think?

4

Education

What you know is the one thing no one can take away from you.

You probably know that Jews value education above almost everything else, and we consider the education of women as important as the education of men. As Jewish mothers, we pride ourselves on knowing everything that is important to know. Of course, we decide what is important. While the Jewish people as a whole are called the "People of the Book" for our traditional devotion to the Torah, perhaps a more appropriate name should be the "People Who Read Everything," in honor of our well-developed affection for hardcovers, paperbacks, newspapers, magazines and whatever we find on the Internet. No Jewish home is complete without a small library in every lavatory. Wherever we are, we read.

We joke that if you put two Jews in a room, you get three opinions. In our family, maybe even four. Opinions, arguments, commentary—they are an integral part of family. What good is an education if we can't argue at the dinner table about who is right about the topic of the day? We take great pride in the members of our tribe who have contributed some of the most profound philosophical, scientific, artistic and medical advancements in human history, from Sigmund Freud, Albert Einstein and Jonas Salk, to

Ayn Rand, Gloria Steinem, Richard Rodgers and George Gershwin. Explore any sphere of learning and you are bound to find a Jew.

The Jewish approach to education is to question authority, not merely accept it. Even in religious school, we are taught to ask why. Often you will find Jews on the front lines of civil rights movements. What are they doing? In effect, they are questioning the status quo. Advocating for justice, finding the courage to speak out—this is what the Jewish mother teaches from the crib.

Why is education so important to us? Because what you know is the one thing no one can take away from you. Jews have survived inquisitions, pogroms and a Holocaust of unparalleled atrocity and scope. Our history is one of persecution and exile—they don't call us the "wandering Jews" for nothing. How did we survive? Think about it—what do lawyers, doctors, teachers, authors and scientists all have in common? They do not make things that a government can take away. We have always relied on what was in our brains, not in our hands. When all fell apart, we took our learning with us to the next place, from wherever we were.

The Grandparents: Education

We are very proud of the level of education achieved by our grandparents and great-grandparents, particularly the women in our family. Ida, Gloria's grandmother, attended business school after high school. Gloria's mother, Sylvia Levy, was part of the first graduating class of Long Island University (and lived long enough to attend her sixtieth class reunion). She then became a teacher in New York City. Her book club lasted more than fifty years, until everyone either died or moved to Florida. Sylvia saw to it that both of her daughters, Gloria and Cooky, graduated from NYU and became licensed teachers.

The best story comes from Grandma Helen, Sol's mother. Helen Goldblatt was born in a shtetl in Lithuania called Ligum. She came through Ellis Island at age 13 and lived to be 106. Grandma Helen told us that the reason her family survived the notorious pogroms in her region was because her mother was the only woman in the town who could read and write. So the non-Jewish women in the town would pay her to read and write letters for them. As a result, Grandma became friendly with them and they would tip her off before a pogrom would come into town. So you see? Education literally saved us, generations ago.

Education: The Mantra

Knowledge is the one thing you will carry with you until the day senile dementia creeps in, bite your tongue three times. The importance of learning is repeated constantly like a mantra by parents, uncles, cousins, grandparents: "Education, education, education." (Yes, this sounds like that other mantra "Location, location, location," which is also repeated in Jewish households, but only *after* you have your degree.)

☀ *Gloria's Philosophy*

I taught my girls that you can lose your gold coins, your fancy clothes, your freedom, your dignity, your position in life, your friends and sometimes even your family. But no one, as long as you are alive on this earth, can take away the knowledge you accumulate in your brains. Learn something, learn it well enough so that you can make a living at it, and make sure it's also something that you can do on your own, so that you won't need to depend on anyone else to make your living, just in case. ■

 Jill's Take

Like a dentist, my mother drilled it into my head: Education is the most important thing to give to my children. I learned this from my mother, from my grandmothers, from everyone.

Even though I practice this as a parent, I have to say, I wasn't particularly interested in school as a kid. I was busy. One day my father showed up at Lawrence High School and asked the principal, "Where is Jill?" He said, "She is in so-and-so class." My father said, "Really? Find her." Oops. I wasn't in class. Where was I? You think I remember? Obviously, my father suspected something was going on, or he wouldn't have shown up. He came home that night and didn't tell me a thing. The next day I was called into the principal's office and sent to the "rubber room" with all these really bad kids. The "rubber room" meant you sat in an empty classroom with no books and nothing to do until one P.M., when a private bus took you home. Some kids might like this but it really freaked me out. I think it was the last time I cut school. At least the last time I got caught.

But even though I didn't always do what my parents wanted, I definitely got the message. Education counts. ■

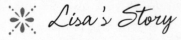

Lisa's Story

I discovered pretty early on that I loved school. I even remember loving my first homework assignment, to write my name four times. Some of my earliest friends were books. The storybooks I read as a child still sit on my shelves so I can look at them and smile, remembering the great adventures they brought me without having to leave my bedroom. In seventh grade, my English teacher inscribed my yearbook, "*To Lisa, my most inquisitive student, but you were a delight.*" After I looked up the word "inquisitive," I knew what she really meant: "Lisa, you interrupted me constantly with questions, but I liked you anyway." Some things never change. ■

ask yourself

1. How important is learning to you?

2. Did you take school seriously when you were there? Do you regret it if not?

3. Do you read the newspaper every day to keep yourself constantly learning?

4. How often do you read an entire book?

5. Do you have a social group that enjoys learning, like a book group or a continuing-education class?

The Rabbi

A rabbi is not like a priest. A priest is usually considered an intermediary between the ordinary people and God. In the Catholic faith, the ultimate priest is the pope, and he is considered by the faithful to be "infallible." Jews have no such person in their faith. Our rabbis are merely teachers—hopefully learned, ethical teachers, but teachers nonetheless. They are considered no closer to God than anyone else. We also use the term "rabbi" to mean a mentor in business; in other words, a person who is looking out for you and teaching you what you need to know to succeed.

As a teacher, the rabbi is revered in the Jewish community. Why? Because he is presumed to know the most. Knowledge is a sacred value.

ABC . . . Easy as 1,2,3 . . .

Jewish mothers believe it is never too early to teach the basics. From the minute we find out we are pregnant, we talk to our children, surrounding them with educational toys, books and music. Don't laugh—Lisa swears both her kids recognized "Edelweiss" from the womb. Read to your children from the day they are born. Don't be put off by thinking your baby can't understand *Winnie the Pooh* yet; none of us know how early our kids begin to understand language. The point is to lay the foundation early for your child to love reading. He will surely love reading if you have begun that experience as a bond together from his earliest memory.

A Word on Television:

Ah, the ubiquitous boob tube. We admit it—we love our television. Gloria and Jill particularly love theirs, and Lisa would find it difficult to survive without classic movies, shown without commercial interruptions. But watching television is no substitute for the experience of reading a book, and you are kidding yourself if you think your child is learning more from a video than he would if he sat on your lap and you read a story to him, one-on-one. Sure, it takes time and patience to read to your child, but we Jewish mothers cannot stress enough how important it is to teach your children by example that book learning is the number one way for a person to absorb information. Lisa was so fed up with fighting about this issue that she and Bill decided to remove all television connections from the home for the entire family. This experiment lasted two years, until the next Olympics, when they kept their promise to televise this occasion. Naturally, the television stayed, but this time, with strict limits. What had been accomplished? Plenty. Jon became an avid reader for life, during the crucial ages of seven to nine, and Joanna benefited as well, living in a house without television from the ages of one through three. You want your kids to be readers? Hide the clicker.

Gloria's Kvelling

We taught Lisa to say her entire alphabet before she was two. I bragged about it to everyone. She also counted on her fingers. We *kvelled*. ∎

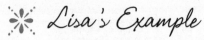

Lisa's Example

The best baby gift we received for our firstborn was a carton of baby books from our cousin Selma. I read to Jon for hours every day in his rocking chair. At two, he could recite his name, address and phone number in case he got lost. At four, Jon could read Dr. Seuss's *Hop on Pop* out loud by himself. We *kvelled*. ■

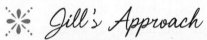

Jill's Approach

I purposely filmed a scene for the show with Allyson reading the op-ed page of *The New York Times* to identify words she didn't know and look them up. I wanted to emphasize how important vocabulary is and how we try to integrate it in the home every day. The Jewish mother is always teaching. ■

ask yourself

1. Are you laying a solid foundation for your children vis-à-vis education?

2. How many hours do you sit your kid in front of a screen? Turn it off!

3. How many books are in your house right now? When is the last time you read one?

4. Do you quiz yourself on the words you don't know? Do you keep a dictionary handy in the kitchen or eat on a place mat of a map? These are easy and fun ways to keep learning all the time.

Public vs. Private:
Which Is Better?

If you are a parent, choosing your child's school is one of the most important decisions you will make. Just as you were shaped by where you attended school, so too will your child be affected not only by what she learns in the classroom but also by the rules of the playground. Unfortunately, when it comes to education, we don't get any do-overs. But also remember that kids are resilient; once they find the right environment in which to learn, they will blossom. What is your job as a parent? To find the learning environment that is best for your child.

Which is better: public or private? Our answer: It all depends, and not only on one's pocketbook. We have friends whose children attend the most elite boarding schools on scholarships; we have others who could afford the most expensive private schools but choose the local public schools. For some families where religious education is paramount, public school is not even an option. The key is to make the decision that is right for your family and your child. First you must evaluate your options.

Jewish mothers are usually experts on the educational choices available in their community for every grade that their own kids have passed through. Ask a Jewish mother about a good preschool, and instead of answers, you will get a series of questions as the interrogation begins: "Are you looking for strong academics, good play space, religious instruction, parental involvement, certified teachers, a nice classroom, a longer day, an anti-bullying program?" These are just some of the factors that skip through her mind in a nanosecond. Really, if you don't have a Jewish friend yet and you are a parent of kids in school, you ought to go find yourself one. It will save you a lot of legwork.

Second, you need to know your child. You need to balance the pros of keeping your kid on the same school bus as the other neighborhood kids versus the cons of knowing that your kid will now have new friends who are a *shlep* away in other towns, and that your kid may now feel excluded from the after-school games on his own block. You need to decide whether the pros of the particular education your child will get in a specific private school outweigh the cons of the education he is receiving right now. We Jewish mothers are pretty good at figuring out the right questions to ask, but only you know the right answer for your family.

Gloria's Take

Forty-five years ago the world was a different place. We moved to Woodmere from Brooklyn for the good public schools, and they worked for Lisa. She did well there and got an excellent education. Jill had some problems, and it might have been wiser for us to move her to get a fresh start, but we kept at it and eventually things got better for her. ■

Jill's Story

We had considered public school for Ally, but private for us in New York City seemed the better option. Someone once told me that the most important thing he could give his children was an education, because it was irreplaceable. He was not Jewish, but it really made an impact on me. We were not rich when I had Allyson and paying for private school in New York City was a big sacrifice. It meant giving up vacations and dinners out and living in a smaller apartment. But it was the best investment I could make for our daughter.

In her current private school, they provide extra help

every day from her teachers if needed, and she has a unique one-on-one relationship with all of her teachers. They taught her not just the action of reading but the love of words. She is engaged in her subjects and looks forward to going to class. New York City public schools are overcrowded and hit-or-miss. Walking into an average middle school in New York City means metal detectors and security. There are wonderful public schools with special programs for gifted students, and I would have sent Ally to one if I couldn't have afforded private school, but I was willing to go without "stuff" before I would do that. ■

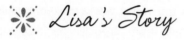

Lisa's Story

My philosophy is this: Every kid has different needs, and those needs change throughout his childhood. Jon received most of his education in public school, but for high school, private seemed a better option. Incidentally, the private school we chose was Episcopalian and they had chapel once a week, but the values of the school were totally in keeping with what we believe, so we had no issue with this. Joanna had an early Montessori education. She was bored in first grade in public school. So we switched her to a Jewish day school with a double curriculum in Hebrew and English. That worked for four years and gave her a great foundation. By sixth grade, the social scene of the same thirty girls had played itself out. She wanted a change. So Joanna re-enrolled in public school, where she is today. The school has an excellent reputation, and so far, it is working for her. But if it stops working for her, we will make a change. Does the money matter? Of course. But, like Jill, we would sacrifice whatever was necessary to find the money we need. ■

What Would Gloria Do?

Jill's Dilemma

Ally was unhappy in a private school that was convenient and familiar. Staying in that school also meant that Ally would be attending fifth grade in a middle school with older kids through eighth grade. However, if Ally transferred, she would most likely have to repeat the grade she was in because she had a November birthday. That didn't seem like the right solution either.

What Would Gloria Do?

1. *Investigate the Options.* After looking around, Jill discovered a private school that valued the uniqueness of each child. That school kept the fifth graders with the lower school, where Jill felt they belonged. And, most important, they would not require Ally to repeat her grade.

2. *Give It a Shot—Apply!* Jill and Ally decided to go for it. If you don't apply, then you never give yourself the opportunity to accept. Better you should do the rejecting than them . . . so apply! What have you got to lose?

3. *Make the Change.* Ally got in! She was relieved and happy to switch. The decision has turned out very well; she will graduate, God willing, from that school in the spring of 2010.

ask yourself

1. Did you attend the right kind of school for you? If not, what would you have changed?

2. Is your child (if you have one) happy in the school he is in?

3. If not, what are the reasons for his unhappiness? Would a fresh start help?

4. Can you afford to make a change? Can you afford not to?

Detours and Doing Your Homework

Educating ourselves and our kids is a major responsibility. Do you suspect that you or your kid might have a learning disability? Is your child having difficulty reading or concentrating on schoolwork? What about math? A Jewish mother pays attention to how her kid is doing in school and intervenes when necessary. She focuses on the early grasp of reading and math concepts. Problems caught early on are a lot easier to fix. You don't have the poor self-esteem layers that begin to pile on when a child is falling behind.

Learning disabilities run in our family. We know what we are talking about here. Our advice is simple. If you suspect your kid might have one, don't wait for the school to get your child tested. Find the money and do the testing yourself, with a private neuropsychologist. These tests are expensive, but every month you waste waiting for someone else to pick up the bill is another month your child is falling further behind. Neither you nor your child can afford the time. Once you get your report, it will come with a "blueprint" for indicated therapeutic services. Then you can go to your school, if necessary, and demand that certain services be offered.

By the way, do not panic. There is a huge range of learning disabilities, and many of them are curable with the right therapy and will not return. Those that don't go away can be compensated for with strategies that really do work. Do not ignore a problem you know is there because you are afraid to find out that your suspicions are true. You are not doing yourself or your kid any favors.

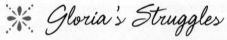 *Gloria's Struggles*

Only a few weeks ago a doctor I saw suggested that I might have had learning disabilities, which is why I could never do math. He is probably right. But in my day, nobody knew anything about these problems, so I just considered myself stupid when it came to math.

When Jill received a low reading score at the age of six, I knew there had to be something wrong: Either the test was wrong or she had a problem. Either way, I insisted on finding out. After we had her evaluated by a reading therapist, we did exercises together and she saw a reading tutor until the problem went away. By the end of second grade, she was reading with her peers. The problem never returned. ■

 *Jill's Story*

I believe now that I had undiagnosed attention deficit disorder, which may not be technically a learning disability but definitely affected my ability to learn in school. I had a hard time sitting still and focusing in a classroom. I once read a list of symptoms and said yes to most of them. If I was growing up today and had medicine to keep me focused, I probably would have excelled in school. Mommy saw I was very smart yet didn't excel. She did everything possible in those years to diagnose me. I went to a child psychologist in first grade and continued to see her on and off as needed. To this day I wonder how I actually graduated from Simmons College. ■

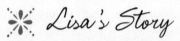

Lisa's Story

Because learning disabilities run in our family, I was on the lookout. When Joanna wrote a couple of letters backward at age four, I ran to a neuropsychologist just to get her tested. I probably overreacted, but it turned out she had a very minor weakness that was cured by just a few one-on-one sessions and some home exercises. No big deal. Caught early, fixed early. ■

ask yourself

1. Did you suffer from learning disabilities yourself?

2. How were you diagnosed? Early or late?

3. What impact did this diagnosis have on your self-esteem?

4. As a parent, are you vigilant with respect to your child's ability to learn?

5. Do you know where to turn for help? (You want a good neuropsychologist to do the initial evaluation; typically this will run about $2,000.)

Jill the Party Girl

It was hard to hold Jill down even back in college. She founded her own company, called JSK Productions, and proceeded to launch huge disco parties all over Boston. She also got in big trouble at Simmons College because, in true entrepreneurial spirit, for Valentine's Day Jill created and sold men's underwear that read "I've been Simmonized" across the backside. Get it? The school didn't. They almost expelled Jill. Fast-forward to winter 2008, when Simmons hosted Jill at an event at Bergdorf's. Funny how that incident never came up . . .

Getting into College:
A Little Luck, a Lot of Moxie

Did we mention that every Jewish child is expected to go to college? And by that we do not mean a two-year school—we mean a four-year degree, even if you begin at a two-year school and receive an associate's degree first and then transfer. There are many good choices out there. Believe it or not, the world is bigger than the Ivy League, which no one can get into today anyway. We're not saying we wouldn't be thrilled if our kids did get into one of these schools, but we're not counting on it.

The Jewish mother makes it her business to know the pros and cons of each college that might be appropriate for her child, especially all those within car-ride distance from home just in case we need to see our son or daughter on the weekend. Just in case. Our mother, in particular, did a lot of extra homework when it came time to help us choose the right colleges. And it really paid off.

 Jill's Story

How was I as a student? I didn't pay much attention through high school, that I can tell you. Surprisingly I did very well on my SATs. I have to give all the credit to Mommy for guiding me the right way when it came to my education. She knew I wasn't an academic and she looked for a program that would fit my personality and interests. We chose Simmons College because they had an internship program. My internship experience launched my career and gave me a great job. It didn't hurt that Harvard Medical School was next door. I remember Mommy telling me to sit on the steps after school so I could meet a doctor. ■

Lisa's college application experience was unique. Here's what happened—looking back, Mommy was really pretty amazing.

What Would Gloria Do?

The Situation

Lisa was dejected. It was late May of junior year. She had just lost a big student election that she had counted on winning. This election was her raison d'être for senior year. And all of Lisa's friends were a year older than she and going off to college.

What Would Gloria Do?

1. Gloria took charge of the situation, a Jewish mother specialty. Gloria had already decided that Lisa had outgrown high school anyway; this presented a perfect opportunity to act.

2. Gloria investigated the options. She had discovered by reading a magazine that Johns Hopkins had a special program for kids who had not graduated from high school yet. The same afternoon that Lisa lost that election, Gloria picked up the phone, called Johns Hopkins, spoke with an admissions officer and talked him into granting Lisa a personal interview with him on campus that following weekend. The conversation itself is part of our family folklore—it begins with "I am telling you not as a mother, but as an educator, my daughter Lisa is the [insert your choice of superlative adjective, then insert three more] student you have ever seen." The Jewish mother is nothing if not persuasive.

3. Lisa applied. During the interview, Lisa was asked what she would do if she didn't get in. She said, "I'll roll with the punches. I'll apply next year." Lisa handwrote the application in the office, submitted it and followed it with a one-page typed essay within the week.

The Outcome?

Lisa was accepted, on her seventeenth birthday no less, skipped her senior year of high school and graduated near the top of her class at Johns Hopkins.

The Lesson?

Failure can always be viewed as an opportunity: If Lisa hadn't lost the election, she never would have gone to Johns Hopkins the following fall. Gloria seized the opportunity. The Jewish mother believes in her children and is not afraid to intervene and advocate for her kids, especially when it comes to education. Education is too important!

Lisa's Reflection

It helps to have a mom who isn't afraid to pick up the phone and brag about her kids. I remember sitting on the bed, open-mouthed, as she carried on with the admissions officer about how she wasn't talking "as a mother, but rather as a teacher." Mommy, you are something else.

ask yourself

1. Did anyone guide you about post–high school choices? Were your choices the right ones?

2. If you had to do it again, would you make the same choice? Why or why not?

3. What should you have done differently? Who should you have asked to help you?

Our View on the Ivy League

Let's face it: You can get a good education anywhere. If you graduate college, you are already within the top 1 percent of human beings on this earth in terms of your level of education. So what's the big deal about the Ivy League? We know you will make "connections." But that's not the only reason to go to an Ivy—you'll meet people everywhere in life. The nice thing about having gone to a "good school"—and we include plenty of non-Ivies in this—is that you don't have to prove that you are smart afterward. People assume you are smart. This is a huge advantage in life. Can you do without it? Of course. Most people do! But for the ones who have that ticket, they know they've been given a pass of entry into better jobs simply because of the name on their degree. Do they deserve it? Not necessarily. But who said life was fair? Certainly not Jewish mothers; we know more than anyone that life isn't fair. So what's our point? If you study hard when you are young, it pays off in the long run.

Lifelong Learning

Jewish mothers believe in education at every age and for every stage. We reinvent ourselves to keep life fresh, and we continue to learn because it keeps life interesting. Sitting in a classroom keeps those gray cells moving, and going to school usually means interaction with young people. Having some young friends keeps you young too.

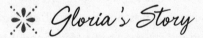

Gloria's Story

I went back to school to get my master's degree in my forties. It took me four years and I went at night, but I finished. I was really proud of myself. I met some fascinating people. Having that degree gave me the credentials I needed to teach as an adjunct professor in a few community colleges, which was the only teaching job that I really enjoyed. ■

☀ *Lisa's Story*

After I walked out of my bar exam, back in the summer of 1984, I vowed that would be the last exam I would ever take. I hated law school, and studying for that exam ruined my eyesight—my eyes went into spasms and never recovered. So I kept learning in a different way. When I moved to Westport, I started a book club with some friends. Twenty years later, we are still meeting monthly. That gave me a steady date to have an intellectual discussion in the midst of diapers and tantrums. Practicing law meant that I was always learning as a practical matter, plus we have continuing legal education requirements. But the biggest learning curve has been the new radio career, and I am still learning that as I go. As far as exams, though, I'm done. ■

☀ *Jill's Story*

I have often thought about getting an executive MBA someplace. I hear Harvard has a three-month program, so if Allyson goes to school in Boston, maybe I'll go there too! I have taken various classes at the New School for fun, including cooking, pottery and a famous movie class where you watch the film and speak with the director or actor afterward. Allyson has even gone outside her high school for continuing education courses in fashion and photography, which were not offered there. I love to learn and encourage Allyson to do the same. ■

In Conclusion

We really have a simple message in this chapter, but Jewish mothers are nothing if not repetitive, so we appreciate your having read this far. We sum it up thusly: Learn as much as you can for as long as you can. Learning enriches your life and the lives of your family and friends. Take your learning and fight for what you believe in. Your education is a privilege that few on this earth possess; you have a duty to spread it around and share what you know.

5

Career

Careers are where you realize your potential and fulfill your dreams.

Jewish mothers believe in careers, for themselves, their families and their friends. We are fortunate to have been born women in America in the late twentieth century and lucky to have been born into a family that valued the education of women as a means to earn a decent livelihood. Nonetheless, not everything in our lives was the result of luck and happenstance. We worked very hard to achieve success early in our careers and now find we are working even harder as our careers have shifted directions. We made some conscious choices too—choosing between career and family obligations, between jobs that would require travel and those that would allow us to work at home. We all chose to work, at various times and for various reasons. Why? We work for money, self-esteem, achievement and intellectual rewards. We work because we like to work, even if we don't always like the work we are doing.

To be fair, we three are not exactly what you would call career mavens. Mommy ended up in a career she hated, Lisa felt relief after quitting her fancy law firm job on Wall Street and Jill stopped climbing up the corporate ladder as soon as she realized that she could afford to stop working and spend more time with Allyson after she married Bobby.

....

So this book will not teach you how to climb the corporate ladder to success, or how to maneuver yourself into the plum corner office. Jewish mothers, in general, are a lot simpler than that. We are really just trying to figure out how to keep our families in reasonably good shape while preventing our brains from dissolving into mush. That said, we do feel qualified to share some career advice. Why? Because we made mistakes that we've learned from, and we were willing to take risks to try something new. We all had winding paths in our working lives, and found our niche later in life—Lisa with her radio show, Mommy with her newfound career as an advice columnist and Jill, using a career in the media to circulate back to her original love, retailing and merchandising.

"Career" is a bigger word than "job." Jobs are what you do to make money. Careers are what you engage in to realize your potential and fulfill your dreams. Making money is an important element of a successful career, but you can have a very successful career without earning a lot of money. To the Jewish mother, the success of one's career is determined by one's status in one's chosen field. So, for example, a tenured professor at a prestigious university may not make as much money as the owner of a local dry cleaner's, but to the Jewish mother, writing and teaching are far higher on the scale of success than turning out a well-pressed shirt. On the other hand, if you are the best dry cleaner in the country and have won awards for your skill and expertise, then *mazel tov* to you. Jewish mothers appreciate excellence wherever we can find it.

The Jewish mother is well aware of the discrepancy in America between what we pay our baseball players and what we pay our doctors. It's a *shanda*, an outright disgrace! On the scale of human endeavors, we ask you—which is more worthy: hitting a ball, or saving a life? Of course, we admit to a little self-interest here. Jewish kids are far more likely to become doctors than professional athletes. We know this, we accept this and we are actually rather proud of this fact.

As you now know, the Jewish mother is a matchmaker, but not only for people. We are always making connections, and one of the most important is connecting someone's natural talents with a career that would allow those talents to flourish. Jewish mothers want everyone to be happy, and you cannot be happy unless you put your time and energy toward attaining a goal that gives meaning to your life. Careers fulfill that need in us to achieve something worthy.

After College: You Are Not Allowed to Waste Your Brains

Jewish mothers do not believe in wasting one's brains. We believe in the inherent value of working or volunteering your time and skills. Idleness is neither tolerated nor respected in our group. If you are lucky enough to go to college, make sure you put what you learn to good use.

Not many people know what they want to do in life, even by the time they graduate college. But since most of us have to pay our own bills, we usually take the first good job that comes along. So take that job, but examine your life. Don't settle for spending years doing something that does not make you happy. Aim for a career you can love, no matter how long it takes you to get there. A dream is a terrible thing to waste.

The Small Things Are Important

Basic work habits are essential to success. Here are a few: Show up on time, or call if you will be late. Act responsibly and return your messages, preferably within twenty-four hours. Never address people by their first names unless you have asked their permission, or they have already used your first name in conversation. Also, remember that people appreciate a thank-you note after an interview, and make sure you do not have any typos on your résumé.

Jill's Path

The Jewish mother pushes—it's either work *or* school, but preferably work *and* school. Lazy is not an option in the Jewish house. I've been working since I was fourteen. My first job was as a cashier at a Chinese take-out restaurant. After ringing in soda as $45 instead of 45 cents three times, I was fired for the first and the last time. Once I got my first job at a local clothing store after school, I knew I wanted a career in the retail industry. I wanted to become a women's-wear buyer.

Sometimes the job you think you want isn't the job you should have. After I attended the Retail Management School at Simmons College in Boston, I was accepted into the Filene's Department Store training program as an intern. During training I was assigned to men's dress shirts, under Jeff Kantor. We worked hard and had fun, but I was looking at this as a stepping-stone to my goal, women's wear. After the internship, I got placed back in men's dress shirts and was very disappointed. I later found out from

Jeff that since I did such a good job as an intern, he had specifically requested me. It turned out to be the best thing that ever happened to me professionally. I had the privilege of working for some of the greatest minds in retailing. My managers became the people who later ran May Department Stores and Federated Department Stores. And Jeff Kantor? He is now the president of Macy's Home. He and his wife are two of my closest friends.

When I moved back to New York to marry Steven, I continued to work, eventually ending up as national sales manager for Jockey Hosiery. I had a great job and a great boss, Dean Norman, and would have continued to work there had I not married Bobby. The funny thing is that as a result of my participation in the show, I now have the opportunity to create a brand and use my expertise in merchandising. As of this writing, I am planning to launch an entire bedding line to be nationally distributed. ∎

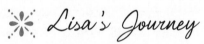

Lisa's Journey

I became a lawyer because I didn't know what to do with myself after college. It was the safe choice. Go to school, get good grades, get into a good law school, get good grades again and then get a good job. All good. Plus, Daddy was an attorney and I had loved my constitutional law classes at Johns Hopkins. At the NYU School of Law, I quickly realized I was among many smart, ambitious women. In an earlier generation, we would all have become teachers. After law school, we all dutifully got jobs at the most prestigious Wall Street firms, places where our dads had been turned down twenty years earlier because they were either Jewish, black or Hispanic, or didn't live in Darien. Poetic justice, American style.

Most of us didn't last at those law firms for more than a few years. I had purposely trained in real estate law so I could one day practice law from my own home and eventually did just that for many years. Those slave factories, I mean law firms, were not designed for anyone to have a life that balanced career and family. The day I quit that firm I was so happy that everyone asked if I was pregnant. I glowed that much. Practicing law didn't satisfy my soul, but I learned to write, to advocate for causes I believed in and to express myself clearly. Today I am still teaching, advocating and communicating on the radio; it's all the same thing, just done in a different forum. Everything in life you learn, you use. ■

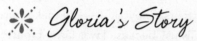 ## Gloria's Story

The irony of my career is that I was a really good teacher, even though I hated it. Teaching suited my personality, but the problem was that I never did teach something I really loved, like fashion design. So I took my regrets and tried to make sure my daughters would make better choices. ■

ask yourself

1. How did you end up in your career—by design or by chance?

2. Does your career maximize your natural talents, or is it merely a way to earn a paycheck?

3. If money was not your sole consideration, what would you do with your working life?

4. Are you a person who fantasizes about not working? It's OK as a fantasy, but how will you pay the bills?

5. Do you respect people who work, who contribute to society?

On the Job:
Are You Being Treated Fairly?

Did you know that women still earn approximately 66 cents for every dollar earned by a man? It isn't that we can't do the job; it's that we do the job and accept less money for it. We should all stop doing that, don't you think? It's time we spoke up, like Jill did, years ago.

Jill's Fight

I've learned the most about life from working. I once worked for three partners. They all used to make fun of me and call me "the Twins" because I was large-breasted. I was so naïve at the time that I thought it was cute and that they loved me. Looking back, I should have sued them for sexual harassment. Their behavior was demeaning and condescending. In spite of their behavior, I was their best salesperson and I earned them more money than anyone else did. On one deal my commission alone was $40,000—enough for us to build our country home in Pennsylvania. Nevertheless, they never wanted to pay me what I was worth. Every time I made them more money, they would cut my commission rate.

One day, I walked into their office and said, "You can make jokes about my breasts, carry on about my figure, you can say whatever you want about my looks, but don't screw with me over money." That one time, they gave me what I was owed.

Eventually I quit when, among other things, they wrongfully docked my pay for three days when I was sick. I was terribly hurt because I really thought these partners cared about me as a person. I was wrong, but in retrospect the signs were all there. They never showed me any respect.

However, there is a good ending to this story. While I had been working there, I met a really good manager who left because of the same problems I had. After I quit, I contacted this man and he hired me for an even better job. I always say, we make plans and God laughs. God was giggling again. ∎

What Would Gloria Do?

The Situation

You are doing a great job, but you are not appreciated. You are getting paid less than you deserve.

What Would Gloria Do?

1. *Assess the situation with a clear eye.* Are there special perks about this job that make it convenient for you, even if the boss doesn't appreciate you? Can you get hired by a competitor in this market? What are your other realistic options?

2. *Do not act impulsively.* Do not quit until you have another job lined up if you are depending on the income. Interview and bide your time. Quit when the time is right for you, not them.

3. *Give it a shot with your company, then move on.* Unless your boss is a total jerk, give him or her a chance to appreciate you. Make your case. Speak up. Be specific about what you want. Then, if the answer is no, move on.

4. *Never telegraph your punches.* Thinking of leaving? Don't be a fool; tell no one until your other job offer is in your hand.

Advocating for compensation is tough for all of us and tougher for women than for men. We need to ignore the little voices in our heads that tell us that classy ladies don't haggle over money. Class has nothing to do with money when it comes to getting paid what you are worth. In business, money is the ultimate sign of respect.

ask yourself

1. Do you know if you are getting paid what you should be? Have you dared ask others in your position what they get paid? Money is the last taboo. . . .

2. If you are unsure whether you are being paid fairly, can you find out by calling headhunters? Headhunters will tell you what you would get paid elsewhere. Once you know, don't cry. Or rather, cry it all out and then do something.

3. Do you know how to negotiate a fair raise? If not, ask someone in your life who earns substantial money to tell you his salary-negotiating tactics, or buy a book on the subject. There are tricks, tools you can use. Learn them.

4. Do you worry whether you have the guts to make the big speech? If so, concentrate on one good point about yourself you want your boss to remember. Just one. Practice your speech in front of a mirror. Then practice in front of your friend.

5. Are you being sexually harassed? Years ago, it was something you either had to put up with or quit over. Today, there is no reason to accept this kind of behavior, and he (or she) knows it. Speak up. Sexual harassment is all about power—even the score.

The Power of the Mentor: Your Very Own "Rabbi"

All successful people achieved because other people helped them. It's not just what you know that makes you successful, it's who your mentor is. We actually call our mentors rabbis because "rabbi" is another word for "teacher." Find one. Your mentor should be someone you like as a person and who likes you too. Ideally, it would be nice if she works in the same organization as you and could help you rise up the ladder on the rung right under hers, but that is not essential. If no mentor comes to mind, join a networking organization in your field and ask around. Jill actually had two rabbis: One was Karen Gillespie, Gloria's friend whom you met in the friendship chapter and who mentored Jill throughout her education. The other was Jill's first boss, Jeff Kantor, who is still a good friend.

What should a mentor teach you? The "hidden curriculum," by which we mean the myriad network of unwritten rules in any industry designed to trip up the unsuspecting. These are the rules you discover only after you have broken them and have gotten punished for doing so. Trust us, we've been there. If you are lucky enough to find a good mentor, take his advice. Don't make him tell you a second time. And finally, every person has a duty to "pay it forward." Don't forget to mentor somebody else; it's a *mitzvah* to pass along the knowledge you have learned.

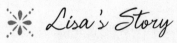 *Lisa's Story*

After twenty-five years as an attorney, I finally found my way to the career I was born to have—creating my own radio show. Ironically, if I had not been working as an attorney, I never would have found my "radio rabbi." One day, out of the blue, a longtime client called me up to ask me a real estate question. I was distracted, since the name I saw on the caller ID said "XYZ Radio Company." At the time, I didn't know a soul in radio, but I knew I wanted to be on the radio. So I interrupted my client to ask about the caller ID and discovered that in fact he was in the radio business. I asked if he would give me some advice. We made a date in New York for the very next day. This self-effacing man turned out to be the CEO of a major radio syndication firm. Major. CEO. I never would have known had his caller ID not shown up on my phone.

I promptly appointed this client as my "radio rabbi," my mentor. I do not make a move without consulting him first. I take his advice. He told me to get on the air; I got on the air. He told me to keep going; I kept going. I told him that he is going to nationally syndicate me one day, and he told me . . . you never know. You never know, indeed. ■

ask yourself

1. How did you end up in your career?

2. Do you love it?

3. Does your career suit your talents?

4. Do you work even if you don't have to? Why or why not?

5. Have you found your "rabbi" yet? Your mentor?

6. If there is no one obvious available to be your mentor, what organizations can you find to help you get one? There are plenty out there—try Google.

Finding the Right Career— Don't Just Stand There

Accepted wisdom permits parents to guide and shape their children's higher education. However, there is less cultural consensus on the amount of guidance parents should give their kids with respect to their career choices. Perhaps that is because we as a society presume that by the time our kids graduate, these young adults can figure it out on their own. To this we say, "Are you kidding?" Have you seen the level of anxiety in the kids graduating college today? Historically "safe" careers, like medicine and law, are no longer guarantees of financial security or intellectual reward. We've outsourced almost every occupation and profession. Small businesses are having trouble staying afloat, much less hiring young, inexperienced employees. Even the Peace Corps has a two-year wait list, and last time we checked, they don't pay enough to make a dent in those college loans.

What to do? As you can imagine, Jewish mothers take the same active approach to career choices as we do with college choices. Ideally, we do not push our kids into doing anything they wouldn't be happy doing. But we are not above giving a shove in the right direction.

Other Jews Who Have Made It

Jews take inordinate pride in the accomplishments of other Jews. We take *kvelling* to a whole new level when it comes to Jewish Nobel Prize winners. Famous musicians, great authors, brilliant doctors, the occasional sports figure—if they have a Jewish parent, we know about it. When Jews hear that anyone has done something great, the first question they ask is, Is that person Jewish? If the answer is yes, well, then, it's a reaffirmation of just how great we all are, isn't it?

FINDING THE RIGHT CAREER, STEP 1: THE ACADEMIC WORLD

We are rather snobbish when it comes to achievement in life. The Jewish people are the People of the Book, and we admire professions that depend upon learning. Here is how a Jewish mother would sound if she were giving advice to a young person deciding what to study.

"I understand you are good at math and science—do I hear 'the doctor is in'? What about teeth? Dentistry is an excellent choice, especially for women (fewer emergencies), but you must have good hands. And speaking of mouths, you can use your big mouth to an advantage if you want to consider law. Sure, we know lawyers are a dime a dozen, but it's so *flexible*, you can do so much with that degree, and let's face it, you do love to argue. All the time. How about accounting? We could use a good accountant in the family; God knows you'll never run out of work with all the changes they are always making to the tax code. And let's not forget teaching. It is still the best job to have while you are raising a family, and teachers are finally getting the respect they deserve, not to mention all those vacation days and benefits. An MBA? What is that exactly? Can't you learn those skills while actually working for a living? Okay, whatever, education is education. Good choice."

All stereotypes aside, it is important to make the most of your time in college, whether it leads you to a fulfilling career immediately afterward or is a time for intellectual growth that you store and make use of sometime later in life. College today is an enormous commitment of time and money, averaging over four years for most students and often leaving you and your family in debt. You owe it to yourself and those who have supported you to make the best possible use of all your opportunities to learn.

FINDING THE RIGHT CAREER, STEP 2: START A BUSINESS

In business, you either work for yourself, or you work for someone else. We recognize that not every person can manage to save or borrow enough to begin her own business, but historically, Jewish people try very hard to do so, even though entrepreneurship does not guarantee success and comes with many pressures. Why? Because if we are going to spend our lives working, we might as well have something to show for it at the end of the day—meaning something we can sell to someone else, whether it be shares or assets of a business. Look at all those poor *schmucks* who slaved for years at companies that went bankrupt. Now what have they got? *Bubkes*. If we are going to have *bubkes*, it might as well be because we blew it ourselves, not because we relied on someone else who ruined everything for us.

Also, we'll be perfectly honest. Jews prefer not to work for other people because we do not like being told what to do. Have you ever tried to tell a Jewish mother what to do? Our point exactly—it's not worth the aggravation for either one of you. Telling other people what to do? Now, that's a Jewish mother's specialty. So, if you can, start your own business. When you make mistakes, you can mutter out loud to yourself the way we do. When somebody else makes mistakes that affect you, we'll step out of your way.

....

Deep in her heart the Jewish mother believes all of her children can be Bill Gates. Especially the college dropout, the one with *real* potential—Bill Gates dropped *out* of Harvard, didn't you know? Jewish parents save money for two things: their children's education, and anything else their children might need. If they can, many parents put money away to help their child achieve a dream. They love to say, "Come to me with an idea, my son, my daughter, and let's figure it out together." That's what our mom and dad did with each of us.

Jill's Story

I had an idea to start a business to sell "samples," which were the clothes that were used by stores to decide what they would buy from the manufacturers. We would buy them at 40 percent off "cost" and sell them at wholesale prices six months before they even hit the stores! I had a partner and we needed money to get started. I asked Mommy and Daddy to help me. I was all of twenty-two years old and had never done anything like this in my life. They gave me $10,000 outright, no questions asked. It was a lot of money then, and it's a lot of money now. And you have to remember that my parents never had a lot of money—they had good and bad years, but they were never multimillionaires. Yet they believed in me. Always have. Can you imagine? I learned a lot from that first business venture and we were quite successful, even as each of us was working elsewhere at another full-time job. When I met my first husband, Steven, I moved to New York and we closed the business. I paid back every dime to my parents. Today, I look back with awe at how much faith my parents had in me. ■

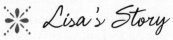

Lisa's Story

I thought investing in real estate was a good idea ten years ago. I had some money, but not enough. Without question, my parents gave me the money I needed. By then, they were retired in Florida and living on savings, but they insisted that I take their money to make the deal happen. We were partners, but I managed everything. Eventually I was able to buy them out, at a profit. They trusted me, period. I believe that their trust in me made me capable. Income from that investment still helps support our family. I hope one day my two kids will come to me with an idea for a business venture and I will be able to say, "Here, take this money. I believe in you." ■

ask yourself

1. Has anyone ever helped you with a business venture?

2. How did that make you feel?

3. Was the venture successful?

4. Would you help someone else in a business venture if asked?

FINDING THE RIGHT CAREER, STEP 3:
IT'S WHO YOU KNOW

Looking for a job? Applying to a special program? Connections matter. Putting a face on a résumé is everything. If you don't help yourself, who will? Call in those favors—didn't you do a favor for him when he asked you to? Do not be shy. Find the right connection and ask nicely, "Are you looking for anyone to help you?" What's the worst that can happen? They say no. But often your connection will say, "I can't use you, but I know someone who can. . . ." Business is built on relationships, even when you are first starting out. Use every connection you can to get in the door. This is how life really works.

FINDING THE RIGHT CAREER, STEP 4:
HIRE A CAREER COUNSELOR

Why not hire a career counselor? It seems to us that choosing a career is just as important as choosing a college—in fact, probably more so. Wouldn't it be great if we could save ourselves time and frustration and just figure out what it is we really want to do? As they sang in *Flashdance*, "Take your passion, and make it happen."

A Word on Employment

Not everyone is meant to be an entrepreneur, and moreover, there are many occupations, like teaching, that are simply not typically entrepreneurial. Unemployment levels are unusually high right now. If you are searching for a job, take anything that you can live with, even if the job is significantly short of perfect. Our philosophy? Working is better than not working. Like eating. Just don't get either too loyal or too complacent. Your boss is neither one.

ask yourself

1. Are you pursuing a line of study that will help you achieve your career goals? If not, then redirect your energy.

2. Do you have the inclination to start your own business? If so, create a plan, and look to your own savings as well as investors. Investing in yourself might be the best decision you ever make.

3. What connections do you have that can help you succeed in your chosen career? Use them, no matter how tangential the connection might be.

4. Have you ever hired a career counselor? What have you got to lose?

Second Chances: Changing Your Mind

For whatever reason, you may find yourself in a job or career that you hate. You dread the thought of going there day after day, year after year, as the price of supporting your family. Your job bores you, it doesn't fulfill you, it doesn't pay you enough, whatever. How long do you want to spend your life doing something you hate?

God knows it is complicated to change careers. But guess what? Life is short! (Maybe shorter than you think.) Not happy? Break out of your trap. It's never too late to chase your dream. Never. Ever. You will feel truly successful only if you love what you do.

Lisa has given a lot of thought to the subject of changing careers. If you know you need to change but you are not sure what specific career might be right for you, then find a therapist, life coach or career counselor to help you. If you do know what career you seek, the following advice may help.

Lisa's Advice for Career Changers

1. The most important thing to remember is that real change comes slowly, not all at once. Relax; take a deep breath. First, accept one thing—you can't quit your day job, at least not now. Quitting your job is the last step. I still haven't stopped practicing law, although I do it a lot less now.

2. Tell people what you want to do. Unexpected doors will open. People you know will surprise you by revealing their experience and connections in your new field. I promise.

3. Carve out a little bit of time to work on getting credentials or experience in your new field. Maybe sign up for a continuing-education class in Excel to improve your computer skills. If your dream is to act, perhaps you can audition for a community play.

4. Read about your new career. Trade magazines will teach you a great deal about the business and the people who are the big names in your field.

5. If you are feeling gutsy, make some cold calls to some of those people who are named in the trades. You'd be surprised how many people would love to help an enthusiastic person who is willing to work hard.

6. Give yourself some clear goals within achievable time frames, and stick to them. For example, "In the next six

months, I will call ten people in my new field and ask them certain questions. I will follow their advice to the letter."

7. Go to the conventions where the top people in your chosen field meet and learn. Spend the money, spend the time. Walk around like a wandering soul and just say hello to people. That's how I brought my show to Yale radio. People at these meetings are generally really friendly if you just smile and tell them you'd like to belong to their group.

8. Aunt Cooky always says that it's about the journey, not the destination. Sometimes it doesn't seem as if you are getting anywhere until you look back at where you started. Remember to enjoy making your dream come true.

 *Lisa's Second Act*

After twenty years as a practicing attorney, I resented it. I started thinking to myself, Why should I spend my time solving your problems? You created them, you solve them. Meanwhile, I spent my years chauffeuring my kids around while talking back to talk radio. I decided I could do a better job on the radio than most of the people I was hearing. I had a vision of a show that would bridge NPR and commercial radio, of providing real information in a down-to-earth and relatable way. I also felt very strongly about certain political issues. It was almost as if I needed my voice to be heard.

With Bill's financial and moral support, I scaled down my law practice and went to the Connecticut School of Broadcasting. I knew I needed to update my skills since my college radio days. Months later, I auditioned at my local radio station, and as luck would have it, a spot had just opened up on Saturday mornings. I grabbed the slot and set aside savings from my law practice to fund my new company. My show aired September 30, 2006. Connecticut Governor Jodi Rell was my first guest. As soon as I got behind the mike on live radio, I knew that I had finally found the thing at which I was a "natural." It was the easiest thing I had ever done, and by far the most fun.

Radio has given me an excuse to talk to fascinating, interesting, accomplished people. More than that, some of them have become my friends, my mentors and my inspirations. I feel that I am doing something meaningful with my life. In July of 2009, I was honored to accept an award for Gold Coast Best Radio Personality. ■

 Jill's New Career

Most people ask me two questions: "How did you get on the show?" and "Why would you do a show like this?"

In September 2006, I got a phone call from someone casting a new reality show called *Manhattan Moms*. I saved the message and still have it on my answering machine. It was supposed to be a show about "glamorous New York City moms and their family and friends." I was intrigued and went through the casting process. My parents and sister thought I had nothing to gain and everything to lose. Bobby and Allyson were 100 percent supportive. My priority was to protect Allyson, and to this day I remain very controlling over when and what she films. The producers eventually said I was perfect and the show would get "green-lit" by December of 2006.

Months went by and I never heard a thing. Then Allyson and I were having lunch in June of 2007 when I got a call that the show was green-lit and ready to go.

The answer to "Why would you do a show like this?" is simple. I saw it as an opportunity to promote our business and promote the charity work we do. Zarin Fabrics has been a landmark destination for discount drapery and upholstery fabrics since 1936. How many companies get an opportunity like this to promote their business on national TV? I am a spokesperson for Kodak and have written a book with my family. I travel the country for speaking appearances and have never had more fun. How many people get a chance to cook their grandmother's latkes recipe on the *Today* show, gossip with Joy Behar about current events and have their photo in the Best Dressed pages of weekly magazines? Yes . . . it could go to my head, but I have Lisa and Mommy to keep me grounded, don't worry!

I can't say that being on a reality show was a dream of mine, but it has opened up doors and let me become even more of a connector. I now have a much larger network for fixing people up or helping them get a job or giving relationship advice. ■

Gloria's Take

I never thought both of my daughters would end up in the media. But I can see they are both naturally talented at what they do. I do think they got their verbal skills from me. To tell the truth, the whole journey has been amazing to watch and participate in. I am very proud of both of my girls. ■

ask yourself

1. Have you thought about changing your career?

2. What is stopping you? Think about that carefully. If it's money, how much money do you really need to get started? Most schools have scholarships—investigate.

3. Can you take a baby step forward to your next career?

4. If you do nothing, how unhappy will you be a year from now?

5. Are you afraid of success? This is common. Our advice: You should only have that problem. Don't create barriers that aren't there; real life is hard enough.

6. Are you afraid of failure? Also common. But is it worse to have never even tried than to have tried and failed? Sol says that the only things he regrets are the things in life he didn't do. He doesn't regret one thing he tried to do and failed. He wishes he had made more mistakes—it would have meant that he had tried more things.

In Conclusion

Most people in the world do not have the luxury of being able to choose a "career." Some women live in a society where their roles are so restricted that their real job is to take care of their family. Circumstances drive others into a boring job that they need to support their family. It is a blessing to be able to discuss career options. We are enormously grateful for the opportunities we have been given in this life, by our society as well as by our parents, spouses and children. We take none of this for granted.

Most people don't start out doing what they were "born to

do." But many people do discover a talent or ambition they secretly hope to accomplish. Be brave. Take one step at a time. If you are meant to achieve this goal, there will be signs along the way. Look for them.

As we said at the start of this chapter, career experts we are not. We've made lots of mistakes, too many to list in this chapter or in this entire book. But here is what we have done—in this, the middle of our adult lives, we find ourselves with careers that are fun and rewarding. They aren't the careers we started out with, and that's our lesson. If it wasn't too late for us to find careers we love, it's certainly not too late for you.

6

Marriage

If anyone who has been married
a long time tells you her
marriage is and always has
been perfect, she is lying.

We come from a long line of long marriages. Our paternal grandparents, Ben and Helen, had sixty-six years together (and celebrated number sixty at Café Baba in Queens, complete with belly dancers . . . don't ask), and our maternal ones, Sylvia and Jack, fifty-three years. Mommy and Daddy celebrated fifty-two years this past December, and Aunt Cooky and Uncle Sy count over forty. Lisa and Bill are in their twenty-ninth year, and Jill and Bobby just celebrated their ninth anniversary. In today's world of fragmented families, we truly count our blessings (and spit a lot).

All of our Jewish mothers knew how to keep their marriages intact, if not always blissful. Looking back, every couple made compromises and faced unique challenges. No one in our family became very rich; no one starved. Everyone put family first, ahead of themselves. Maybe one reason they stayed together for life was partly generational; people didn't view their lives strictly through the prism of happiness. We were taught that it is normal to go through bad times in a marriage, even bad years. But if you have shared values, shared goals and an underlying affection for each other, you stick it out and pray that the good years will return.

What secrets did they know? What qualities did these women possess? They knew when to push and when to pull back. They knew when to spend and when to save. They knew enough to know that a lot of life is just plain luck, and some of it depends on the luck you make for yourself. We, Lisa and Jill, have been lucky enough to learn these secrets and more. Our mother's voice is the voice in our heads, and occasionally the voice that comes out of our lips too. Even as we recognize them, we can't believe we are actually repeating those same words. . . .

Why Even Bother Getting Married?

Historically, marriage for women meant property rights, protection of her children and the legitimacy conferred on her relationship by society. It still does. Women who fool themselves into thinking that being someone's mistress is the equivalent of being someone's wife are just that—fools.

Hence the oldest trick in the book—getting pregnant to get the ring. This ploy still works a lot of the time; we don't approve of it as a trap, but we've seen it work. If you are thinking of getting pregnant merely to hook your man into marriage, ask yourself what you will do if it doesn't work—are you prepared to raise that baby alone, if necessary?

If you have decided to marry and have convinced the man in your life that it is time to walk down the aisle, and he meets all the criteria we laid out in the dating chapter, we say *mazel tov!* Being married in our view is a great and important thing. A strong marriage is the basis of a strong family.

More and more people today are having kids without the commitment of marriage. Although we are not sociologists, we are opinionated, commonsense women. It seems pretty clear to us that two parents are better than one. Men are not disposable commodities in a family unit; the influence our father had on our characters and choices was profound. And men who marry, who live with their wives and children, as opposed to those who do not, are far more likely to commit to consistent parenting and providing obligations. Kids really do need men in their lives, much as we Jewish mothers sometimes hate to admit it. Marriage is never perfect, but often it is the best we can do to give our children the best chance of becoming well-adjusted and competent adults.

If you don't intend to have children, then why get married? Societal respect, legal issues and moral convictions may be your reasons. Love may be your reason. We don't care why you get married, but if you do get married, we wish you lots of *mazel* (luck). Other than love, *mazel* is the most important ingredient.

Jill's View

Does everyone need to be married or want to be married? I know I did. It is in my DNA. Since I was a little girl, I was set on a life path—get good grades in school (I might have ignored that one), go to college, have a career and get married. Getting divorced was not part of the plan. I thought my first marriage would last forever, but if I had not married Steven I would not have had Allyson, so I will never call it a mistake. I knew Bobby a few years before we got married. Is our relationship exactly the same now as it was then? No. I admit it was more sexual in the beginning. All relationships are and should be. Then you should settle into a comfortable relationship that always involves great sex but also has layers of friendship, love and, most important, trust. Bobby has taught me that a marriage is like a book. You have different chapters in your marriage. If you are in a rut, like anyone who's been married long enough has been at times, you need to turn the page and get to another chapter. Embrace the "life is a book" concept and work together to turn the page. ■

The Jewish Wedding

Have you been to a Jewish wedding? Did you ever wonder why the groom smashes a glass with his foot at the end of the ceremony? The reason? Jews want you to remember that even in the midst of a wedding, the happiest ceremony of life, our Second Temple was destroyed. The smashing of glass is a symbol of that destruction. Wherever there is joy, there is also sadness. You see? We Jews can't be unconditionally happy for even one moment. No wonder we are always laughing and crying at the same time.

Keeping a Man . . . Happy?

If anyone who has been married a long time tells you her marriage is and always has been perfect, she is lying. If she is not lying to you, she is lying to herself, but she is surely lying. Relationships take work. The Jewish mother understands that very well.

❋ *Gloria's Story*

I'm no starry-eyed romantic on the subject of marriage, even though I love Sol deeply. Disappointment is often a part of life. You keep expecting and hoping for one thing, and then you get shocked or surprised or dismayed by another. For example, Sol and I had a rather large interest in a silver mine many years ago. We flew to Arizona to inspect the mine and thought it looked great. For one evening, we were "paper millionaires." The next week we found out the ore was practically worthless and so was the stock. But during that brief time when the stock was sky-high, Sol seemed to change before my eyes. He became quite arrogant and not very nice. When the stock fell, he turned back into the nice guy I married. Maybe that episode was a blessing in disguise; perhaps our marriage would not have been strong enough to handle sudden great wealth at that age. Too bad we never did have the chance to find out. ■

> **From Jill and Lisa: Gloria's story about the silver mine reminds us of another secret we'd like to share—beware the man who makes a lot of money while still young enough to really enjoy it. It usually goes to his head, and by that we mean the wrong one.**

Do not get the wrong impression here. Despite the occasional disappointments, shouting matches (Mommy shouts, Daddy runs away) and long stretches of the silent treatment, Mom and Dad finish each other's sentences. They cannot be apart. They adore each other, when they are not complaining about each other.

Mommy has observed more marriages than we have. She also is part of the generation in which a wife had a more clearly defined role in marriage. Sometimes that was a good thing; other times, not so good. Here is our mother's advice to us on how to keep a man—did we say "keep him happy"? No, we just said "keep"....

GLORIA'S RULES TO KEEP A MAN AFTER YOU ARE MARRIED

1. *Your Looks Count*: Keep up your appearance. If you gain fifty pounds during your pregnancy and lose forty of them, you'll feel better about yourself and he'll still have the girl he married.

2. *Get Away Together as a Couple*: Sol and I used to go away for weekends in Westchester when the girls were young. It wasn't expensive, it wasn't too far away—but it was away from our ordinary routine and we got to be alone together.

3. *Be Afraid of Virginia Woolf*: Try to find fairly happy couples to socialize with, not the kind who fight in front of you all night long. Not only is that kind of behavior unpleasant; it can also be contagious.

4. *Pretend a Little*: If your spouse has a hobby he loves, like sports, you should try to seem a little interested once in a while. (Personally, I never did that, but it sounds like a good idea.)

5. *Keep on Your Toes*: Do not be naïve about other women taking an interest in your husband! A friend of mine was definitely after Sol for a very short time, during a time when she was fighting with her first husband and before

she found the man who was to be her second husband. I was gullible and stupid; that can be a dangerous combination. Every woman has to stay on her toes.

6. *For Better or for Worse Includes Richer and Poorer:* If fortune fails you, don't give up. Be understanding of his plight. Pitch in and help where you can. I realize many women today contribute significantly to household income, but in my day those women were rare. Men need to work and earn money to feel valuable. When their earnings dip, their ego drops too. Be gentle during the rough times.

Gloria's Example

Marriage is a partnership in the truest sense of the word. When one is having troubles of any kind, the other steps in to help. Sol was having financial difficulties when Lisa was ready for college. I was out on leave from teaching and had no desire to return; in fact, I hated teaching in New York City public high schools. But we needed the money to pay Lisa's tuition, so I went back to work until Lisa finished college. You do whatever it takes to get through. That's why I always felt it was so important for my daughters to have their own way of making a living, even in those days when men were expected to bring home the paycheck. ∎

ask yourself

1. How much *do* you resemble the girl in the wedding photo? If not, is there something within your control that you can work on to be that woman again?

2. Do you make time just for the two of you? How often?

3. When was the last time you got away alone for a little time together?

4. Are you mentally prepared to stay for the long haul? If not, is marriage the right choice for you?

5. When money is tight, do you pitch in and work to help?

6. Do you show an interest in the things he is interested in?

Who Said Your Husband Has to Know Everything?

We love our husbands. Most of the time, we even like our husbands. But our husbands are not our sisters. Hell, they're not even our girlfriends. Are they best friends, in the sense of being there for us, supportive and kind, loyal and true? Yes, they are. But does that mean they are entitled to know what we spend at the hairdresser, how often we go for touch-ups at the dermatologist and the details of how much it really costs for our children to get all the tutoring they need? Uh . . . no. That's why we have girlfriends.

What about when your friend or family member tells you a secret? It is usually understood that you can tell your husband, but what if your friend asks you not to? Do you tell him anyway?

We say no way. A confidence is a confidence; if you don't want to keep any secrets from your husband, fool that you are, let your friend know this ahead of time so she can decide whether or not she still wants to tell you. Don't you know that some men are the *worst* gossips? There is *no* way some men can keep a secret.

Our Aunt Cooky believes she has to tell her husband, our Uncle Sy, everything. This irks Mommy, whose feeling is: "Why start trouble? You are just going to do what you want anyway, so do it."

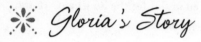

Gloria's Story

Years ago we were invited to a family Bar Mitzvah. There I met a very good-looking, newly married couple who were very good friends with our cousin. I danced with the guy, we talked and that was that. A few days later the phone rings and this same guy asks if he could send a limo for me to take me to New York City. After getting over my shock, I said quite nicely that I was very flattered by the offer but would not accept the invitation since I was a very happily married woman. I should have been quite angry with him, but I must say that I was flattered, even though I thought he was a piece of trash and pitied his wife. Ultimately, I decided against telling Sol since this guy was our cousin's close friend. Why start trouble? ■

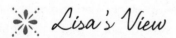

Lisa's View

Daddy had a wooden valet hanger for his pants in our parents' bedroom. Mommy used to go into Daddy's pants pockets and take money out of his wallet. She did this often and without asking. In fact, it used to look like stealing, because Mommy always did it with a little sneaky look on her face, as if Daddy wasn't going to notice he was missing twenty dollars. When I asked Mommy about this surreptitious ritual, she always said, "Your father doesn't have to know everything." Later, I learned that most of this money went to pay for Jill's reading therapist. Mommy felt Daddy wouldn't want to pay for the lessons if she told him how much they really cost, so she told him they cost much less and gave Daddy the satisfaction of thinking the check he wrote paid for the whole therapy. But you have to wonder where Dad thought all those twenties were going. . . . Maybe the hairdresser?

And speaking of secrets, I was a little miffed recently when I found out my husband kept one of his own. A mutual friend of ours had confided to my husband that his wife had filed for divorce, but I only found out about it much later, after the wife finally got around to telling me. I thought that Bill should have shared the husband's secret with me, since we both knew the couple well. But Bill honored the request his friend had made not to tell anyone about it, and for Bill that "anyone" included me. So you see? Don't be a fool. You think you have to tell him everything? Why? I guarantee your husband does not share this philosophy. Most men have plenty of secrets. Give yourself permission to have one or two yourself. ■

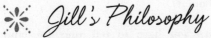

Jill's Philosophy

Let me start with the fact that Bobby has never said no to me. Come to think of it, neither did my dad. (Sorry, Mom, I now know how you hated being the "bad cop.") Well, Dad may have initially said no, but I always worked on him to turn it into a yes. I think that is my gift in life, to never take no for an answer. With that said . . . it is easy for me to be open and not have secrets. I think if Bobby said no to me about things, I would do them anyway and just not tell him. I admit there have been times that I thought he would say no and lied at first. But I can't keep a secret from him too long and always fess up. I think that one lie leads to more lies, and then they become hard to keep track of. Plus, marriages based on lies never last. ■

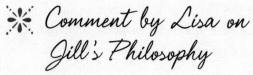

Comment by Lisa on Jill's Philosophy

Let's not even get started on all the things you don't bother to tell Bobby. Even Bobby admitted on the first season of the *Housewives* television show that he was "on a need-to-know basis." Guess who decides what and when he needs to know something? You do, Jill. ■

ask yourself

1. Have you ever kept a secret from your husband?

2. Was it about you or someone else?

3. Did he ever find out? What happened?

4. Did you feel guilty about it?

5. Why do you believe you have to tell your husband everything?

What Would Gloria Do?

The Situation

Your marriage has not been so good lately, although you love your husband. At work, an attractive man strikes up a flirtation and you respond. One day, you find yourself in a compromising situation. You don't exactly break your marriage vows, but you come close. You feel guilty and vow you will never do it again.

The Question

Do you tell your husband? Do you confess your behavior to him?

What Would Gloria Do?

Why do you want to confess? To make yourself feel better? To alleviate your own guilt? Too bad. If you intend to stay with your husband and work on your marriage, then shut up and don't say a word. You would be hurting your husband needlessly and causing mistrust where there was none before. Fooling around was your sin; your punishment is that you have to live with what you did. Every time you look at your husband and feel so close to him that you think you could tell him anything, bite that tongue and keep your mouth shut. If you do confess, your marriage will never be the same.

"He Who Payeth Sayeth": The Value of a *Knipple*

He who payeth sayeth. Was there ever uttered a truer statement? Surely the one who controls the purse strings controls so much in life. *Money is power. Money is control.* When a woman has no control over what she can spend, she has little control over her life. This is a core belief of the Jewish mother. Although many households are now two-income, in most cases a man's earnings are still greater than a woman's. The disparity usually grows when children are born. Let's face the truth: Even in modern, two-parent relationships where the goal is to share every aspect of child-rearing, Mom still does the lion's share of the work. She is also usually the first to sacrifice, or at least scale down, her career during those early years. That's why it's so important that she have a *knipple* of her own, to spend as she likes, without having to answer to her husband.

Leo Rosten's *The Joys of Yiddish* defines *knipple* as the money saved up by a married woman out of the household funds her husband gives her; a nest egg, so to speak.

As Mr. Rosten comments, "Women fiercely guarded as earnings the small amounts their careful management of the household made it possible for them to divert to personal, undisclosed causes. My wife claims that when I married her she had already saved up her own little [*knipple*], which I was not to consider divvies, which is not Yiddish but Chicagoese for anything to be divvied up." Leo Rosten wrote this in 1968. Some things never change.

Every family creates its own version of financial fairness. To us, the way you arrange your saving and spending of money says volumes about your relationship and also is an indicator of its long-term success. Living in an adult relationship requires trusting the other person to behave like one.

Mommy taught us that a woman must have the ability to spend money without having to report to her husband about it. Too many issues arise in life in which you simply do not want to have to ask your husband's permission to spend money. It might be the $3,000 Bar Mitzvah gown that your husband would flip over, so you tell him it cost $1,500. Or it might be a new kind of neurotherapy that insurance won't cover and your husband doesn't really think is necessary but you think is worth a try for your daughter. Or it might be that your dearest friend needs you to send her an airplane ticket to come visit you because she doesn't have any money and desperately needs a vacation. It doesn't really matter what it is—it matters that in your life, he who payeth for most of it doesn't get to sayeth for all of it. You must have some degree of financial control over the things that are important to you.

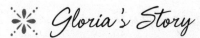

Gloria's Story

My grandfather was very cheap. It's one thing not to have money. It's another thing to have the money and not to give it. If a man is the one who is cheap, the woman is doomed. I was very close to my grandmother. I watched my grandparents scream at each other all the time, often over money. My grandmother used to somehow squirrel away money to give me presents. I could see it made her happy to do so, like she had gotten something over on my grandfather. When Sol and I got engaged, my grandfather came over to me and asked if he could give me something. He had not even known that my grandmother had already given us our engagement gift. I think it was my experience with my grandparents that seared this lesson of financial independence upon me. Never would I be completely financially dependent on a man. Never would I let my daughters become that way either. ■

✳ *Lisa's Story*

I had a friend whose husband used to ask her about every ATM withdrawal she made from their account. Why did you take out the money? What did you spend it on? If my husband ever interrogated me about money like this, I'd fly out the door with no regrets. Too many women have come into my law office with no money and no resources whatsoever, sometimes after a marriage of thirty years. These women could provide for neither themselves nor their children. If there is one lesson I insist on Joanna learning, it is that she must learn a skill for which she will get paid so that she can always support herself and her family. ■

✳ *Jill's Arrangement*

Bobby and I are financial partners. Whether I earned it or he did, we pool our money together. I admit I still have my own 401(k) from a previous job (I guess you could call that my *knipple*), but other than that we joined all our funds. Bobby trusts me and I him. I saw how he treated his family when he got divorced and know if anything ever happened to us he would do the same with me (God forbid, bite your tongue three times). Bobby is a man of integrity, loyalty and trust, which is why I married him. Do I have a backup plan? Yes. We have a prenuptial agreement, which I strongly believe in, so I don't have to worry. I also have two arms, two legs and a big brain (and mouth), so I can always earn a living. I don't believe I am entitled to anything in this life and was taught always to be prepared. Bobby worked for more than thirty years and now I, too, am adding to our nest egg. I always confer with Bobby for the big purchases, but overall, I buy what we need or want and I decide what to give to charity. Our marriage works because even though I have the ability to spend freely, I don't abuse the privilege. I also know that if necessary, I can always rely on myself. I do think it is essential that every woman have access to money she and her husband earn so that she has freedom. I couldn't live any other way. ■

ask yourself

1. In your relationship, who makes more money?

2. Do you have access to your money? Do you also have access to his money?

3. Who decides how the money is spent? Are you comfortable with this situation?

4. Do you think you have enough influence over decisions about money?

5. Have you fallen into a pattern where only one of you pays all the bills and knows how much money you have?

6. Do you feel you are not able to spend money as you think fit? If so, start withdrawing money anyway. Either spend it or save it in your own name. In other words, start your *knipple*.

7. Do you have access to some money that is solely in your own name? Make sure you have your own account. You never know when you may need it.

What's His Is Yours, What's Yours Is Yours

This is the classic Jewish statement on marital finances, incidentally uttered by both Jewish mothers *and* fathers to their daughters. Not to their sons, mind you, only to their daughters. We've never heard "What's hers is yours." That would be distinctly ungentlemanly.

We concede that some secrets of a Jewish mother are sexist. This one is downright paternalistic. (We do love our daddies!) But note the obvious lesson—men and women are not the same. Men and women deserve equal rights, but they are not the same. Therefore, some rules must be bent to favor women over men because the realities of life usually mean:

1. Women get pregnant or decide to adopt children.

2. Women usually take over more of the everyday responsibilities of raising children than men do.

3. While women are raising their children, they are usually not earning as much money.

4. Women should not be deprived of their share of income because they have chosen to use their time to raise children.

Are there exceptions to this advice? Sure. You can be the one who says, "Whatever you earn is yours, honey, keep it in your name, I trust you. And tell you what, I'll deposit my paycheck into our joint account too because I love you so much." And we have a name for you—it begins with an *s* and ends with a *k* (and it isn't Salma Hayek). If you haven't figured it out yet, you can look it up in our Yiddish glossary.

You can also be the woman who holds everything in a joint account with both names on it, which means everything that's his is yours and everything that's yours is his. That works too, but make sure you still have a *knipple*, just in case. . . .

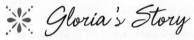

Gloria's Story

Sol has always considered any money I earn to be money I can spend however I want. I don't argue. And he is very generous—it should be this way for every woman. ■

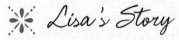

Lisa's Story

I have been earning money since the day I got married, and the beauty of it is that Bill has always looked at that money as my money, not our money. We never fought about it. His money is our money and my money is my money, exactly as each of us was raised. (Thank you, Mom and Dad Wexler!) Of course, much of my money has been spent on the family, but after all these years, I've saved a nice-size *knipple*, which we are both proud of. Make sure you have a *knipple* for your own rainy day, may it never come. ■

Jill's Story

I may be in a unique situation with Bobby, or simply too trusting, but I don't feel the need to squirrel away my own funds. On the other hand, I also know that I can get to our money whenever I need to, since our accounts are in both our names. Of course, in case of a real emergency, I do have that 401(k) . . . God forbid, bite my tongue three times, I should ever really need to use it. ■

ask yourself

1. Do you still have money in your own name, alone?

2. How is his paycheck deposited—into a joint account or another way?

3. Do you have to account for the way you spend your money?

4. Does he understand that you are allowed to save money on your own but that you are also allowed full access to spend his?

The Prenup

If Jewish mothers could make prenuptial agreements go away with the wave of a diamond-studded hand, they would. Prenups? How unromantic. How untrusting. How unfair. Unfortunately, how common.

Signing a prenuptial agreement means negotiating the divorce before you eat your wedding cake. But for some couples, especially those in which one of the partners has already been married, a prenup is an essential security blanket to enable them to move forward with a marital commitment. They may have children from their first marriage they are worried about protecting or obligations to others that could go awry in case of a divorce. Sometimes, people simply want the security of knowing they can walk out of a bad marriage and not have to leave behind the property they have earned or inherited.

For Mom and Dad, and Lisa and Bill, the issue of prenups never arose. Both couples started out young, poor and full of romantic love. The only "baggage" they brought into the marriages consisted of the honeymoon trousseau. For Jill and Bobby, however, the prenup was definitely an issue.

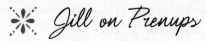

Jill on Prenups

Bobby raised the issue of a prenup several months before we got married. When I met Bobby, he was a man of substantial financial success, and it was his second marriage. I understood his concerns about protecting his three children. I wasn't marrying Bobby for his money; I was madly in love with him and in the marriage for the long run. So I really didn't mind signing a prenup, provided it was fair. For women planning to marry men who have been divorced, I always tell them to look at the way their prospective husband is treating his ex-wife. If he was the breadwinner, how fairly did he share the wealth? How hard did he fight to keep what he thought was his? Don't marry someone else's cheap, mean ex-husband. He might be yours someday! In the case of my prenup, I wanted Lisa to represent me as my attorney, but she refused. She said that even if this was her area of expertise, which it wasn't, she didn't want such a big responsibility in case things went wrong. However, she did insist I get my own attorney, even though I didn't think I needed one.

My advice is that if you believe in your relationship and you trust the guy you are going to marry, then don't be afraid of a prenup. When presented with the contract, examine it from his point of view as well as yours to ask the all-important question: Is it fair? Fair is the criterion I use when negotiating any deal, business or personal. For example, the longer you are married, the more equity you should get. Do you really think you deserve half his wealth if you only stay married a few years and have no children together? Do you think you should never have to work again if you were only married for a few months or if you cheated on your spouse? It makes me crazy when I read about these high-profile divorce cases where the woman demands $60,000 a month in child support. Even I couldn't spend that much. This works both ways—I read of men who go after their wives for outrageous sums in alimony, when they seem perfectly capable of making a living on their own. Remember that if you stay married until your spouse dies, the will supersedes the prenup. Make sure your estate planning is fair too, because if your marriage lasted and was a good one, you'll want to spend your remaining years in comfort. ■

"Five Minutes of Understanding"

Gloria uses this phrase with Sol to calm the waters, those churning, turbulent waters that threaten to overwhelm us. When things are really bad and it seems like communication has stopped, with each person stuck in his or her corner of the boxing ring nursing his or her wounds, Mom will speak up in a small voice. "Sol, can I have five minutes of understanding?" It usually does the trick. If somebody asked it of you, wouldn't you listen?

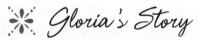 *Gloria's Story*

In the beginning of our marriage, every time we had a fight, Sol used to stop talking to me and treat me to a wall of silence. I had come from a very loud and fairly angry family, but at least we knew when one of us was angry with another. At first, I didn't know how to react and was quite upset. As the years went on, however, I started to do the same thing to Sol that he did to me, which didn't satisfy either one of us.

Now Sol gets very unhappy when I don't respond. The five minutes of understanding allow us both to calm down and collect ourselves. We make up a little more quickly than we used to also. We are not as strong as we once were, and it is healthier to be happy. ∎

ask yourself

1. What words do you use to communicate that you need your spouse's attention? Are they effective?

2. How effective are you at asking your spouse for advice about something or telling your spouse something you know will upset him?

3. Do you occasionally need those five minutes of understanding?

Stay or Go? The List of Pros and Cons . . . and When It Really Is Time to Leave

The Jewish mother believes in marriage and believes in divorce. She may not like divorce, but she believes that in certain circumstances, divorce is desirable, even occasionally necessary. We do not need to go into the particulars; there are the obvious ones, like violence and drug abuse, and the not-so-obvious ones, like a relationship that has essentially been dead for years. No Jewish mother wants to see her kid suffer in a loveless life. Are you going to sit out your own life waiting for him or her to change? Forget it. Move on.

How do we know what your breaking point is? We don't. Obviously there are many, many breaking points right now because more than one out of every two marriages today will end in divorce in this country. That is simply staggering, isn't it?

Personally, we wouldn't tolerate philandering. Although we have heard *theoretically* there are people who have been able to kiss and make up and move on after this kind of behavior, in real life, we don't know any couples who actually did. We know couples who stayed together for a long time after the cheating and who appeared to the outside world as if everything was peachy, but eventually those couples separated. All of them. Anyway, we think too much of ourselves to stay with a guy who would cheat.

Jill's Story

I come from a family that stays married. Both my grandparents and parents and close relatives all stayed married. Getting divorced was not an easy choice for me. My mother knew I was unhappy and that I needed to make a change. This was very hard for her to watch and for me to do. I was crying all the time during this period. I wanted to give it one more chance and went to therapy. I took Steven to a session I will never forget. In that room, Steven said I was the same person, but that he had changed. At my next session alone, the therapist told me I could leave and move on now without guilt. My advice is this: Try everything, including therapy, to stay in your marriage. For a second, I even thought about having another child to "save my marriage," but I knew that wouldn't solve our problems and would only create more stress for everyone. But if your marriage must end, make sure you both agree to put your children first. ■

*G*loria and Lisa, 1960

*S*ol, Gloria, Lisa and Jill, Christmas vacation in the Catskills, 1972

*J*ill, Gloria and Lisa, Woodmere, 1969

*L*isa teaching Jill how to ride a bike, Woodmere, June 1969

*J*ill at age seven in front of her house, August 1970

*E*thel, Sol, Gloria, Jill and Lisa, at Lisa's Bat Mitzvah, Woodmere, May 1973

*J*ill and Lisa, Camp Kinni-Kinnic, Vermont, 1972

*L*isa and Bill, graduating from Johns Hopkins University together, Baltimore, May 1981

$\mathcal{G}$randma Syl, Aunt Cooky and Gloria, Gloria and Sol's wedding, Bell Harbor, New York, Christmas Day, 1957

$\mathcal{J}$ill and Bobby, Hamptons, 2009

$\mathcal{G}$loria and Sol on the cruise ship the *Leonardo da Vinci*, 1969

$\mathcal{L}$isa and Bill's wedding, with Bill's sisters, Debby (Wexler) Dombrowski and Laurie (Wexler) Stolowitz, and his parents, Joan and Jerry Wexler, Lawrence, New York, 1982

*G*loria with Aunt Gloria at Jonathan's Bar Mitzvah, 2000

*J*ill with her two oldest friends, Elisa (Staple) Rosen and Jill (Clare) Kirschenburg, Central Park, 1995

*T*he four "Golden Girls": Lisa, Jill and their cousins Sharon (Bronheim) Caputo and Debby (Bronheim) Hofmann, Westport, 2000

*L*isa with her close college friend Sandy (White) Braem at the JCC, Norwalk, Connecticut, 1991

𝒜llyson at her Bat Mitzvah, New York,
New York, November 5, 2005

ℒisa and Jill at Joanna's Bat Mitzvah,
2005

ℒisa, Allyson and Joanna,
Chanukah, Westport, 2000

𝒥oanna and Jonathan at Jon's
Bar Mitzvah, Bridgeport,
Connecticut, 2000

*J*oanna, Jill and Ally, World Trade Center
Windows on the World, 2000

*A*llyson and Grandma Helen,
Far Rockaway, New York, 1999

*L*isa and Jonathan,
Brookline, Massachusetts, 1989

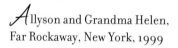

*B*obby's family
on the boat,
Hamptons, early
2000

*L*isa and Jill at Lisa's Radio Studio, AM WSTC/ WNLK, 2008

*B*ill, Joanna, Lisa and Jon, November 2009

*A*llyson, Jill and Bobby at Bryant Park skating rink, New York, New York, fall 2009

*J*onathan Zarin, Jill and David Zarin, Jill, Allyson, Jennifer and Bobby, ARTRageous, 2009

*K*elly Killoren Bensimon, Luann de Lesseps, Jill, Bethenny
Frankel, Ramona Singer and Alex McCord, premiere party for *The
Real Housewives of New York City* Season 2, March 2009

*J*ill, Lisa, Aunt Cooky and Gloria,
Fourth of July, 2008

*L*isa, Sol, Gloria and Jill, October 2009

We've given you these secrets of a Jewish mother so that your married life can be a happy one. But the bottom line is you can control only what you do; you can't control what anyone else does. So if you are unhappy, go into marriage counseling. We look at counseling as giving your relationship a touch-up, like redoing your house. Everyone could use it now and then, even couples who think their marriage is just fine. If your husband loves you, he will go with you into counseling because he will be scared to lose you. Good counseling helps you fall in love again and rediscover why you got married in the first place. Even if you go alone, counseling is a place for you to sort out your own feelings and gives you space in which to grow.

Here's the real message we are trying to share with you—marriage is work, but if it isn't working in ways you can tolerate, then leave. You'll know when you get to that point. But we really hope you never do.

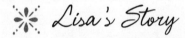 *Lisa's Story*

I have so many friends whose marriages broke up over the years, and the one thing they have in common is that these were always the couples I swore were so happy! You can never tell what is really happening in anyone's marriage.

Why have Bill and I stayed together all these years? I think it's because both of us never gave up on the marriage at the exact same moment. God knows, there have been times when each of us has wanted to walk out; I think that's normal. Life is stressful, and parenting throws curves at you that you didn't expect when it was just the two of you. I'm sure living with me isn't wonderful all of the time; I get busy and distracted easily. Bill had a severe obesity problem for many years. I was in despair that I had lost the man I married. But God was good to us; Bill turned fifty and turned his life around. At this stage when we are just starting to see what an empty nest might look like, I have my Bill back again. As Aunt Nessie says, what is a Jew without hope? We live on it. ∎

ask yourself

1. Are you seriously thinking of leaving your marriage?

2. If so, have you received marriage counseling?

3. Have you made the list of pros and cons?

4. Is this problem something that you can never see yourself forgiving?

5. Have you stowed away any cash? Remember, you'll need money.

The Final Secret: Love Means Talking Even When He's the Last Person on Earth You Ever Want to Talk to Again

Jewish mothers are famous for keeping it real—too real, in fact, for some people. Indeed we can be brutally, tactlessly, in-your-face real. But just because we see it like it is, and often tell it that way too, does not mean we don't laugh about life. We sometimes laugh ourselves into hysteria (when we're not crying, yelling, complaining, criticizing or telling other people what to do). An intelligent wife knows when, what and how to communicate.

First, do not be a bore. No one is interested in every minute detail of your day. (Admit it; are you? Even if you can remember?) Discern what is important and make sure you regularly talk about those things with your husband. What should you tell him? Start with the kids, if you have them. If his eyes glaze over when you discuss the details of the orthodontia, okay. But watch how excited he gets about buying the Little League uniform. Parenting is a two-person job, so include him as much as possible.

Of course, wise wives know when to mention that your son had a fight on the bus, your mother is coming to stay for a month or your daughter didn't get invited to the big birthday party. Picking the right time to have difficult conversations is an art. Sometimes there is no right time, and sometimes you'll impulsively choose the wrong time, but pay attention to that. Part of working at a marriage is knowing which buttons you can push and when.

What else should you communicate? Your feelings. Are you happy with your routine? Do you like your job? Are you excited about a new friend you just met? Are your parents, or his, causing you stress? Most important, how are you feeling about him? This is the conversation that keeps marriages alive. Remember that.

By the way, we fully know that getting most men to discuss their own feelings is like pulling teeth. It's in the man-code, transmitted from generation to generation. However, you know in your heart that the reason he married *you*, as opposed to anyone else on this earth, is because you are the *only* person he can talk to about his feelings. Therefore, make him exercise this muscle often. It's good for both of you.

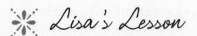

Lisa's Lesson

At my best friend Sandy's bridal shower in Guadalajara, Mexico, Sandy's mother had us play a game where we threw little bits of paper into a hat. Each contained a bit of advice we wrote to the married couple, and all were read aloud. I thought Sandy's mother, who was married to a minister and had been a missionary for decades, would offer some platitude like "Love each other always" or "Never skip church." Instead, she wrote "Communicate." So simple, so elegant, such incredibly good advice. No wonder her marriage lasted sixty years. ■

As far as when it's best to communicate, Jill has her own philosophy on the subject.

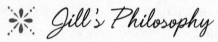

Jill's Philosophy

I believe a man is hard when he is soft and soft when he is hard. If I have to translate, what I'm saying is that it's easier to get what you want from your man when you have put him in a really good mood, so don't be afraid to get out those candles, dim the lights and put on a sexy negligee. "Men are really very simple creatures," as Grandma Syl used to say. ■

Another secret to keeping your marriage alive is to keep your lives interesting. You are on this journey together, so defy expectations. Keep your sense of humor; laugh together. Keep your sense of wonder and share it with each other. Read the newspapers and talk about what they say. Follow your passions. Work on a political campaign, teach music, create a garden, go back to business school—whatever. Have an opinion. Encourage your husband to do these things too; otherwise, you may lose interest in him.

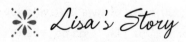

Lisa's Story

Bill travels frequently—either I could sit home and pine and whine, or I could start a book club, run for local elective office and keep my law practice alive. Each of those activities gave me a reason to be out in the world, satisfied my need for intellectual stimulation and kept our conversations interesting. When Jon went to college, I pursued my dream of creating my own radio show. I figured that gave me the ultimate excuse to speak to fascinating people. Bill has been incredibly supportive. It has been the beginning of a new chapter in our marriage as well as my career. ■

ask yourself

1. On a scale of 1 to 10, how good is your marriage right now?

2. Are you an interesting person? Is he?

3. What makes your marriage work?

4. What doesn't work for you?

5. Have you been to marriage counseling before? Did it help?

In Conclusion

Is this all we need to know to keep our marriages alive? How would we know? But it has worked for us. We are thankful that our guys, Daddy (Sol), Bill and Bobby, have put up with us this long. We counted, and between the three of us we are working on a grand total of eighty-nine years of wedded . . . bliss? Let's not kid ourselves. Some bliss, some *tsuris*, but always, always, a lot of laughter and love.

(You want to know what *tsuris* is? Go directly to the parenting chapter. It starts as soon as the kids are born.)

7

Family Focus—
The Non-negotiables

You are a bride today and a
mother-in-law tomorrow. Be kind.
What goes around, comes around.

Our Jewish mother philosophy on family is pretty simple. Even though your family may drive you insane at times, you should stay as emotionally close to them as possible. We even recommend living nearby (maybe not next door, but nearby), but we know that is not always an option. Why do we feel this way? Because of all the people in the world, your family is the group most likely to support you when you need them. We always say, "You only dump on the ones you love." Who, except your family, knows the real you? More important, after knowing you, who still loves you? Usually, that's your family.

Our particular family resembles a Neil Simon/Woody Allen dynamic, complete with dramatic gestures, eccentric personalities and loud voices. Of course we fight, a lot. We also try to make up, quickly. Mommy thinks grudges fester like untreated wounds and the infection gets deeper until you end up having to cut off a limb, or sever the relationship. She taught us that it is better to air the grievance, clean out the wound, make or accept the apology and move on. With a kiss. Always with a kiss.

Even though you cannot choose your family the way you can your friends, you can choose the battles you pick with them. You can even choose to embrace your family, despite their faults. You do not have to continue the feuds and the intergenerational grudges that you might have inherited. We have reconnected with long-estranged cousins years after everyone has forgotten why our families were fighting in the first place. But it's a shame about those lost years. We were deprived of the shared histories that bind families, like our uncle's incredibly loud snore, which began right after dessert, or the particular cackle emitted by our great-aunt. Take a survey of your family tree. Is there anyone there you miss? Someone you never got to know? It's not too late. Why not invite someone to a holiday dinner? Holiday dinners are great places to begin making memories you can laugh over years from now.

Nonetheless, Jewish mothers are not Pollyannas. We realize there are situations in life where you need to give up, walk away and make your family from other people you love. Some people are not worth the aggravation, even if they are family. If you have given a family member so many chances that you are worn out, then sometimes you must say good-bye to preserve your own health and sanity. If the relationship is meant to rekindle, it will; if not, there is someone else in your life who loves and appreciates you. For us, our close friends are our family too. For many people, close friends are their only family. Treasure and nurture those relationships that mean the most to you.

The Jewish mother uses a "*mensch*" yardstick to evaluate behavior. Was he a *mensch* or not? Was that a *menschlich* thing to do, or not? A *mensch* is a person—traditionally a man, though we apply the yardstick to women as well—who acts like "a real person," someone with integrity and a sense of morals. A *mensch* does not talk about doing the right thing; a *mensch* does the right thing. There are certain responsibilities in life that define whether or not you are a *mensch*. You can try to weasel out of these obligations, but a weasel you will be. We call these commitments "non-negotiables," even though we negotiate our way through them every day. Though many of our non-negotiables stem from our Jewish heritage, they are based on universal ideas—what we may require for a Bar Mitzvah, you may require for a baptism. The goal is always the same: Do the right thing, be there for your family and try not to hurt anyone else in the process.

Do the Right Thing: Holidays

Remember Spike Lee's seminal film *Do the Right Thing*? Well, none of us saw the movie, but we know the motto. Spike must have borrowed it from Aunt Nessie or Aunt Cooky. Daddy always says it. Jill thinks she invented the line too. Everyone wants credit.

Doing the right thing begins with fulfilling your obligations to family and friends, starting with the holidays. We build our entire calendar around the Jewish holidays. Maybe you do the same with Christmas and Easter. For us, it's Rosh Hashanah and Yom Kippur in the fall (known as the High Holidays) and Passover in the spring. On the Jewish New Year, which begins in the fall with Rosh Hashanah, we take stock of the past year, make our apologies to people and God, set some new goals and hope the Book of Life will be sealed again for all our loved ones. On Passover we hold a Seder to commemorate the Jews' exodus from slavery in Egypt, because pretty much every Jewish holiday has the same theme: "They tried to kill us. They failed. Let's eat."

All kidding aside, the Jewish holidays are a very serious and important time for us. Sometimes we wish our lives slowed down during the rest of the year the way they do during these holidays. Time stops for these occasions. Appearances are mandatory. Missing a holiday is acceptable only if you are gravely ill, God forbid, or if you have to go to your in-laws. On that note, your in-laws are always welcome at our homes, but we would be extremely upset if you chose to spend the Jewish holidays with your in-laws on a regular basis, instead of with us. On the other hand, if your in-laws choose to invite us too, then we can alternate to make everyone happy. We'll even bring the wine.

For many years, Mommy "made" all the holidays for our family, every single one. Those were the days when we lived close enough to walk to and from temple, and most of our close relatives lived a five-minute drive away. Now Lisa makes the first day of Rosh Hashanah and Passover, and Aunt Cooky makes the second. We are definitely a "two-day" family; less observant Jews celebrate only one day of each of these High Holidays. Jill tries to host the "break fast" for Yom Kippur. All the food is kosher and cooked from scratch. Lisa's chicken soup and Mommy's pot roast are the traditional menu and the big draws. It doesn't matter that we are now physically spread out, living in Connecticut, Florida, Manhattan, Dix Hills and Hewlett. It doesn't matter that it can take three hours to get to the host's house if the traffic is bad. We are summoned. We appear.

Our Jewish holidays are always shared with close friends, many of whom are not Jewish. We don't happen to think someone's religion is especially relevant when it comes to sharing our holidays. These are special times for our family and we want our close friends to be with us. Also, we always make room for another seat at the table if we discover someone has no place to go. For us, the holidays are about enjoying good food, intense political conversations and lots of love. With every year, these occasions become more important, not less. As we slow down, the years speed up.

✳ *Gloria's Story*

My grandmother had eight siblings. Everyone lived within walking distance of each other in Brooklyn. Every holiday we were together at the "compound," which is what we called the Fifty-fifth Street house where my grandparents lived. All nineteen cousins and assorted friends would come together for the holidays. I remember all the men sitting at the huge dining table, being waited on by a bevy of women. The kids had their tables in an adjoining room. It was very comforting. We felt so cocooned and totally secure within our family structure. Those were indeed the good old days.

I taught my children that the Jewish holidays are a "cannot miss" event. Sol and I make reservations from Florida to fly north every fall and spring to spend these holidays with everyone. Getting together on holidays is a sign of respect as well as love. ■

✳ *Jill and Lisa's Take*

The Jewish holidays mean a lot to us. When we were growing up, we used to walk to and from temple, in the way that Orthodox Jews do, instead of driving there. At our synagogue, the High Holidays were also an annual fashion show. Daddy and the other men would hang out outside in the cool, fall weather watching the women pass by, dressed up in hats and the latest styles. Once in a while they would go in and pray.

Our Papa Benny, Daddy's father, was very religious. He

never drove on the Jewish Sabbath, which was from sundown Friday to sunset on Saturday. Lisa's Bat Mitzvah was held on a Friday night. Papa had a choice—either he would have to drive to *shul* or miss the Bat Mitzvah. What to do? He always said this was an easy decision. Do you see him in the picture, cutting the *challah* with our Papa Jack, Mommy's father? Papa was so proud to be there; he wouldn't have missed his granddaughter's Bat Mitzvah for the world. The lesson he taught us? Religion is always more about the spirit of the law than the letter of the law. ■

The Bris

Here's an old joke: "Jews are barbaric. First they cut off your penis, and then they say, 'Let's eat.'"

We say, "Let's eat," pretty much after everything; why should a circumcision be different? The "Bris," the Yiddish pronunciation of the Brit Milah, in other words, circumcision, is one of the oldest and most sacred commandments in the Jewish faith. It's what separates the men from the boys, so to speak, or at least the Jewish men from all others whose faiths or customs do not perform this rite. Jews do this on the eighth day after birth, unless there is a health reason to delay.

If you have a Jewish friend who is giving birth to a boy, don't expect to be invited to the Bris. Don't be insulted either. Our custom holds that no one is invited to the Bris. Because this ritual always happens at short notice, you make it your business to find out where and when it is happening and you show up if possible. Your appearance isn't mandatory, unless the baby is close family. After the ceremony, expect a nice lunch. You do not need to bring a baby gift with you to a Bris; your presence is gift enough. You can send a gift later.

ask yourself

1. Are family holidays a priority for you?

2. Do you dread the holidays or look forward to them?

3. What childhood customs, religious or otherwise, do you want to continue with your own family?

4. **What are your holiday traditions?**

5. **Have you told your family that these traditions are a priority for you?**

Do the Right Thing: Funerals and Hospitals

Outside of holidays, funerals are the other occasion where family attendance is mandatory. You attend a funeral to comfort the living, not merely to pay your respects to the deceased. Daddy says Aunt Cooky has attended more funerals for more people than have most rabbis because she considers it a special *mitzvah* to be there for a friend who is grieving. If, for some reason, you cannot attend the funeral to comfort a loved one, be it friend or family, then we recommend you pay a condolence call. Jews call this a "*shiva* call," because we "sit *shiva*" in mourning together for a week after the burial. Handwritten sympathy cards are always appreciated as well. If you want to send something to a grieving family, send food, not flowers. Jews like to eat; they hate to watch flowers die. It's depressing.

Mommy is also big on hospital visits to friends and family, having unfortunately spent too many nights in hospitals over the years herself. She has a rule for visitors, though: Try to look nice when you go. Put a little lipstick on. Why? Because lying in a hospital is sad; seeing you look pretty will lift your loved one's spirits. We really are such a superficial group; we always get happy looking at people who look good. Don't you?

Also, we always bring gifts to patients, like magazines, mints or a cute stuffed animal. The only happy reason to be in a hospital is to have a baby; anything else is simply not fun. Visiting your loved one in the hospital is an important *mitzvah*.

What Would Gloria Do?

This was a real discussion that occurred in our family. Thank God the worst scenario never came to pass, but the point of the conversation has become family folklore.

Jill's Potential Dilemma

Jill and her first husband, Steven, had planned a vacation in Europe. They knew Steven's grandfather was very sick, so the question was raised: If something were to happen to Steven's grandfather while they were gone, what should they do, continue the vacation or come back for the funeral? Steven's parents were adamant: Do not interrupt your vacation. You can mourn when you come home.

What Would Gloria Do?

Mommy was adamant as well: Should Steven's grandfather pass away, God forbid, Jill and Steven were to come home immediately. Mommy felt strongly that their duty was to be with their family, to comfort them during this time. Vacations are a second priority to grief.

The Punchline

Steven's response to Jill was, "Let's make a deal; if I don't have to go to your grandparents' funerals, you don't have to come to mine." As you may imagine, that went over really big with Mommy. Thank goodness nobody died while anybody was on vacation.

ask yourself

1. Do you go out of your way to visit hospitals, attend funerals, wakes, etc?

2. What do you expect people to do when you suffer a loss or are sick?

3. Do you owe a visit, *shiva* call, sympathy note or get-well-soon card to anyone?

Grandma Helen

There aren't many people who can say they lived during three centuries. Sol's mother, our Grandma Helen, was born in 1899 and lived until April of 2005. Until the day she died, she ate with her own teeth, read the paper without glasses and did not spend one night, ever, in a nursing home. On her 106th birthday, Mayor Bloomberg issued a proclamation in her honor. After her husband, Ben, died, she used to say: "What am I still doing here?" We told her that God intended for her to be here as an example to the next generation, to Jon, Ally and Joanna. And she was. What was her secret? God knows, it had to be the genes. Genes, and a diet that consisted of chicken and fresh vegetables every day of her life. Must it always come down to the matzoh ball soup? Apparently so.

Bar Mitzvahs, Weddings, Family Gatherings: The Grudge Starts Here

We build our lives around major events that start with dreams from childhood. Yet these same milestones are also minefields of misunderstandings, miscommunications and unmet expectations. The clash of fantasy and reality can be devastating. Often, our disappointments turn into righteous indignation, followed by anger and ending with "I'm never speaking to or seeing you again." And for what? Wasn't this originally supposed to be a happy occasion, or a solemn one? Why do we often end up being so petty about the things that are meant to commemorate the larger aspects of life, like love, commitment and the importance of faith?

Jews plan Bar Mitzvahs more than three years in advance. Nowadays, there are engagements that also take that long. For all major events, invitation lists are divided into the "want-tos" versus the "have-tos." Cross off a "have-to" and watch the feud begin.

So many family relationships have fallen apart as a result of the unanswered invitation, the unsent invitation, the inadequate gift and the incorrect event attire. Who can forget that classic scene in the film *Avalon*, when the uncle said, "And you didn't wait for me to cut the turkey!" thereby ending the family tradition of spending Thanksgiving together. We've got a few of those stories to share. Lessons to come later. . . .

Gloria's Tales

I was engaged to Sol and went to Bonwit Teller to try on a wedding gown. It was made of heavy satin, simple and quite lovely. I tried it on and started to cry because I was so taken aback at how lovely I looked and felt. I came home and told my mother. She told me she would not pay for a new dress and I would have to wear my cousin's dress, made of chiffon for her May wedding. We were getting married in December; this dress was the wrong style, the wrong fabric and not especially flattering on me. I know money was tight but I believe that if she had liked Sol she would have bought me my own wedding dress. I wore the damn chiffon dress and never forgot or forgave.

Weddings cause more problems and more long-term grudges than any other single function in life. My parents didn't speak to Sol's parents for ten years as a result of our wedding. The details are not important—it's all crap. I begged Sol to elope, but he would not do it. So instead, I got married in a dress in December that I resented wearing. My mother did not allow me to invite my friends to the dinner, only for cocktails. When Lisa got married, I begged her to take $25,000, which was the cost of a beautiful wedding then, and just walk away. She wouldn't do it. I worked really hard to make sure Lisa wouldn't suffer the same regrets I did. Luckily, that wedding turned out okay. ■

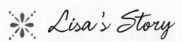

Lisa's Story

I can think of quite a few stories about grudges in our family that started when someone wore the wrong dress, or gave a really cheap gift, or decided to cancel at the last minute, or didn't show up altogether, but the problem is that if I give you the details, then the ugliness starts all over again. So you know what? Here's a story about how I unwittingly hurt one of my dearest friends, instead.

When Joanna's Bat Mitzvah came, I made my list and decided not to invite a very close friend from law school with whom I had lost touch. I figured she didn't know Joanna anyway, I hadn't seen her in a long time, blah blah blah. Recently, I had dreams about her and called her up, because it had been so long and I missed her. We talked, and she told me that she realized the Bat Mitzvah had come and gone and said how much I had hurt her feelings by not inviting her to such an important *simcha*. She figured that since I had excluded her from such an important occasion, our friendship could never be repaired. I felt awful; I had made a terrible mistake. You can't go back, you can only hope to be forgiven and move forward. Mommy is right. No matter what, these affairs end up causing hurt feelings. ■

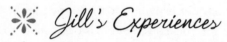 *Jill's Experiences*

Michele and I grew up together. We were always competitive. I went to college and she didn't. She was very rich and I wasn't. She had a hot body and I thought I was fat (it's a family thing . . . we always think we are fat). After college we stayed distant "friends" because I lived in Boston. When I got engaged to Steven, I didn't want to invite Michele to the wedding. I thought she was jealous of me and wished me the dreaded "evil eye." Was I crazy? Who knows? But I got married and did not invite her. I felt terribly guilty and had nightmares after the wedding. I finally called her so my nightmares would stop. It was hard, but I called and apologized. I was sorry. I couldn't change the past, but I was determined to make an effort to be friends. Michele started dating someone special and we went out with them often. She got engaged. I was thrilled. When the invitations went out to her wedding, I did not receive one. Spite? Tit for tat? Michele got even; she hurt me back. We are not friends today.

For my second wedding, to Bobby, I had the smallest possible wedding. Only twenty-five members of our immediate families attended. We held the ceremony in the rabbi's office and hosted an elegant lunch reception at a five-star restaurant in New York. I did not invite one friend. If I had, the others would have been insulted. Everyone understood. I felt strongly that for my second marriage, I wanted to minimize any stress that might occur in planning a wedding. Our original plan was to organize a reception afterward in which we could celebrate with all our friends, but it never happened. Instead, we ended up celebrating at many smaller gatherings with our friends. This was definitely the right decision for us. ■

The Bar Mitzvah

The Bar Mitzvah has become such a significant subject of American cultural scrutiny that we have even read that some Christians do "faux" Bar Mitzvahs just to get in on the party scene. They are missing the big picture. Yes, we do love to party. As Daddy says, "Which would you rather spend your money on? Celebrating a Bar Mitzvah or a hospital bill?" Daddy prefers to dance. But the Bar Mitzvah is more than a party; it truly is a rite of passage, and not just for the kid.

The Jewish mother is literally counting down the days until the next Bar or Bat Mitzvah from the moment of birth. We kid you not: As soon as our cousin's first son was born, Mommy called and said, "We've got a Bar Mitzvah in thirteen years!" Like it was going to be tomorrow. For you who are not Jewish, here is the basic Bar Mitzvah drill:

1. For a boy, the word is Bar Mitzvah, for a girl, we call it Bat (or Bas) Mitzvah. The age is usually thirteen, but it can be twelve for girls.

2. The ceremony is a Jewish coming-of-age. It means that the child is considered responsible to perform the *mitzvoth* (the commandments) of the Torah (the first five books of Moses). Unfortunately, what this often also means is the end of a Jewish child's formal religious education, instead of the beginning.

3. The Bar Mitzvah itself is usually a two-part event—the religious service followed by a party of some kind. The party can be a luncheon at the synagogue, a teenagers-only party or a gala at the Plaza Hotel, complete with Yankee baseball centerpieces. Anything goes and anything has gone.

4. If your kid is invited to a Bar Mitzvah, any gift is considered appropriate. Nobody judges gifts teenagers give each other, at least they shouldn't. If you are invited as an adult, it is always safe to give money. For girls, jewelry is a nice choice, as are watches and cameras for boys and girls. We also like Judaica, like candlesticks or special books. Anything handmade is incredibly special and will be most appreciated.

ask yourself

1. Have you ever felt wronged by not being invited to an event you expected to go to?

2. Do you remember not inviting someone you should have? Did you apologize?

3. Which family relationships in your group were damaged after one of these affairs? Are they worth repairing?

4. How many grudges can you name in your family that were started as a result of a missed communication or hurt feelings as the result of a wedding or other special occasion?

So Is the Grudge Worth It?

We have endless experience with grudges. The stories never end. We've got the cousins who stopped talking for ten years because she came late to a family wedding and accidentally got left out of some wedding pictures. How about the one we've all heard where she wasn't picked to be the bridesmaid so she dropped the friendship altogether? There's a really, good kind friend. She has turned what should be a time of joy for someone else into a portrait of "What about me? I'm left out, my feelings are hurt." There are lessons from these lessons. So here are a few basic rules to consider before holding the grudge that will sever a relationship for life. Learn from our mistakes; we've made plenty.

1. How important is that person to you altogether? If she is someone you see only at weddings and funerals, then don't expect too much in the way of gifts or thoughtful gestures. Do not make more of the relationship than is

there. If you accidentally insult her or she insults you, who cares?

2. If the person is very important to you, never let a gift come between you. Period. If he or she came to your event, that is all that matters. Showing up is always much more important than a gift (though of course both are appreciated!).

3. Do not confuse the amount of money someone gives you with his respect for you. People do this all the time with gifts at weddings or Bat Mitzvahs, but it is wrong. Not everybody can afford the "going rate."

4. Decide what was really insulted—your vanity? Your pride? Think about this and how much it will take out of *you* to stay angry.

5. Try to see things from her point of view; it's possible that both your hormones are working overtime. Stress can do that.

6. Have you told the person that you are holding a grudge against her? At least give her the chance to feel guilty about what she did wrong. Remember that most of the time, people are preoccupied with their own problems, not yours.

For Siblings:
You Only Have Each Other

There is nothing more important to the Jewish mother than making sure her kids understand that one day she will be gone and they will only have each other. Yes, her children may (in fact, should) move on to get married and have children of their own, but to the Jewish mother, her offspring are accompanied on this life's journey by their siblings, not their spouses and children. In other words, the Jewish mother makes sure there is always someone looking out for her chicks. After all, You Only Have Each Other. By the way, even if you hate each other, You Only Have Each Other. So, please, stop hating each other.

We know siblings who are not close at all. Some live far apart; others have very different personalities. There are thousands of reasons why sisters and brothers choose not to be friends as adults. But we believe that though sibling relationships may be difficult and complicated, they are worth nurturing. We have two reasons for this: First, who else will really understand your complaints about your parents? Second, as you age, who else will remember your childhood? That shared history alone makes your siblings worth cherishing. We know plenty of exceptions to this rule, plenty of people who have very good reasons why they stopped talking to their brothers and sisters. But this doesn't make the Jewish mother very happy.

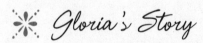

Gloria's Story

Sol was always very close to his only sister, Nessie. Nessie was married to Bernie, who controlled her in many aspects of her life. For example, after Nessie once got into a minor car accident, he told her she couldn't drive anymore. She didn't drive for many years, until Bernie passed away. Bernie hated Sol and despised me. He once threw me out of their house. Later, he refused to let Sol enter as well.

Nevertheless, the one thing Bernie could not control in Nessie's life was her relationship with her brother. After Bernie threw both of us out of their house, Nessie stayed close to Sol, calling him every week. Even though we spent no holidays together and had no social life together as couples, Nessie kept the relationship strong. After Bernie died, it is sad to say, the families became close once again.

I tell my girls, no matter who your spouses are, you only have each other. I expect them to listen. ■

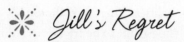

Jill's Regret

My biggest regret in life was not having a second child to grow up with Allyson, even though Ally has three half siblings and three step-siblings. As my marriage to Steven got worse, I didn't want to contemplate being single with two children. I thought I would have more children later. Bobby has three children, and when we first got married we talked about having a child together. We could have done this, and in hindsight I think we should have. It would be easier if Ally had someone to share the burden of caring for me when I am older. ■

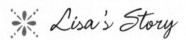

Lisa's Story

I told my parents to make me a sister. When Jill was born, it never occurred to me that I might get a brother instead. I have always felt very protective of my sister. We used to have rules for our daily fights in our upstairs playroom: no biting, punching or pulling hair. No kicking either. As an adult, Jill brings fun into my life.

In my own family, I thought Jon would have a better life if he had a sibling, probably because I am so close to my sister. We got our dog, Snuggles, because I was having trouble conceiving. I wanted Jon to share our attention with another "person" in the house, and thought it was important to teach him the care and love of animals early. We were lucky to conceive Joanna, but if we hadn't, Bill and I would have been happy to adopt. I try to impress in my own children the importance of taking care of each other, but I always include Ally in the mix. I think of her as my own. ■

A Word on Sibling Rivalry

Sibling rivalry can be ugly and destructive. It is a huge subject in families, but we are not going to address it in detail in this book because we, Jill and Lisa, never really felt competitive with each other growing up. Thanks to our parents, we believe in building each other up, not tearing each other down. Our parents celebrated our different talents. Lisa was the academic, Jill the business girl. Though others now ask us whether we feel competitive with each other, we look at our recent careers in media as opportunities to help each other grow and become more successful. We are having more fun together watching each other's talents develop than we would if only one of us had achieved success.

ask yourself

1. Are you lucky enough to have a sibling?

2. How hard do you work to maintain that relationship?

3. Over the years, have you gotten closer or further apart? Why?

4. Did your parents stress to you the importance of staying close to your siblings?

5. If you are estranged, does the reason for your estrangement still make sense to you? If you were a parent yourself, would you want your kids estranged over this issue?

6. If you do not have any siblings, is there someone else in your life who fulfills that role for you?

You Invite One; You Invite the Other

This isn't a hard rule; it should be fairly obvious. Either you invite all the kids, or no kids. Of course, there are exceptions. With your children's friendships, sometimes only one child is friendly with someone, and parents should not always have to entertain their children's friend's siblings. We get that. But for family affairs, it's all or nothing. Someone in Sol's family didn't pay attention to this rule. Watch what happened.

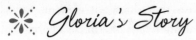

Gloria's Story

Sol's first cousin was giving a party for the family. My mother and father-in-law, Helen and Ben, were invited, as were Sol's sister, Nessie, and her husband. Helen looked around the room and noticed that we weren't there. She asked the host where we were. He replied that he didn't invite us, at which point my mother-in-law said: "Benny, we are leaving now." They just got up and left. They were insulted that one of their children was specifically excluded from the invitation. If you invite one, you invite the other. ■

ask yourself

1. Was your sister or brother ever invited to an event without you where it hurt your feelings? What happened? Did you say anything?

2. Do you ever split up families when inviting? What is your reason?

The In-Law

How many stories have you heard about a nasty, insensitive, stingy, interfering mother-in-law? Too many. Talk about a minefield of miscommunications—the possibilities are endless, especially when two people of different cultures marry. "A daughter is a daughter for the rest of your life; a son is a son until he takes a wife." Why? Because you can say anything to your daughter, and you'll still see the grandchildren. Say one wrong thing to your daughter-in-law and you risk being disinvited to your son's home forever.

We have a word in Yiddish that does not exist in English, which describes the relationship between the bride's parents and the groom's parents. They are called one's *machatunim*. They are related, but only through the marriage of their children to each other. When you think about it, *machatunim* share a huge bond, but our society does not set expectations for that relationship. People must navigate that one on their own.

Mommy only had daughters, and her mother only had daughters, and her mother-in-law only had Daddy and one daughter, and Aunt Nessie only had two daughters . . . you see where we are going here? So, of course, we don't have too many problems with being the mother-in-law of daughters-in-law because we don't have any. Only Aunt Cooky has a son, and she has gone out of her way to invite her *machatunim* to every single holiday in her home, and to cultivate a close relationship with her daughter-in-law. But she always has to remember that she is not the mother; she is only the mother-in-law, and that makes a big difference.

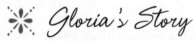

Gloria's Story

As I said, my mother didn't care too much for Sol, and the feeling was mutual. But Sol was a good son-in-law, and as my mother aged, he took care of her finances when she needed him to help. For my part, I respected Sol's parents, but our relationship was not that close. My mother-in-law, Helen, was very old-fashioned and believed that she should stay closer to her daughter's family than to ours. I appreciated that my in-laws never tried to interfere in our lives, and, when asked about Sol and me, she always said, "It's a love affair." ■

❋ Lisa's Story

Aunt Cooky threw me a surprise bridal shower at her house. Years ago, people didn't register for everything from soup ladles to armoires. You just bought something at a store and hoped the bride liked your taste. Anyway, I spied an expensive new vacuum cleaner in the room. The card was from Bill's mother, Joan. I'm thinking, "Yes, this is a nice present, but who wants to receive a vacuum cleaner from her mother-in-law? Exactly what is she getting at here?" My hackles were slightly raised. You know what Joan said in the card? "Dear Lisa, Enjoy this beautiful vacuum cleaner. May you never have to use it yourself." I had a friend for life.

I married Bill when he was just twenty-two years old. You would think his parents might have objected. But from the moment Joan and Jerry Wexler met me, they never treated me as anything other than a third daughter. I call them Mom and Dad to this day. When I became engaged, Joan gave me the most beautiful diamond pendant, which she was given by her mother-in-law when she got married. I treasure it. ∎

❋ Jill's Story on In-Laws

Despite my divorce from Steven, I am still quite close to Steven's parents, and I still refer to them as my in-laws. I call them for the holidays and encourage them to see Allyson as often as they can. I can always count on them to show up at school concerts and anything important. I consider myself very lucky to have such a loving relationship with them. Bobby's father passed away, and his mother lives in an assisted-living facility near us. We see her often and have always had a warm relationship. ■

Sorry, if you were looking for a good, juicy story about a mean mother-in-law, you've come to the wrong book. We got lucky. Obviously, we married men who were the sons of wise Jewish mothers, who knew how to welcome us daughters-in-law with open arms. We wish you the same luck.

ask yourself

1. How do you expect to be treated by your in-laws? Do you expect to be invited to all the holidays? Do you expect them to initiate contact, or for you to do that?

2. What kind of an in-law are you?

3. Do you encourage your spouse to stay close to his parents, even if you are not?

The Kids Come First (Assuming You Have No Pets)

The Jewish mother does not live in a vacuum. On the contrary, she is well versed in all the latest sociological studies on what makes a successful and harmonious family. Many studies say you should put your spouse first, even defer to him on occasion, in order to have well-adjusted children and a good marriage. In theory, this makes sense to her. In practice, um . . . not so much. Like mothers everywhere, we believe the kids are the first priority, at least while they are growing up and living under your roof.

Why bother mentioning that we believe our kids should come first? Because we live in a world of all kinds of families—nuclear, extended, blended, step, gay, foster—all kinds of combinations of people living together and hopefully loving each other. Sometimes there are conflicting emotions and even priorities. In a second marriage, in the flush of new love, it's easy and tempting to take your minds and eyes off your kids for a while. Not a good idea. Not fair to the kids. Their childhood is not within their control. Their experiences and their perceptions depend upon adults; if we as parents do not act in their interests, who will?

Gloria's Story

Sol's friend used to openly admit that he cared about his children more than his wife. He used to say, "After all, they are my blood and she's not." He didn't care that his wife was standing right there when he said it. He was an unusually devoted father. Sol is a very devoted father as well. I understand that. Both of us have made the kids a priority over each other at times. ■

Jill's Story

Bobby treats Ally the same as he treats his own children, and even Ally will admit that. But Bobby feels I am always trying to please Ally, especially when it comes to how we spend our vacations. I don't care. I tell both of them they are my first, my last and my everything. ■

Okay, We Still Have to Talk about Our Pets

First the pets, then the kids, then the husbands—this is the actual order of priority in many a Jewish home. Bill's grandmother used to joke that she wanted to come back to this world as her own dog—that's how well her pet was cared for. Our kids tell us we would sooner cook dinner for our dogs than for them. You may ask, "How can this be?" To which we would reply, "If you accidentally close the trunk of your car and lock your husband, kids and dog inside, who is going to be happy to see you when you open the trunk?" Enough said.

Of course, we are kidding about our pets being more important than our kids. Sort of. Jewish families do adore their pets. A pet provides the focus for the unconditional love in a family. You may hate your mother, but you still love your dog. You may despise your sister, but your cat understands you.

 *Gloria on Pets*

We had an episode with a stray dog we took in and couldn't handle, and that scared us away from ever having another dog. So we made sure Lisa and Jill each had her own cat. When Lisa's cat got killed by a dog while she was away at college, I cried, even though I hated that cat. I knew how much that pet meant to Lisa. After Jill went away to college, her cat moved across the street. She preferred to live with our neighbors. I wonder what that says? ■

✳ Lisa's Take

My first dog, our beloved Snuggles, was sixteen when she passed. For the last couple of years, I changed her diaper several times a day. Someone once made the insensitive comment to me that when the dog's bladder went, it was "time for her to go." Really? Will it be time for you to go when someone has to change your diaper? I think not. Our bichon, Sugar, is aptly named; I've never seen a sweeter disposition on an animal. Sugar comes with me to the studio every day. I tell my kids, "God will punish you if you put me in a home without a dog." One day I may live without people, but I will never live without a dog again. I need all that unconditional love. ■

✳ Jill's Pets

I am still holding a grudge against my parents for lying to me about our first and only dog, a stray Samoyed that we found in the neighborhood and named Taffy. He lasted two days in the house before my mother told me he had to go back home to his farm. I found out thirty years later that she gave it to the vet. None of us really know what happened to that beautiful dog.

My first dog was Hercules, a seven-pound Chihuahua. I shared her with my friend Monique, who was a traveling nurse. Then Monique got engaged, moved to Alabama and took Hercules with her. On Mother's Day 2005, she showed up at my door at 11 P.M. with a six-week-old puppy we named Ginger. Ginger never grew to more than four pounds. I fell in love with her instantly. She has some mental problems and still nips at people's ankles even though she knows them. Nevertheless, I take her with me wherever I go, whenever I can. ∎

ask yourself

1. Who comes first in your household? Is it as it should be?

2. Who thinks they come first?

3. Do you have a pet? Why not? There are more than ten million dogs and cats in shelters right now. Go rescue one who needs you. You need him too. Trust us.

In Conclusion

There is nothing in life that causes the Jewish mother more heartache than family friction, even if she knows that she herself is the cause of that friction. Navigating family relationships takes much skill. If you want to generate harmony, you won't talk too much. As this tactic is impossible for the Jewish mother, we need to find the alternate route, which is to talk to the right people, who won't repeat what we said. That's what our friends are for.

Years ago, our rabbi gave a sermon on *sinat chinom*, which is translated as "needless hatred." Jewish scholars interpret that in a larger, global context, but our rabbi's message was that the real needless hatred in the world was the kind that caused parents and children, and brothers and sisters, to despise each other for years. Before we can ever move forward as a civilization, we need to mend our individual families.

We are all judgmental about what other people say and do. We judge people on what they are wearing, the kind of gift they gave and whether or not they said thank you. We judge our in-laws, our siblings, and of course, our parents and children, on the basis of their manners, looks, accomplishments, and the way they act with their own children. The Jewish mother relishes the analysis and the judgment but does not let that get in the way of the overriding goal, which is to nurture and repair relationships. We all get tripped up by the events in life that should be the most joyful but end up being the most stressful, like weddings. If you live fully, you can't avoid some conflict. Nevertheless, you can remember that as you are a bride today, you will, God willing, be a mother-in-law tomorrow. Be kind. What goes around, comes around.

8

Money

Money is round.
It comes and goes in life.

"I don't care too much for money. Money can't buy me love."
Paul McCartney wrote that line, and he is one of the richest
men in the world. So do you believe that he doesn't care too
much for money? No? Neither do we. Money may not buy you
love, but it buys a nice diamond ring and a lovely wedding. Plus
health insurance and a good education. Money is not everything,
but it plays a significant role in many life decisions.

Whenever you hear people say "It's not about the money, it's
the principle of the thing!" watch out; it's usually about the
money. Money causes more relationships to rupture than does
anything else. What is the number one cause of divorce? Not
sex—it's (the lack of) money. Loaned any money to friends lately?
Say good-bye to that friendship. We live in a society obsessed with
cash, with the accretion of it, the hoarding of it and the spending
of it. Money fascinates us. Who wants to be a millionaire? Obviously, everybody.

Being rich is a relative term. Daddy defines a rich man as the
one whose income exceeds his expenses. Of course, the trick is to
keep your expenses lower than your income, which is difficult for
us and apparently impossible for our government. In our family,

there are no trust fund babies, no inherited wealth. We don't snicker at those trust funds; we just don't have any. Thank God everyone is healthy enough (pooh, pooh, *kaynahorah*) to be able to work to support themselves.

Many families are secretive about how much wealth they do have. They would sooner tell their own children the intimate confessions of their sex lives than confide their net worth. Elderly parents facing medical issues do not divulge their financial situation to grown children who worry about whether their parents can afford the attention they need. Maybe these parents don't trust their kids. Maybe they have good reason not to trust them. We don't subscribe to this attitude about money. In our family, the subject of money is as much an open book as everything else. Because our parents talked to us about money, we not only learned how to manage our own finances, we were given the message that when it comes to money, our parents trust us.

One of Mommy's favorite phrases is "Money is round," by which she means that money comes and goes throughout life. Few of us are either fabulously rich or desperately poor forever. Most of us experience times when we feel rich as well as other times when we worry about money. Money does not define character. Nor is money a basis for choosing friends or lovers. Coming into a lot of money at one time may seem like a blessing, but it can be a curse too. All of a sudden you question people's motives—do they like me for me, or do they pretend to like me for the money they want from me?

One thing we have learned is you should never judge people by how much money they have or how they choose to spend it. One person's necessity is another's frivolity. Would you spend your last hundred dollars on a new haircut? Some people would. Some of our friends who cry that they are broke somehow manage to lease a luxury car that we can't afford. Economic decisions are not rational—people spend on impulse and allocate their resources in unpredictable ways. Don't get into the trap of losing respect for people because you don't like the way they handle their money. It's their money! Only worry about it if they ask you for some of your money!

The Richest Man in the Room

The best lyric in *Fiddler on the Roof*, in our opinion, is "When you're rich, they think you really know." Profound thought, indeed. How many times have you been in a business meeting or social gathering when a very rich person walks in and the waters part like the Red Sea? The room is hushed—people are talking to each other while surreptitiously trying to listen to what "the great one" is saying. Really? Why so great? Making money in and of itself is one kind of achievement, but why we attribute wisdom to that skill is beyond our comprehension. You want wisdom? Let's hear from your best teacher, your spiritual leader, your parents. Part the waters for them.

How Much Do You Care about Money?

The three of us have different attitudes about money. Lisa doesn't worry about it enough and then panics. Jill worries about it too much and then second-guesses herself. Mommy takes the long view and the practical one.

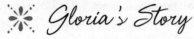 Gloria's Story

Money may make the world go around, but when there is less of it, the world may seem to come to a halt. Most of us have periods of financial struggle. When that happens, you should get a job, any job, and try to earn what you can. What you shouldn't do is sit back and just cry and feel sorry for yourself. That gets you *nowhere!* Every single person has something to offer this world, no matter how much money he makes. It doesn't matter whether you clean a house or design the next great computer system. When Sol's business went down, the last thing I wanted to do was reenter the public school system as a full-time teacher. But I did it anyway. We needed the money. ■

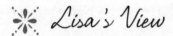 Lisa's View

I have never been primarily motivated by money, even though I always worked. Every time I had some to spare, I gave it away. I think that is because in the back of my mind, I was able to rely on Bill to pay for food, rent and the other essentials. I acted as if I could afford to do a lot of pro bono work, but what I was really doing was shifting all the monetary stress to Bill, which wasn't fair.

Recently, I have reassessed my approach to money. I don't agree with Malcolm Forbes's famous comment that "He Who Dies with the Most Toys, Wins." I will never be primarily motivated by money for its own sake. But I recognize that money can buy you respect in your field, freedom of choice and peace of mind. Grandma Syl used to say that you need more money when you are old than when you are young. Of course, she also referred to the "golden years" as the "tarnished years." But I know what she meant—the last thing you want when you are old is to be dependent on anyone else to pay your bills. ∎

Jill's View

I definitely have a lot of money "noise" in my head. I am very aware of what things cost, and some say I am a human calculator. The only reason I got into a good college was my high math SAT score. I am not sure if this is a good thing or a bad thing. On the positive side, people trust me with money and financial advice. On the negative side, my obsession with spending money and knowing what things cost made me appear showy and braggy growing up. My parents always made me think we were rich. I had a house charge account at every store in town. I obsessed over money. Lisa never did. Neither does Ally. I still do. I wonder why?

When I married Bobby, my life changed, of course. Bobby was a very successful retailer and real estate investor and was extremely generous. But deep down I am still very insecure about money, and so after we married I wanted to go back to work. Even though Bobby has never once questioned me about a bill or said no to me (about anything!), I wanted to contribute. I went to work for Bobby the Donald Trump way (Ivana worked at the Plaza for one dollar a year but got all the dresses she wanted) until I was cast on the show.

My father did talk to me about money probably more than he talked with Lisa about it (simply because I always wanted to know the price of everything). My motto: "Spend less than you have and you will always be rich." Period. The best advice I could give is to think of money like food. If you want to go on a diet, leave some of the food on your plate. If you want to have some money left over, leave some of your paycheck in the bank. ■

ask yourself

1. Do you judge people by their finances?

2. Why do you think our society is so obsessed with money for its own sake? Are you?

3. Have there been times in your life when you were richer versus poorer? Was that your own fault or the fault of circumstances beyond your control?

4. Is money a motivator for you?

5. How many decisions in your life have you had to make because of the lack of money?

6. Do you think you are responsible when it comes to matters of spending and saving money?

What's Mine Is Yours . . .

Daddy was self-employed, with no steady paycheck, no parents to rely on for money "just in case" and no retirement savings. Mommy worked sporadically when we were young. There were a lot of financial "almosts"—investment opportunities where our parents were convinced they were going to hit it big. The money went up; the money went down. There must have been times of enormous stress, but as kids we didn't know about it. Mom and Dad thought it better for adults to have adult worries.

Our parents kept their priorities firm despite the lack of money in the bank. They went ahead with all the plans for Jill's Bat Mitzvah even though afterward they knew they would have only $316 left in their bank account. Why? They couldn't bear to give one daughter a wonderful party and not the other, even though their financial situation was different when Jill had her event than when Lisa had hers. And they had faith that somehow the money would return.

Jill had tutoring, sleepaway camp and private ice-skating lessons. Lisa had tennis, sleepaway camp and art class. Both of us attended Hebrew school three times a week. Neither of us ever felt deprived of anything. On Friday nights Daddy routinely brought home a toy of some kind, sometimes just a pen. Every Jewish New Year, we had new outfits to wear to temple.

Why are these details relevant to the conversation about money? In our family, we used money to enjoy life, and we didn't hoard away vast savings for a rainy day that never happened. Money, clothing, gifts, advice—all were freely given away. Our parents often gave money to friends and family down on their luck. Our family sees money as a means to an end, not an end in and of itself. It is a means to freedom of choice, not merely in material goods but in health care, education, recreation—life in general.

Mommy believes that what is hers belongs to her children. As a matter of principle, everything she owns belongs to her family. This is also the philosophy of Daddy, and of our Aunt Cooky and Aunt Nessie. All of them regularly and sincerely offer to their children, their siblings and their nieces whatever money they have. We believe that money also goes up, down and sideways, from children to parents and from siblings to each other. We believe that whoever needs financial help should get it.

Here is our Jewish mother secret to money—our parents made us feel as if we were rich. Lack of money may have been a reality, but it was never an obstacle. We lived as if the world belonged to us and we were just as entitled as anyone else to a big slice of that great American apple pie.

✳ Gloria's History

My mother watched every penny. She wasn't stingy, but she was careful. She never bought something without making sure she paid the lowest price she could. She once took Lisa shopping all day for a raincoat at Macy's, Gimbel's and B. Altman, only to decide at the end of that long day not to buy anything. I did not inherit that trait from her. Of course, I came of age in a postwar boom time and she was a bride during the Depression. Big difference.

I buy what I like, if I can afford it. I have no patience to *shlep* around and compare prices. I didn't want Lisa and Jill to worry about money or to know when we worried about money. I heard too many of those conversations myself growing up. ■

✳ Lisa's Thoughts on Stereotypes

One of the reasons our parents purposely raised us in their version of a "Jewish ghetto" was that they didn't want to subject us to bigotry. We heard no lousy jokes about Jews and money, no off-color remarks implying that we were either stingy or stinking rich.

Those jokes about Jews and money are in bad taste and have made quite a comeback. I don't like them. The irony for me is that these stereotypes are so far from my own experience. I'm sure there are stingy Jews, like there are stingy people in any group. But my family was never stingy.

I was born into a generous family and I married into a generous family. Because we were raised this way, Jill and I really did believe anything was possible, and we never saw lack of money as an impediment to our dreams. ▪

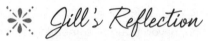

Jill's Reflection

I am really glad my parents gave me the impression we had plenty of money. I think all parents should give children the illusion of security and not share with them financial stresses. Kids need to know that they can't get everything they want, but they also don't need burdens. ▪

Jews, Money and Anti-Semitism

Did you know that in some slang, to "Jew someone down" means to bargain with them to bring the price lower? We take offense at that, obviously. We take offense at other negative stereotypes about Jews, just as our Italian friends do when people assume they are "connected" to the Mafia. Prejudice against the Jewish people, based on lies, ignorance and exaggerations, is a very dangerous thing. We assume you don't need us to give you a historical dissertation on the damage anti-Semitism has inflicted on Jews and so many others. However, even though each of us, to some degree, has been affected by prejudice, we largely heed Ethel's advice and "pay it no mind." Thank God we live in the United States of America, which none of us take for granted. We know there are ignorant and vicious people in this world, and we step over, around and through them when we encounter them. As far as the stereotypes themselves go, we Jews love nothing more than a good joke, even if it's at our own expense. But "Jewing someone down"? Not funny.

ask yourself

1. Did you feel rich or poor growing up?

2. Did your parents make you feel insecure about money?

3. Did you feel that the lack of money prevented you from doing something important to you?

4. How would you describe your parents' attitudes toward money?

5. Were your parents generous? With you? Others?

6. Do your parents today trust you with money issues?

7. Do your parents ask your advice about money? Do you seek theirs?

8. Do you feel left out when it comes to matters of money in your family?

9. As an adult, have you passed on the attitudes you learned from your parents to your children?

Don't Be a *Schmuck*: Know Your Money

The Jewish mother has one rule for personal finance—try not to be a complete *schmuck*. A woman should always know where her money is being kept. Don't laugh; countless spouses do not know the locations of their joint bank accounts, much less the amount in them and the account numbers. Find your safety deposit key and tell someone else you trust where it is. Keep a file of life insurance policies. Know who has the original copy of your will. And if you don't have a will, make one. The last thing you want is for the court to appoint someone else to take care of your estate when you are gone. There are plenty of great books out there to help you organize your money. Buy one and spend some time organizing your finances. It is absolutely essential that you know how much money you have, where it is, who technically owns the asset and who has access to it. Make a plan for your financial future if you don't have one. The most important thing is not how much money you have, but how you manage what you do have for the long term.

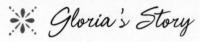

Gloria's Story

Women of my generation were particularly naïve when it came to money, because so many of us didn't have our own. Even now, Sol doesn't share all the decisions he makes about our money. It is a source of great frustration for me. However, I do know where all of our assets are. ■

ask yourself

1. Do you know where your assets are?

2. Do you have access to all your assets?

3. Do you have a smart plan for your financial future? If not, why not?

What Will You Do for Money?

It is a sad fact that some people will do anything for money. Some of those people end up in jail, others in the biggest mansion in town. Who are we to know what you are willing to do to get rich?

Only you know where your lines are drawn. When it comes to money, very often your moral compass will be called upon to give you a direction. We advise you to let your conscience tell you where to go. Here is the dilemma Daddy once had, as told by Mommy.

Sol's Dilemma:

Sol was a licensed attorney as well as stockbroker. He had started his own underwriting firm and achieved some financial success. In the early 1970s, Sol was approached by some men to become the president of a New York Stock Exchange securities firm. Wow! Prestige, recognition and money. We were so excited. Sol took the job and closed his own firm to join this one.

On Sol's first day at the new job, the men asked him to do something unethical. We don't even know the specifics; they are not important. Can you imagine Sol's dilemma? He had just closed down his company and had a family to support.

What Did Sol Do?

Sol quit his job that first day in the office. He came home and told me he felt he had no choice. Then he contacted his old law partner and the two of them started new business ventures together. Even though he was in shock for a while, Sol never looked back.

What Happened to the Firm?

Years later, the SEC investigated wrongdoing at this firm. Eventually the people who did wrong got punished. They usually do.

As we said elsewhere, Daddy believes people know when they are doing the wrong thing, even though they choose to do it anyway. We believe in being able to sleep at night, which means avoiding doing something that will trouble our consciences. If you are ever in doubt, look at the example of Bernie Madoff. He had so much money, but it wasn't enough. He had to lie and cheat and steal to get more. And in the end, did the money bring him or anyone else happiness? It only brought misery—to so many people.

ask yourself

1. Can you recall a situation where you were asked to do something unethical at work? How did you handle it? Looking back on your decision, do you have regrets?

2. What are you willing to do to make money?

3. What are you unwilling to do to make money?

4. Who is your "moral compass," the person whose counsel you seek as your extra conscience in this world?

Pigs Eat Shit

Mommy insisted we put this phrase in the book. As coarse as it is, Mommy repeats it frequently. We are talking about greed here, not animal farms.

We are fond of a particular expression in Yiddish: "*Gornisht mit gornisht iz gornisht,*" which literally means "Nothing with nothing is nothing," but is better translated as meaning "a little bit of something is better than a lot of nothing." In other words, don't be greedy. Let's say your salesperson requests a high commission to sell your widgets. We say, wonderful. Pay him his commission and hope he does a good job. Otherwise, if you are greedy and do not pay him, then you have no sales. You get to keep 100 percent of nothing. *Mazel tov.*

Some people cross ethical lines because they are afraid they will lose their job if they do not obey orders, and some people are so consumed by greed that their lust for more overwhelms any moral compunctions they may have had. We think greed is an affliction of our modern American culture, and it has permeated and distorted our notions of what we really need versus what we think we need to keep up with our neighbors. How else can you explain why in recent years our top corporate officers earn approximately five hundred times more than the lowest paid employees at the same firm, when, fifty years ago, they earned only twenty times more? Are they so much better executives now than they were years ago? We doubt it. Let's just admit it: Ever since *Wall Street*'s Gordon Gekko famously said, "Greed is good," too many people believe precisely that. We do not agree.

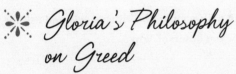

Gloria's Philosophy on Greed

Greed will do you in! I have seen that many people seem to lose their grasp on reality when suddenly coming into a lot of money, like winning the lottery. I feel very lucky that I hit the jackpot with what really counts in life, namely, my children, a kind and good husband and being surrounded by people who care about me. That is what money can *never* buy. Everyone wants a nice home, a good education for their kids and nice clothes. That's all great, and people should strive to achieve that, but the question really is, "What is enough?" To some there is never enough of anything that they want. I think we have to sit back and revise what is important to us. "I have to have . . . " is a mantra to too many people. ■

Jill's View

Greed and competition—to me they do seem connected. I was the "it's never enough" kid. I never took no for an answer and always wanted more. I am very competitive—with myself. Does that make me greedy? Not really. I don't think someone else should go without something so that I can have it—my philosophy is the world is big enough for everybody to have what they want! ■

ask yourself

1. How much money is enough for you?

2. Do you ever feel content with what you have?

3. Do you negotiate with people until it gets ugly and ask for more than you know you deserve? Why?

Giving Back: The Selfish Reason

Aunt Cooky doesn't believe in true altruism. She believes that giving makes you feel good, and therefore there is no such thing as completely unselfish giving. Jill takes it a step further—she believes that when you give, you get back much more than you give, not just in good feelings but in the connections you make in this world that lead to other opportunities. Whatever you choose to believe about giving, here's the message: Just do it!

We all believe in paying it forward. We are all connected in this world and the universe wants us to join together to do good deeds. We believe in giving back, with both time and money. There are unending opportunities to help other people, advance causes and aid animals. Pick at least one and begin, if you haven't already.

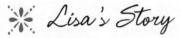

Lisa's Story

My best friend Sandy was going on a church mission trip to the Dominican Republic to teach "Vacation Bible School," which was a term I had never heard of. So, I invited myself, and they were happy to have me. I figured I could teach math and English while everyone else taught scripture. Joanna was eight years old, and I brought her with me. We stayed at a very primitive and extremely poor boys' orphanage in Esperanza, a town not too far from Haiti. Huge insects climbed up the walls. Joanna was terrified, but she got through it. My non-Spanish-speaking eight-year-old taught the boys basic arithmetic and made some great friends.

This experience changed my life. I couldn't get these kids out of my mind. I continued to send clothing and medical supplies to them long after I returned home. Joanna and I visited them almost every year. I took two boys under my wing and sponsored their educations. I made at least one lifelong friend.

Last February, Joanna and I brought Jill and Ally with us to visit all the kids. They loved meeting everyone. You can't help but be extremely generous when you get there. When you see how little others have, compared to what we take for granted, you want to do everything possible. There is no doubt in my mind that I received much more from these experiences than I gave. ∎

Jill's Story

Bobby always says, "We make a living by what we get but we make a life by what we give." Every charity needs support and exposure, but sadly I can use my resources only on what is meaningful to us. Over the past few years we helped raise money for Help for Orphans, which aids poor children in Africa, and Creakyjoints.org, to promote health and education for arthritis. My philosophy is if someone asks for it, they probably need it. So yes, we do give money to people on the street. This is controversial, but if a small gift can make a sad person smile . . . it is certainly worth more than a few dollars to me. ∎

ask yourself

1. Do you make it a priority to volunteer your time or give money to charity? Why or why not?

2. Do you know anyone who needs you? It doesn't have to be an organization; how about an acquaintance who could use a friend?

Don't Wait Till You Are Dead to Give It Away

When Grandma Helen passed away, Mommy said there was one very good thing about being poor—nobody was rushing you out the door. Mommy made a very good point. Nobody was waiting with open palms for the estate that they never earned but to which they still felt entitled. As the baby boomers of this nation age and inherit their parents' wealth, the largest amount of money in human history is beginning to change hands. Because this earlier generation benefited from the largest postwar economic boom this country ever enjoyed, many people will now be affected by issues surrounding whom all this money should go to, in what amounts and when. Mommy's answer to all of this is simple: Don't wait until you are dead to give it away. Don't give anyone a reason to push you out the door before your time.

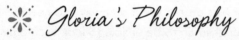

Gloria's Philosophy

I never understood people who hold on to their stemware and sterling silver long after they stop giving dinner parties. What for? To look at it in a drawer? Same thing with jewelry. After a time, my pearls looked better on my daughter's neck than on mine. So I gave them to her. Exactly what was I saving them for? I much prefer to see my daughters look beautiful during my lifetime than have them wait until after I have gone to enjoy my things. I don't understand mothers who feel differently about this.

When it comes to an estate, a parent has to be very careful. There is a philosophy that says if you have one rich child and two poor children then you should give the poor ones more money because they need it more. I do not agree with this. I've seen that money is round; the rich son today can be poorer than the daughter tomorrow. You can't know in advance how much money your children will need. Unless there is another very good reason to treat kids differently, I believe every child should have an equal share of a parent's estate. If you are really worried about the financial situation of one of your kids, then give her some money now. It is that simple. ∎

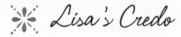

Lisa's Credo

As a practicing probate attorney, I have counseled many families on this issue. Parents have poured their hearts out to me, and the situations vary widely.

When it comes to estates, money is love. Pure and simple. You can rationalize all you want that your daughter is married to a no-goodnik and needs your money, while your big-shot son is a hedge fund millionaire, but I am telling you that your kids do not see it that way and never will. If you want your children to be unable to look each other in the eye after the funeral, then by all means, give them unequal shares in your will. But if you want them to stay close, or at least hold on to the idea that you loved them equally, then give them equal shares in your will. Anything else will be interpreted by them as "you loved her more than you loved me." Are there exceptions to this rule? Yes, but they are rare. If a client comes to me and simply wants to leave one child more money than the other because of financial circumstances, I advise them against it. I agree with my mother; money is round. In this case, money is also love. ■

ask yourself

1. Why are you holding on to belongings that your family might enjoy?

2. Are you in a situation in which you could give money to those who need it now? Why are you waiting?

In Conclusion

Money is complicated. People have written tomes on the psychology of money—some yearn for money to replace love they need; others use money to control and demoralize people in order to satisfy their own insecurities. We, Jewish mothers, believe that the secret is to treat money seriously enough to make sure you can provide what you need in this world, but not so seriously that greed corrupts your values. Money should never stand in the way of love, friendship and trust.

Life is short. As our friend once told us, there are no luggage racks on the hearse. We believe you might as well enjoy spending what you want and saving what you want, with no regrets. Give away as much as you are comfortable with while you are still alive so you can enjoy seeing your loved ones appreciate and enjoy the money too. Remember that money is round, and don't judge people by their pocketbooks. When you leave this world, you take with you your reputation, and you leave your bank account behind. Your good name is more important.

9

Parenting

Make sure your children know
you love them, every day and
in as many ways as you can.

The most important thing in life you will ever do is parent a child, and that is the one thing you can't learn in school. Even if someone teaches you how to change a diaper, she will never be able to teach you how to manage things when your first-born won't stop crying in the middle of the night. It is a law of nature that you will be the giver and your children will be the takers. They will take the *kishkes* out of you. Count on it. You will also worry about them from the day they are born until the day you die. You will worry more about them than they will ever worry about you. This is the way God made us. We Jewish mothers accept this. So should you.

If you are lucky, you learn the dos and don'ts of parenting from a set of good, loving parents. Our parents believed that we were the most important human beings on the planet. Sacrifices made for our welfare were as natural as breathing; they were unspoken and unforced. This is a value we hope we have passed on to our children; good parents put their children ahead of themselves. If your own parents weren't the best, then find a parenting mentor. That person could be another relative, a teacher, a friend or the parent of a friend.

Parenting advice abounds. Some rules you will make up as you go along. Here is what we know: The most important thing parents can do is communicate love to their child. Love makes up for a lot of personal flaws. It makes up for a parent who is busy, distracted, worried and forgetful. It compensates for a parent who is messy, is a lousy cook and comes late to parent-teacher night—can you tell we've all been there? Luckily, kids are resilient. They will forgive you again and again for your mistakes. The absence of love is the one thing that will cripple children. So make sure your children know you love them, every day and in as many ways as you can.

If you are interested in becoming a parent, you should ask yourself why. Do not have children if you are seeking happiness. It's not that having kids automatically makes you unhappy, although it can—it's just that *your* happiness is not the point of raising children. Being a parent means feeling such overwhelming love for your child that it can leave you breathless, but it can also make you feel that same level of despair. The experience of raising a child guarantees that you will feel joy, anger, pride, frustration, wonder, disappointment and awe. It isn't for everyone. It doesn't need to be for everyone—we see nothing wrong with choosing not to have children. We are convinced that people without kids end up with the fewest lines on their forehead and the most money saved in their bank account.

Nevertheless, all three of us wanted to be mothers. In our view, raising a child completes the human experience, whether or not that child is someone to whom you gave birth or someone you adopted. There is nothing quite so humbling in this world as watching your own child grow up to become a person who is not you—a person who, despite your best efforts, has a soul, spirit and mind of her own. That soul will defy you, contradict you and ultimately teach you more about yourself than any other person can. Just as you are meant to teach lessons to your children, so are you meant to learn from them. Also, we happen to come from a long line of really good mothers. What's the sense of having all that wisdom if we can't force it onto the next generation?

No child is easy, but some are definitely easier than others. What we attempt to do in this chapter is provide you with a set of guidelines that you may not learn in parenting books. This advice comes straight from our hearts and guts—and by guts, we mean *kishkes*.

As you will see, to avoid being too preachy, not to mention hypocritical (guilty, guilty!), we have separated several of these sections into "What We Should Do" and "What We Really Do." Hey, life is full of compromises.

Commonsense Parenting Basics

The following are our basic parenting precepts. To us, these are classic "no-brainers," commonsense, simple rules that need no extra explanations.

1. *Two parents are better than one.* Don't holler—of course, there are exceptions to this rule. But it's still a good rule. Two parents *are* better than one. If you don't believe us, look up the statistics on how the kids of divorce do later in life when it comes to making their own commitments to marriage. If you are a new mother, you are lucky that in the last ten years the expectations of fathers have changed. Neither Sol nor Bobby nor Bill changed a number two diaper—that we can tell you. Today's father no longer gets away with walking out of the room merely holding his nose.

2. *Extended family makes a child feel secure.* Grandparents, aunts, cousins—being surrounded by family who care enough to cluck and discipline is good for a child. It's good for the parents too.

3. *Kids will do what they see you do, not what you tell them to do.* You should parent by example. So play nice with your friends, don't tell petty lies, and read the newspaper to see what is going on with the world. And don't forget to call your mother, often.

4. *Act like a grown-up.* You are one, remember?

5. *Kids need structure.* This doesn't mean your house needs to function like an army base, but your children should be able to count on three meals a day and someone to nag them to brush their teeth and do their homework. Routines give kids security.

6. *Kids need chores.* We expect our kids to pitch in to help with the basics, like setting and clearing the table, taking out the trash, making their beds and putting away groceries. Basic chores make children feel they are contributing to the family.

7. *Say no.* It's your job to say no to your kids. When they do what they want anyway, be prepared with a reasonable consequence for disobeying you. Then enforce the consequence. (For goodness' sakes, get up and take the kids out of the theater when they carry on—don't spoil everyone else's show). We've all drawn a blank or overreacted when our kids have done something unexpected and we can't figure out an effective "punishment" for the "crime." Good parenting requires thinking ahead.

8. *Boundaries.* All children need boundaries and must be told the rules. Consistency is difficult, but crucial.

9. *Apologize When Wrong.* We've all lost our temper. We've all said and done things to our children for which we are instantly sorry. Guess what? If we are wrong, we should apologize. It doesn't make us weak to apologize; rather, it tells the kids we are human and we make mistakes, just like they do. So when they make mistakes, they need to apologize too.

Helicopter Parents

In the spectrum of the "sturdy child versus the vulnerable child," we think the pendulum has swung wildly in the wrong direction. We used to assume that our kids are sturdy creatures, capable of learning from their own mistakes. Now society tells us that our children are vulnerable to all sorts of injuries, and therefore our job as parents is to protect our kids from every possible risk of harm. We feel sorry for those tots in knee pads, elbow pads and helmets on their trikes. They won't even know what a skinned knee feels like, much less have a scar to which they can point proudly one day. Which doesn't mean you shouldn't make your kid wear a helmet on a bicycle or ski slope. Of course you should.

But, in general, you need to teach your kids that they can fall down and get back up. If your son doesn't learn this as a child, he'll have a much harder time as an adult. What's worse, he'll always be looking to someone else to cushion his fall. Life doesn't work that way. You are not doing your kid any favors to pretend that it does.

Don't Take the Credit;
Don't Take the Blame

Our society blames parents for their children's transgressions and praises them for their children's accomplishments. We'd rather take less blame and less credit. We can all see that there are great parents who have lousy kids and there are horrid parents who end up with wonderful children. For every neglected child who grows up to win a Nobel Prize, there are children from privileged and protected homes whose adulthood is spent in isolation and misery. Also, two kids who grow up in the same house with the same parents more often than not have completely different perspectives on their childhood. Even as you read this book, you will find Jill saying to Lisa, "Did we grow up in the same house?" Yes. And no.

If you are not yet a parent, you should know that kids are born the way they are born. Relax. You can't control much of anything, and you probably can't change that much either, especially when it comes to their temperament. If they are willful and stubborn as toddlers, they will probably stay that way. You can influence the books your kids read and the television shows they watch, and try to set the best example humanly possible, but if they start running with the wrong crowd, you are in trouble. Peers exert a greater influence than you do, and you won't even know it until your children are all grown up and confide in you all the things you missed along the way. Do not fret about this—you are not supposed to know everything. Your child's journey into adulthood is meant to contain secrets from you.

You are probably thinking, then why read this chapter at all? If the whole thing is a crapshoot anyway, then why bother following anyone's advice? Just because you probably can't change the outcome of a situation, are you then supposed to abandon the struggle? Absolutely not! If there is one thing the Jewish mother believes, it is that despite the outcome, the battle must be fought.

Obviously, some things make a huge difference in a child's well-being—showing love, giving plenty of attention and setting a good example. So do your best; don't shirk your responsibilities. But if you have done your best, don't flog yourself if the child you raised didn't grow up to be the adult you envisioned. The universe plays funny tricks on all of us. We are meant to learn lessons from every significant relationship. If your relationship with your child or parent is less than wonderful, examine your behavior. If you can look at yourself and absolve yourself of blame, then absolve yourself of guilt. If not, then fix what is fixable before it's too late. People don't live forever.

Gloria

My mother used to tell me that if I had only had Lisa, I would have bragged my whole life about how easy it was to parent a child. We never had to worry about Lisa, look at her homework or wonder where she was going at night. On the other hand, it's no secret that Jill gave us difficult years. She was and is a risk taker, and never took no for an answer. Those traits may have served her well as an adult, but they were tough on Sol and me. After Jill, I knew that a parent's influence can take you only so far. ■

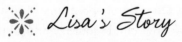

Lisa's Story

Recently, I complimented an acquaintance on the conduct of her thirteen-year-old daughter. At first, her mother accepted the compliment graciously, with a simple thank-you. Then she corrected herself and went on at length to tell me that she, the mother, deserved the credit because of all the efforts she had put into that child. I thought to myself, "This mother is a jerk." She should count her blessings, instead of patting herself on the back. ■

ask yourself

1. Why did you decide to have kids?

2. So far, is parenting kids what you expected it to be?

3. Who is your best parental role model? Do you seek his or her advice? As often as you should?

4. Who is more responsible for your child's good grades in school, you or your child? Why?

5. In what ways has your child's nature been the same since birth?

6. In what ways has your child's nature changed since birth? Do you think the changes are due to your interventions?

7. Do you blame your parents for your own worst attributes? Is that fair?

8. What behaviors in your child do you think your parenting could affect?

When Your Child Is Hurting

Usually we do not know when kids get their feelings hurt. But once in a while, we are there. Then the question becomes, what do we do about it? Do we rush to their defense to prevent more harm, or let them handle the situation to give them confidence in themselves? As parents, when should we intervene, and how?

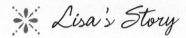

Lisa's Story

All the kids on our street always played together, both outside and inside. Sure, they didn't always get along, but they always worked it out. One day, a new kid moved into the neighborhood and told the others that he didn't want to play ball with one of the kids. I think this new boy was trying to exercise some kind of power over what went on in the neighborhood. When my daughter told me about it, I didn't think it was fair. I could see that this was already leading to all sorts of hurt feelings—one kid "in the game" one day, out another. So I approached this new boy myself and told him that we had a neighborhood rule—and the rule was that if you played outside, no kid could be excluded. If you wanted to invite somebody inside your house, that was different, but the outside belonged to everyone. I also told all the other parents on the street about this rule, and they agreed that it was fair. I think I saved us a lot of *tsuris*. After the rule was explained to all the kids, no one excluded anybody else from playing outside again.

It's interesting to me now that a new generation of little ones is growing up in our neighborhood with the exact same issues. I heard about it, and once again interfered and told them our neighborhood rule. I hope it works for them the way it worked for our kids.

The moral of this story? If we see any kid get hurt, ours or somebody else's, we should speak up. When our kids get cut, we bleed. ∎

WHAT WE SHOULD DO WHEN OUR KIDS GET HURT, EMOTIONALLY OR OTHERWISE

Listen to our kids and assess the severity of the hurt. If the child is handling the situation well, we should back off. However, if a particular incident is either quite severe or becomes a repetitive pattern, then we parents need to interfere. If a bullying pattern is happening in school, we should insist that the administration provide some counseling to the grade, without singling out either the victim or the perpetrator. Studies show it really works.

WHAT WE REALLY DO

Underreact or overreact. We make speeches in our heads at night that nobody ever hears, or sue somebody.

What the Jewish Mother Cannot Fix

In general the Jewish mother will try everything and anything to make things right for her kids, but she understands that the one thing she cannot fix for her child is the heartache that comes from a broken love affair. She can be there, but she cannot fix it. She does not try to fix it. However, she will make the food.

ask yourself

1. Have you ever seen your child bullied or mocked? What did you feel like doing? What did you actually do?

2. Have you ever seen your child taunt or bully another child? What did you do about it?

3. How did you react when your child had his or her heart broken? What did you cook?

Parenting More Than One Child: Fair Is Not Always Equal; Equal Is Not Always Fair

A secret to being a great parent, as opposed to being an average parent, is to give each of your children a separate, customized parenting approach. In other words, if you have more than one child, you need to be a different parent to each one. Changing your reactions to respond to your individual children's character traits is hard work. But if you can figure out how to reach your kid based on their personality, rather than your personality, then you will learn how to unlock that child's potential. You'll also get along better.

In our family, we say "Fair is not always equal and equal is not always fair." By this we mean that every child must be treated as an individual. What's good for the goose is *not* always good for the gander. Just because Johnny gets tennis lessons does not necessarily mean that Janie should get them too, *but* Janie should get lessons in something else that will develop her individual talent.

Good parenting means not feeling guilty when your children try to manipulate you by saying, "That's not fair." Fairness requires judgment. Judgment requires the understanding of nuance and the discernment of the right solution appropriate for the situation. Adults use their judgment to show their children how to grow up.

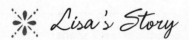 *Lisa's Story*

I had gone to Kinni-Kinnic, a sleepaway girl's camp in Vermont, for five years. I loved that camp; it still comes to me in dreams. Jill had come with me for the last two of those years. I assumed we would be going back together for a sixth summer. This was in the fall of 1973, the height of a terrible recession. As it turned out, Mom and Dad could not afford to send both of us back to camp. So what did they do? They sat me down and told me that Jill was going to camp without me. They had decided that she was entitled to one more summer there because I had already had five summers of camp. I remember feeling both resentful and shocked when they first told me. I didn't think it was fair. I was the one who loved camp more.

But after a few weeks, I adjusted. By the time summer arrived, my reaction had changed. I rationalized that I was getting too old for camp anyway. I took a kind of pride in the fact that I had been asked to sacrifice my last summer at camp so that Jill could have one more summer there. It made me feel good, not bad. Plus I learned to type that summer, the most useful skill I ever learned in school. ■

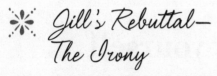

Jill's Rebuttal— The Irony

Until I read Lisa's story as we were writing this book, I had no idea about any of this. I didn't know about our parents' finances that summer, nor did I know that Lisa was told she couldn't go to camp so I could go instead. If I had known, I would have told my parents not to send me! I had the worst bunk ever; the other girls tortured me. I spent most of the summer being punished, sitting under the flagpole. ■

What's the moral of this story? Even if you do something for the right reason with the best of intentions, sometimes you get it wrong.

Our parents might have been better off saving all their money and not sending either one of us to camp, but at least they taught us this lesson about the difference between fairness and equality.

WHAT WE SHOULD DO IF WE HAVE MORE THAN ONE CHILD

Figure out each child's strengths or interests and develop those to the fullest potential. React to each child's personality in a different way by thinking ahead to what might be the most effective reward, or in some cases, consequence.

WHAT WE REALLY DO

Throw a few lessons of each sport at each kid and hope something sticks. Stick both of them in a time-out when it is obvious that only one really is responsible for the trouble. Adhere to our usual reactions to their behavior, even if it is obvious that it isn't working, or that one kid responds better than the other to the same disciplinary strategy.

ask yourself

1. In what ways were you treated unfairly when it came to your siblings?

2. How did unfair treatment by your parents affect your relationship with your siblings?

3. What do you do as a parent that is unequal but still fair?

4. Do you have a favorite child? What makes that child your favorite? Do you think your other kids know? How do you think it makes the other kids feel?

Explain Your Important Decisions to Your Children and Include Their Input

We firmly believe that you should explain to your children why you make important decisions that affect their lives. Loving your children means respecting them too—every Jewish mother will tell you that. Examples of those big decisions include moving, changing schools or changing who lives in your household. As your kids age, we think they should in general be given more control over the important decisions that affect their lives, but this totally depends on the circumstances and your individual child's maturity level.

This approach helps your children accept your choices. All people are more willing to accept a decision if they know the reason it was made, even if they disagree with the decision itself. Your children may still believe you made the wrong decision, but an explanation of the rationale goes a long way toward helping them to accept it. By explaining a decision to your children, you are also giving them respect. A Jewish mother believes children are entitled to respect at every age. And of course, children learn by example. In explaining why you made a particular decision, you are modeling good parenting skills for your children to apply when they become parents.

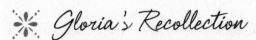

Gloria's Recollection

When I was growing up, parents did not include their children in any decisions, important or otherwise. I always thought that was a mistake. I decided to do it differently when I had my own children. ■

Jill's Story

A question I get asked frequently is, "Why did you decide to do a reality TV show?" I always answer, "We" decided to do the show, not "I." It was a family decision. With respect to Allyson, she was fourteen at the time and I felt she was old enough to understand what her role would be. Allyson herself decided she wanted to tell the world that she has a form of arthritis, which is often referred to as "an old person's disease." People still tell me they never knew children could be afflicted with it. Thousands of fans have contacted me to share their own stories of living with arthritis. Allyson wanted to help other children by sharing her story. She lives with pain every day and works twice as hard to overcome it. The production company was extremely respectful of her privacy and feelings. Allyson is a wonderful girl, and I am very pleased with how she has been portrayed. ■

WHAT WE SHOULD DO WHEN A MAJOR CHANGE WILL AFFECT OUR KIDS' LIVES

Sit down with your children, discuss the change with them and give them the respect they deserve. Be sure to solicit their input over any aspect of the decision in which they can exert some control.

WHAT WE REALLY DO

We're pretty good on this one. We really do these things.

ask yourself

1. As a kid, did something happen to your family that you wish you had been informed of ahead of time? Would it have helped you to adjust better if you had been informed?

2. As a parent, have you made a unilateral decision that had a substantial impact on your child over which your child felt he had no control? Could you have handled that situation differently? Should you have?

3. Are you afraid of letting your kids know what is happening because you would prefer to avoid their reaction? How mature does that make you?

4. How easy is it for you to sit down and talk to your kids? If it's not easy, why? What are you afraid of?

5. How well do you communicate the rationale of your decisions to your children?

Pay Attention: Sit on the Bed

Jewish mothers are always paying attention. They may seem as if they are on the phone with their mothers while their child is snatching that fourth cookie, but their eyes are everywhere. They see that cookie; they know who ate it. They even know how many calories it has. Do we believe that our children must believe in our all-knowing, omniscient power? Of course. We tell our children that no matter what they try to get away with, somehow we will find out. You remember that cliché about our eyes being in the backs of our heads? Each of us has four. Nevertheless, despite vigilant attention, all kids feel neglected sometimes and feel that their parents are not paying enough attention to them or their feelings.

Some people are action oriented and wake their families up at the crack of dawn for that five-mile jog. Not our group. We are bed people. We would rather stay in bed and do the puzzle. We cuddle a lot. We buy small dogs so that they can cuddle with us. When you are having trouble communicating with your kid, sit on her bed while she is in the room. Just plant yourself there. Create a vibe around you that is serene and patient—make it seem like you've got all the time in the world. This is your time to fully focus on your child when she is ready for you. Read a magazine to pass the time while you are waiting for her to look up from her computer. Eventually she will. Here is the predictable course of events:

1. Your child inevitably screams: "What are you doing in my room? Get out of my room. This is *my* room." Do not be deterred; it may be her room, but you are still paying the rent.

2. After an attempt to keep you out of the room has failed, your child will now ignore you. No problem, you've got all the time in the world.

3. Eventually, your child will start the conversation. Wait for it—it will come.

4. Take your cue and watch your words. This is not your time to lecture; this is your time to listen.

5. By the end of the conversation, your kid will probably have asked you for some guidance about some issue in his or her life.

The message that you give by sitting on their beds is simple: "I am your mother; you are the most important person in the world to me. No phone call is more important than you are; no television program or e-mail is more interesting to me than what is on your mind."

Try it. You too, dads. It works every time. Every time you do this you will discover something new about what is going on in your kids' lives. If you do it often, your kids will actually look forward to it, though they may not admit it.

WHAT WE SHOULD DO

Sit on the bed every night. Really pay attention during the few moments alone we have with our kids.

WHAT WE REALLY DO

Sit on the bed when we suspect something is going wrong.

ask yourself

1. How often do you turn off all devices and distractions to let your children know that you are there for them, with 100 percent attention?

2. How well do you communicate with your kids?

3. Do you have the feeling your kids confide in you? Why or why not?

4. Do you do as much listening as talking when you do have their attention?

You Don't Have to Like Me;
You Don't Have to Love Me;
You Absolutely *Must Respect* Me

We Jewish mothers absolutely cannot stand to see adults who allow their children to treat them as equals. We are not our children's equals, nor are we our children's friends. Mommy always says, "You get one mother in this world and one father." (Okay, sometimes more than one, but you know what we mean.) What was her point? That parents need to act as parents—supervising, nurturing and disciplining. Tempting as it may be to be your child's friend, that's not your role. If you are lucky, when your child is all grown up, you may have both a friend and a child. But don't rush it, and never mistake the difference between parent and peer.

As Mommy ran after us at various times when we were kids, occasionally screaming at the top of her lungs, she would repeat this phrase: "I don't care if you like me; I don't care if you love me; but you sure as hell will respect me." Whew! Somehow it got into our brains that respect was the be-all and end-all of the parent-child relationship.

Think of that message of respect—it's so contrary to everything we have heard in the last forty years. We are taught that "like" and "love" are the aspects of a parent-child relationship we should covet. But like and love miss the point. Love is natural; it is always there. Like is often a matter of personality. Respect is what a parent must demand; respect of a parent shapes a child's character. Respect gives the parent-child relationship the right kind of distance. Disrespect of a parent engenders disrespect of all authority—teachers, police, bosses, leaders. To raise a good citizen, a parent must demand the respect of her child.

Talking back, or as we call it, "being fresh," is the most common method of showing disrespect. Sadly, it is running rampant today—don't you agree? Disrespect ranges from what we would call a negative "tone" to cursing directly at a parent. Although we recognize that this is a losing battle in today's culture, we still fight the good fight. You can't really love your parents if you don't respect them.

✳ *Gloria's Experience*

If I talked back to Mother when Dad was around he would force me to apologize immediately. I had to say I was sorry, even if I wasn't. In those days, children were more afraid of their parents than we are today. ■

✳ *Jill and Lisa*

When we hear our own kids speak to us sometimes, the first thing we say and think is "We would *never*, in a *million* years, have spoken that way to our parents." Number one, it wouldn't have occurred to us to show such disrespect, and number two, if we had said that to them, we cannot imagine the consequence. It is literally unthinkable.

We couldn't even get away with referring to Mommy as "she" in the third person. For example, we could never say to Dad while Mom was at the table, "She wouldn't let us go out tonight." She? She who? It was considered rude beyond measure and not accepted in our house. ■

WHAT WE SHOULD DO

Neither lose our tempers, nor overreact or threaten punishments we have no intention of enforcing.

WHAT WE REALLY DO

Get angry, either threaten things we don't enforce, shout or give them the ice treatment for a while, and then go back to normal. Once in a while, we get the apology we deserve.

ask yourself

1. Do you show respect to your parents?

2. Do you demand that your children show you respect? How do you do that?

3. What are the consequences of disrespect in your house?

4. Do you allow programs in your home that implicitly condone disrespect of parents? Watch what your kids are watching. If you are not happy, get up from the sofa and turn off the *drek*.

Parents Are Suckers

As a parent, you tolerate behavior in your own children that you would never tolerate in anyone else. If your friend left an open granola bar in the crevice of your sofa more than once, chances are you would mutter to yourself, "Slob," and cross her off the dinner party list. Not if your daughter did that—like the model parent that you are, you will actually make her a hot meal the next night and invite her to join you at the table. If another friend consistently ignored your friendly hellos, which eventually morphed into desperate entreaties to open the door and come down to dinner, you might drop the relationship altogether. Not if your son acts that way. No, he, too, will be invited to join you at a meal. You might even create four separate meals at the same dinner table to cater to all the dislikes and preferences of your family. Admit it. You know who you are. You are us.

Cook Dinner

Who doesn't love a home-cooked dinner? We certainly do. In fact, what time can you come over to start the oven? Cooking for your family is the fundamental way to show you love them. Plus the studies show that kids who sit down with their families for dinner several times a week are less likely to get involved with negative influences like drugs and alcohol. How wonderful it is to walk into the house, smell something yummy and enjoy a good meal together. But the truth is that cooking dinner is a really hard thing to accomplish nowadays. You are the chauffeur from the time school ends until dinnertime, at which point everyone is starving and you haven't had any time to cook. What's left? The local fast-food joint or, if you splurge, the local diner. No wonder we are all fighting battles of the bulge.

Yes, it's "do as we say, not as we do" time. Our advice is great, even if we don't always use it ourselves. Cooking dinner makes a huge difference in family life. Probably the biggest single difference you can make to improve a host of things, from family harmony to education to good nutrition, is to sit down to a home-cooked meal together. But now that we think about it, it really doesn't matter who does the cooking. So maybe you can find a more creative solution than we did. We hear personal chefs are fantastic, if you can afford them.

Growing up, Mommy cooked dinner five nights a week. She had a break on Tuesday night when Ethel made her famous fried chicken, and Wednesdays when it was "Dad's night out" and we ate pizza. On Sundays, once in a while, we had Chinese take-out. Other than that, it was Mom. And speaking of dinner, we thought you might want to know a few of our favorite family recipes.

FROM THE KITCHEN OF

 *Lisa*

LISA'S CHICKEN SOUP WITH MATZOH BALLS:
BE WARNED—THIS TAKES TWO DAYS

1 kosher chicken, cut in quarters (no livers)
1 large pot of water
1 large onion, peeled
1 tbsp. kosher salt

1 5-lb. bag of long carrots, peeled and diced
1 bunch of celery, diced
matzoh ball mix
fresh Italian parsley

1. Wash chicken thoroughly with hot and cold water.
2. Place chicken in full pot of cold water on stove.
3. Add whole onion.
4. Add salt.
5. Boil on high, then reduce to simmer for 4 hours, minimum.
6. Add carrots.
7. Add celery.
8. Bring to a boil, then simmer for 4 more hours.
9. Turn off stove. After pot is cooled down, place in refrigerator, covered.
10. The next morning, skim fat from the top.
11. Debone the chicken and place the meat back into the soup.
12. Make matzoh ball mix as instructed. We like Manischewitz brand. Note: Boil the matzoh balls in half seltzer, half water.
13. Make sure you keep the matzoh balls separate from the soup until a couple of hours before you are ready to serve. Then place cooked matzoh balls into the soup. Reheat.
14. Add fresh chopped parsley to taste right before serving.

FROM THE KITCHEN OF

≈ঌ *Jill* ঌ≈

JILL'S POTATO LATKES,
IN MEMORY OF GRANDMA HELEN

6 white potatoes
1 egg
1 onion, if desired
1 tsp. salt

matzoh meal
vegetable oil (do not use any other kind
   of oil)

Peel potatoes, cut them in half and boil them in water until soft. Put cooked potatoes in a bowl. Add egg, grated onion if desired, and 1 tablespoon from the "dirty" water you boiled the potatoes in. Add salt. Mix until lumpy. Hand-make thick pancakes, about the size of a small hamburger patty, and roll them in matzoh meal on both sides. Heat up ½ inch of vegetable oil on medium. Lightly fry the pancakes until crispy brown on both sides.

FROM THE KITCHEN OF

≈ঌ *Gloria* ঌ≈

GLORIA'S POT ROAST

deckel (This is a fattier cut of meat than
   brisket, and the typical size is 3–4 lbs.
   This will feed about 6 people)
2 packets Goodman's onion soup mix

1 large or 2 small onions
Heinz ketchup (we've tried others; they
   don't come out as well)
1 cup water

1. Preheat oven to 350°F. If your oven is slow, 375°F.

2. With heavy-duty tinfoil, form a cross with two large pieces of it, one overlapping the other. Place the meat on it and take one and a half packets of the soup mix and rub it all over the meat. Place tinfoil in a roasting pan; disposable aluminum trays work perfectly.

3. Cut up onions and place them around the meat.

4. Dot the meat with ketchup. Splatter it all over.

5. Pour water around the meat and seal it up in the tinfoil very tightly. Place the meat in the oven for 4 to 5 hours depending on the weight.

You know the meat is done when you put a fork in it and it is very soft all the way through.

WHAT WE SHOULD DO

This whole section is what we should do—cook dinner.

WHAT WE REALLY DO

The best we can—a combination of home-cooked meals, pizza and restaurants.

The Mommy Wars

Should mothers work or stay at home? We think that is a really dumb question, as if most mothers have a choice. We don't. We resent this debate altogether. We resent it most when women pit themselves against other women, as if one lifestyle automatically results in better mothers than the other. Most mothers must work outside their homes to support their families. And for those few mothers who do have a choice between "working" and staying home, it is still a dumb question. It implies that if you stay at home, you are automatically more attentive to your children. Not true—some moms fill the day without earning any money or spending any quality time with their kids. This question also implies that if you do stay at home, you are not actually working that hard. Also untrue.

The only thing we would urge you to remember is that in the end, you have most of your life to work but you get only about eighteen years with your kids (sixteen if they learn to drive). It flies so fast. You can hardly remember the time after it has passed. So do the best you can to make your kids feel like they are the number one priority in your life, even if you cannot meet them at the bus every day. And remind them, and yourself, that you are juggling a lot of balls in the air. Once in a while, one or two will drop. You'll all live.

ask yourself

1. How often do you eat a home-cooked meal yourself?

2. How often do you cook one for your family?

3. Do you notice the difference in your family's mood when everyone sits down to a meal together?

Interfere When Necessary:
Don't Be Afraid

The bugaboo of all Jewish mothers: They interfere! Yes, they do. Most don't even apologize for it. Why should they? Since when does interference mean a lack of love? The Jewish mother will argue, forcefully (is there any other way to argue?), that the act of interference is in fact one of the sincerest forms of love. Occasionally, phone calls must be eavesdropped upon and rooms must be searched. Sometimes a parent even has to go outside the family unit to remedy a bad situation. Do we believe that parents can set kids on the right path, with the right mix of love, attention and intervention? Yes, we do. We know this; we've done this.

Belief in one's right to interfere in the personal affairs of an adult child, versus an underage son or daughter, may separate many Jewish mothers from other mothers. It definitely separates our mom from almost all other mothers we know. Mommy believes it is her right and her duty to interfere when necessary in her daughters' lives, meaning our lives, no matter how old we are. She does not care that her words or actions will make us angry. Mommy's conviction that she alone knows what is best for us propels her. She does not second-guess her decision, because it is not impulsive to begin with. If Mom has decided to interfere, she will move forward with the certainty that her cause is just and her actions are merited. Our mother firmly believes that we, her daughters, belong to her until she dies. Merely because we happen to be adults, with husbands and children of our own, is no reason for Mommy to stop parenting us as if we still lived under her roof. Metaphorically, we will never stop living under Mommy's roof.

We have some good examples of Mommy's interference. We begin with Jill's love life.

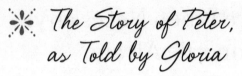

The Story of Peter, as Told by Gloria

I don't believe in tiptoeing around my kids. If I have an opinion, I say it.

Jill was twenty-one years old and dating a chiropractor named Peter. He liked to say he was a doctor, but he wasn't. I've got nothing against chiropractors. I've gone to them for years. But doctors? No.

Jill thought she wanted to marry Peter, but she was really in love with the idea of being in love and getting married. Plus she liked his family. At my niece Rebecca's Bat Mitzvah, Peter started to brag about how he had just graduated school and was going to buy himself an Alfa Romeo. I said, "If you love Jill so much, why don't you get my daughter a ring instead of buying yourself a car?" Peter rose from the table and said to Jill, "We are leaving right now—and I'm leaving with you or without you." So Lisa's husband, Bill, who hates being at all family functions anyway, drove Jill and Peter to LaGuardia for the flight back to Boston. There was only one problem with this plan—the airport was closed due to bad weather. So, they had to come back to our house. That night, Peter told Jill, "I can't marry you. You are going to end up just like your mother."

Their relationship was over. I was happy. I thought Peter was a *shtunk*. The fact that he broke up with Jill because of my mouth confirmed my opinion of him. It meant he never really loved my daughter to begin with. Jill was angry with me about this for a long time. But I know I was right and eventually Jill agreed with me. ■

Jill's Take

The night my mom is referring to is all too true. The irony was the airport was closed and we had to stay over at my parents' house that night. I was very angry at my mother but knew she was right. It is *easy* to say yes to your children about their choices and see what develops in their lives, but my mother never took the easy way out when it came to Lisa and me. She always fought and still does. ■

Here is another example of Mommy interfering, in this case advocating for Lisa.

Gloria's Story on Lisa: The Idiot Principal

Lisa was away on a summer trip after her junior year when her report card arrived at home. I opened it up and saw that the report card said she got a 2 on her Regents exam in biology. A 2. You get a 4 for writing your name. I made an appointment with the principal to straighten out the obvious mistake.

The principal told me that I was mistaken. He said Lisa

was obviously suffering from nervousness and she had too much pressure at school. The fact that she would be attending Johns Hopkins in the fall, leaving high school one year early, was contributing to her mental strain. He didn't want to do anything about the report card. I guess he didn't know whom he was talking to, but he found out. I insisted that the exam be regraded. Finally, he relented. The upshot? Lisa got a 92, not a 2; the computer had erred. What can I tell you? You've got to know your own kids. ■

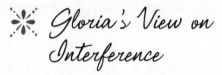

Gloria's View on Interference

I think at times you must interfere, but it's very difficult to know when to do it. You need to trust your mother's intuition if you have a strong feeling inside that something is very wrong. When you know your child is going to be in trouble, you need to interfere to try to stop the situation before it gets out of control. You don't want to have guilt later.

However, you do not have the power to live someone else's life for them. Your obligation is to guide them as best as you can. That child is your responsibility until you die— in every way, financially, morally, everything. We had a situation in our family where Sol's parents did not want to accept that their granddaughter, Nessie's daughter, was marrying out of the faith. They were religious people and they felt that by attending the wedding, they would be condoning the relationship, which they could not do. So they stayed away. After the wedding, they resumed their relationship with their granddaughter and were very close to their great-grandson, whom they dearly loved. Everyone knew Sol's parents were deeply hurt about the interfaith marriage, but as time went on, they were forced to accept it. It wasn't their choice to make.

When it came to Jill's boyfriend Peter, I felt with all my being that this was the wrong boy for Jill. I believed he was not deeply in love with her. Did I start trouble? You bet. Would I do it again? Absolutely. ■

When It's Your Parental Duty to Interfere

Many situations are a matter of judgment. As we said, you have to know your own kid. You could be wrong about that boyfriend you hate—he might be just the right guy for your daughter. If Mommy had listened to her mother, Grandma Syl, she never would have married Daddy, and then where would we be? (Probably with green eyes.) If you radically interfere, you must be ready to suffer the consequences. They can be dire. You might even become estranged. Are you willing to risk it?

We do believe there are some situations where you the parent must interfere, despite the potential risk to your relationship. Here is our incomplete list—we leave you to finish it with your own example:

1. When your child is in danger. Not the obvious kind of danger, but the less obvious kind, like when he is running around with the wrong crowd. If all else fails, take your kid out of school to get a fresh start. Don't wait.

2. When your daughter is dating a married man and she is counting on him to leave his wife for her. Do not let her

waste her life hoping for a happy ending. Call up the guy yourself and find out his intentions, which, in most cases, will scare the living daylights out of him. Your daughter may hate you initially, but your interference will force the situation to a crisis, in which she will finally discover whether or not she has a future with this man.

3. When your child is dating a man, or woman, who is abusive, either physically or emotionally. Do whatever you have to do to break it off. If the abuse is physical, do not hesitate to call the police. Overrule your child, or ignore her altogether. Just do it.

4. When your kid is doing drugs. Everything is at stake; do not hesitate to be aggressive. Drugs are a monster that can take over your child with brutal force and lightning speed.

5. When someone else is giving your kid bad advice. Our advice: counterattack. Let's say, for example, that your daughter has found a new confidante—her best friend's mother. You may not appreciate that this woman doesn't believe in going to college, that she brags about respecting people who come from the "school of hard knocks." Good for her—but your daughter is going to college. How to respond? Stay in the trenches. Keep reminding your daughter of your expectations for her future. If necessary, have a chat with this mom yourself; the chances are that she, too, only wants the best for your daughter. Remember, you have a lot more influence on your own child than she is willing to admit.

6. When there is no one else to advocate for your child, you must be his mouthpiece. You already knew that.

7. If anyone tries to start a fight among your children, you have the right to interfere. You are the mother lioness; she always protects her cubs.

When to Shut Up

We can't think of any examples. And if we could, we probably wouldn't be able to hold ourselves back anyway. You've come to the wrong place if you are looking for restraint.

What Would Gloria Do?

Situation

Your son is dating a girl you despise. This girl has broken up with your son before, breaking his heart, and she has slept around quite a bit as well. She treats your son like a doormat, but every time she says she is available, your son comes running like a little puppy dog. The relationship makes you sick. You are afraid your son will propose to this girl. Your deepest fear is that if you interfere, you will lose him. He will marry her anyway—and then where will you be?

What Would Gloria Do?

I would phone the girl, invite her to lunch, be pleasant but explain very carefully that my son is not for sale, and his affections are not to be played with like a toy. There is little else a boy's mother can say to the girl. If they stay together and she hates you, you will probably never see the grandchildren. If it were my son, I would try to convince him to move to another town, even if that meant moving away from me. I would try to get him to take another job, or persuade him to go to a new school, anything that would entice him to physically remove himself from the scene.

What to Do If Your Kids Are Using Drugs (Hint: Everything You Can!)

The abuse of drugs, alcohol or any substance that is affecting your child's well-being is a situation that calls for a unique kind of interference, one that is drastic. We ourselves do not know a single family who has not in some way been affected by drug or alcohol abuse. We are also aware that many families are affected by mental illness, which is often masked or misdiagnosed and can also result in substance abuse. Unfortunately, this problem has reached epidemic proportions. The damage and the heartache caused to families as a result of substance abuse cannot be overstated.

If you suspect your kids are doing drugs, we congratulate you on your sensitivity. Most parents think they know the choices their kids are making and the situations they are facing, but they probably know only those facts that their kids allow them to know. Some secrets are a step on the road to mature adulthood; others can mean your child is in danger. If your suspicions about drugs have been confirmed, buck yourself up for a very tough ride. You will need all the strength you can muster. If you do harbor suspicions about drugs, here are the guidelines we would follow:

1. Kids have no right to privacy if they are using drugs. Eavesdrop on their phone calls, search their rooms, call their friends and their friends' parents. Gather evidence and confront them. Do not be afraid. God knows, do not be intimidated. This is the one time in your life when they absolutely, positively need you to be a strong parent. This means saying no and setting firm rules with definite consequences for disobedience.

2. If they live under your roof, watch them like a hawk.

3. Drug test them regularly. That means every day until you can stagger it further. If they fail, the consequences must be enforced.

4. Break up the friendships with the kids they do drugs with. Call their parents; tattle, embarrass, be a total asshole in your kid's eyes. Who said it was easy?

5. If necessary, move your kid to a different school. Sometimes a fresh start can work; you won't know unless you try.

6. Get professional assistance to discover the reasons why your kids are seeking an alternative reality. You can't do this alone. Ask for help.

Every situation is different. There are different degrees of drug use; there are kids who are addicted; there are kids who go through an experimental phase; there are kids who might be "self-medicating" for an underlying psychological or physiological problem that was never properly diagnosed. Obviously, each situation requires an individual, appropriate response. If you think your child suffers from a mental illness, then he needs to receive a full medical and psychological evaluation. Fixing the underlying problem may effectively eradicate the substance abuse. Remember that you still love the kid who is still in there. Your child really needs you now.

If mental problems are not driving the substance abuse, then you have to decide whether or not that problem is severe enough to require inpatient treatment, as opposed to outpatient counseling. These are tough, tough issues; they require professional guidance. If you are professionally advised that your child needs an inpatient rehab center, we would suggest that you spare no expense in treatment. There are no guarantees that this will work to cure the problem, but we mention this because money is often the biggest roadblock to getting children into treatment. Good health insurance plans cover a good chunk of the expense, but not all. And many people do not have any health insurance at all. We don't recommend mortgaging your house, but we would if it was the only option left. We would take on three jobs if necessary. Do whatever you have to do to get your child into good treatment.

Our main point is that drugs should never be ignored. You should never assume your child is going through a phase that will pass. If you discover any drug use, and we include marijuana and frequent use of alcohol in that category, then do your best to eradicate it while you still can. Don't feel guilty or like a hypocrite—ignore the fact that you may have experimented yourself. All the studies show that the adolescent brain is at a crucial stage of development. Drugs that meddle with the developing brain do permanent damage. Act as if the whole world is at stake; it very well may be.

We've heard of parents who serve liquor and drugs to minors with the rationale "I'd rather the kids do it in my basement than have them get in trouble in a stranger's home." This is not our motto. We do not believe in sending mixed messages. If our kids do make the mistake and get drunk, they know not to drive. They also know that they can call us any time of the day or night and we will retrieve them, no questions asked—at least not until the next day.

Even though the Jewish mother believes her sovereignty never ends, the law disagrees. Once your kid is over eighteen, your powers are limited. You might be able to exert some financial leverage, but there is little you can do legally to force treatment. So if your child is under eighteen and you suspect something is going on, do not turn a blind eye. Act now while you still can. You will not forgive yourself if there is something you could have done that you did not do.

We know too many stories of kids who got away, whose lives

got derailed too early by drugs and alcohol. We also know many stories of kids whose lives got back on track. These stories belong to those kids and those parents. They are not ours to tell. However, Jill does have one story about speaking up when she was concerned about a particular teenager.

Jill's Story

One summer I invited my friend's son and his friend to stay with me for a country weekend. They were nice boys, young teenagers, and I suspected nothing. When my husband came into the house, he noticed his beer was missing. I thought the kids' backpacks were unusually heavy when I put them back in the trunk of the car to go home on the train. I realized the kids had stolen the beer. I didn't know what to do. Do I forget about it or do I tell my friend? What if something happened to them before they got home that was alcohol induced? I felt I had no choice. I called my friend. What do you think happened? She could not have cared less. She defended her kid and said my husband was wrong and the kids would not steal. Case closed. From my viewpoint, I knew that I had done the right thing in telling her. Now, if anything happened, it would be her responsibility. I have to say that I lost a little respect for her that day, even though I know that it is really hard to accept it when someone tells you your child is doing something wrong. ◼

WHAT WE SHOULD DO

Pay close attention to our kids' mood swings, friendships and overall patterns of behavior. Tell them what we consider to be appropriate behavior when it comes to drug and alcohol use. Check their rooms periodically and eavesdrop on conversations to keep in touch. Pretty much snoop at random.

WHAT WE REALLY DO

We do all that, even though it doesn't give us any illusions that we know everything our kids are doing. But we do it anyway.

ask yourself

1. What is your attitude about drugs and alcohol? You better know it consciously because your kids will pick up on your vibe about both.

2. Did you experiment with drugs and alcohol yourself? How does that affect your attitude when it comes to your own children?

3. Do you think it's OK for your kids to experiment? If so, would you prefer that they experiment in your presence, or at least in your home?

4. Are you prepared for the consequences of having a child who really likes to use drugs or alcohol?

5. Do you suspect your child may be abusing drugs or alcohol? If so, what clues led you to suspect this?

6. Would you prefer not to know? If so, is that a wise decision?

7. What consequences are you prepared to enforce to stop your kids from continuing to abuse drugs and alcohol?

8. Do you have a child with a drug or alcohol problem?

9. If so, what professional help do you have lined up?

Sometimes a Mother Has to Do It Alone

Even though we recognize that perhaps the greatest "secret" of the Jewish mother is to be accompanied as a parent by a great Jewish father, we also firmly believe that sometimes a mother must act in the best interests of her child, regardless of the opposing wishes of her husband.

As three mothers, we know that there will be at least one occasion in your life as a mother in which you will need to spend money on your child for something that your husband does not think is necessary. It may be for swimming lessons, the "best" school, an extra dress, teeth straightening, bleaching or bonding—whatever. At some point, your quite reasonable husband will say "enough" and you will want to do it anyway. It helps if you have your own money and you don't have to lie and sneak around to spend it. But if you have to lie and sneak to help your kid get what he needs, you will. Sometimes it isn't a matter of money; it's a matter of philosophy. Dads in general are a bit more laissez-faire than moms; they think their kids will "grow out of it." Mothers aren't so sure . . . they'd like some insurance, perhaps a little psychotherapy. A mother's gotta do what she's gotta do.

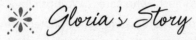 *Gloria's Story*

Sol would never have paid all the money necessary for all those reading lessons for Jill. He is a good man, but he would have said we couldn't afford it. I wasn't working. I took the money from our savings anyway, in cash, and paid what I had to for Jill. He never knew. You have to do what you must for your child. ■

Jill on the Obligations of Divorced Parents

When I reflect on my first marriage, I usually remember only the good times. We did most things together as a team. However, occasionally we disagreed about priorities, and then I would do what I wanted anyway. I guess that is why women need to earn their own money. Freedom. For example, I wanted Allyson to start Hebrew school early. The earlier children start, the more likely it will stick, as Mommy repeatedly told me. Even though we weren't observant, I told my husband that we would sacrifice whatever was necessary to pay for it. When Allyson became a Bat Mitzvah, it was one of the proudest days of my life. Another example was sleepaway summer camp for Ally. By then, we were divorced. My ex-husband had remarried and said he couldn't afford this. I didn't care. I sent her to camp, and Bobby and I paid for it.

I never let money get in the way of my relationship with my ex-husband, Steven. I also don't agree with parents bad-mouthing each other when they get divorced. I was lucky because Bobby is very generous and treats Ally like one of his own children, so Ally was able to grow up in a very comfortable lifestyle. If one parent has to pay more when the other is less flush, who cares? We both love Ally unconditionally and do the best we can. I picked Steven knowing he would be a great father. We might not have agreed on how much "stuff" she should have, but he gives her as much love as he can give. That is really what counts, isn't it? ■

WHAT WE SHOULD DO

Consult with our significant others about every decision as it relates to our children. Make joint decisions about spending money on the children's welfare.

WHAT WE REALLY DO

Consult with our mothers, sisters and friends. If they agree with us that our kids need something, we find the money and do what we have to do.

ask yourself

1. Do you put your child's interests ahead of yours?

2. Do you give your husband veto power over expenditures on your child that you think are necessary?

3. What decisions have you made on your own, without informing your spouse, that related to your kids? Were they justified?

How Critical Can You Be . . . And Can You Stop Yourself Anyway?

The Jewish mother considers it her duty to mother everyone she knows. However, like mothers everywhere, the Jewish mother reserves a special place in her heart for her own children, those lucky few who get to be on the receiving end of her advice, criticism and running commentary. We hereby apologize to our children, and our children's children, for the inevitable insecurities they will suffer with respect to their grades, their posture and in whatever other way we may have unwittingly injured their psyches. However, we do not apologize for criticizing their messy rooms, their procrastination on schoolwork and their "smart mouths." After all, what are mothers for?

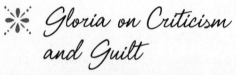

Gloria on Criticism and Guilt

I hate it when I hear parents get their kids to do things by making them feel guilty. My sister Cooky, on the other hand, is a big believer in guilt. She thinks guilt reflects a good moral conscience. I don't agree. I hate guilt. ■

Lisa and Jill on Gloria

With all due respect to our mother, we think Mommy is being a touch self-delusional here. We are constantly being asked to live up to certain standards of behavior. Let's just say, God forbid, we don't call our mother for three days in a row. On the fourth day, we receive the "Gloria hello"—it's really more like "Excuse me, stranger, do I know you?"—instead of hello. We endure a few moments of this, and then all is usually forgiven. We are not criticizing Mom for expecting us to call. We are stating the obvious—our own Jewish mother, perhaps unconsciously, freely exercises her twin powers of guilt and criticism. ■

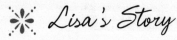
Lisa's Story

In general, my mother built me up more than she put me down. But she always criticized my posture. I still hear her saying "stand up straight" and can feel those "zetzes" in the small of my back, even though we live two thousand miles away from each other. Too bad all those criticisms of my posture didn't take. I still slouch. Only now my back hurts, even when I try to sit up straight. Guess who is now "zetzing" Joanna twenty times a day? I'm glad to be able to pass on the important things in life. ∎

WHAT WE SHOULD DO

Stop criticizing our kids for things they cannot improve immediately, and for things that we see they are trying to improve, like their grades. We should probably stop criticizing altogether. It never works. It just drives them out of the room.

WHAT WE REALLY DO

Nag and torture our kids. Is it genetic?

ask yourself

1. How often do you criticize your kids?

2. What do you criticize them about?

3. Do you have unfair expectations of them? Do you make them feel like they don't "measure up" no matter how hard they try?

4. Do you criticize them about things that are not their fault, such as their appearance?

5. Do you criticize them when you are alone or in front of other people as well?

6. Do you think your criticizing is effective at helping your kids understand how they can improve?

Discipline

Jewish mothers are mavens on the discipline required to do well in life, like showing up on time, going to school and working hard. We are not mavens on the other kind of discipline, like the debates between time-outs and a quick slap on the tushie. As a rule, we tend to intellectualize life, rationalize every one of our kids' transgressions and overthink our kids' behavior. For example, we might spend hours debating the reasons why our kids spend too much time on the computer. We should probably just shut the thing off and make them play outside.

Mommy's discipline was the traditional kind, as in "Just wait until your father gets home." We heard that line a *lot*. Of course, when Daddy came home, nothing happened. We never took Mommy or Daddy too seriously when it came to disciplining us.

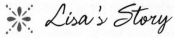 Lisa's Story

Mommy always used to threaten us with "the strap," pointing to the belts hanging in Daddy's closet. As if. Mommy herself never laid a hand on us, but she shouted a lot. We always knew when we did something wrong.

The only time I remember getting spanked was when we had just moved into Woodmere. I must have been about three or four years old. All I recall was Daddy grabbing me in the street and bringing me inside to spank me. He was angry because he had seen me cross the street "alone without looking both ways." Coming from Brooklyn, he must have been so frightened that I would get hit by a car, God forbid. That was the one and only time my dad ever raised a hand to me. Of course, he didn't hurt my body, but he obviously made a strong impression on my psyche. To this day, I look both ways. ■

 Jill's Story

Mom and Dad tried really hard to discipline me. They did. When they would catch me doing something wrong, they always called me on it. They even spied on me sometimes. But they had two problems with me. One, I really didn't hear when they said the word no. My translation of "no" was, "then I have to figure out another way to do it." The second problem they had with me was that I was a really good liar. So I always talked my way out of whatever they accused me of doing. ■

DISCIPLINE: WHAT WE SHOULD DO

Be consistent and firm, but try not to judge ourselves, our kids or others too harshly.

WHAT WE REALLY DO

Overreact or underreact. Act inconsistently, second-guess ourselves, blame ourselves when things do not go perfectly and tell ourselves that there is no way we ever would have allowed our children into that restaurant at that age, especially if they carry on like that!

You Can Never Say "I Love You" Enough

In our family, we take some things for granted, like saying "I love you" before we end every single telephone call, and giving each other kisses and hugs upon saying hello and good-bye. Not every family does this. We think you cannot give your children enough love and affection. Kisses, hugs, "I love yous" every day, for any occasion and no occasion. Even sons appreciate this, though they may not admit it. The great thing is that when you are in the habit of bestowing all this physical affection, you get it back for the rest of your life.

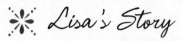

Lisa's Story

My friend Sandy grew up in a loving home, but not in a demonstrative one. She has told me many times over the years that she had to become used to giving my parents a kiss when she saw them. This felt funny to her because she wasn't used to it. But she likes it now.

A very touching thing happened the day Jill, Mom and I posed for a special photo. We brought Dad with us to the elegant Soho loft where the photographer had furnished a delicious lunch for everyone on the set. It was one of those magical moments in life where you take the time to appreciate an event as it is happening. We kept pinching ourselves; we were so grateful to be sharing the experience of being with both of our parents, everyone healthy and happy. We were laughing and kissing and posing the whole day, each of us in pretty outfits with our hair and makeup done to perfection.

At the end of the shoot, the photographer came up to Mom and whispered, "Was all of this real?" Mom said, "What do you mean?" He said, "You know, all this family stuff, all the kissing and affection, was it real?" She said, "Of course," and then the photographer said, "You know, I don't see this very often."

We do fight, we do disagree, we do occasionally yell and even once in a while, we'll go a day or two without speaking to each other, but most of the time, we make sure to tell each other how much we love each other. Try hugging your kids when they are not expecting it. You might be surprised by what you get back. ∎

ask yourself

1. Were you raised in a home with a lot of physical affection? If not, do you feel comfortable giving your family a lot of hugs and kisses?

2. How often do you tell your kids you love them? How often do you hug them?

3. Do you always kiss your kids good night, no matter how old they are?

4. Have you called your parents today? What about your young adult kids?

In Conclusion

We knew as children that not every kid was as lucky as we were to have had the parents we did. Jill used to bring in "strays," other children who didn't get as much love as we did. For a while, Mom and Dad became their surrogate parents too. Even though we are now adults, Mommy still gives advice to many of our friends, on a regular basis. And of course, Daddy. Walking with our dad makes us feel like we are walking on the clouds.

In *Guess Who's Coming to Dinner*, the Sidney Poitier character says to his father something to the effect of, "I don't owe you any-thing . . . You owe me for bringing me into this world and I will owe my kids when I have them." We love that line. It reminds us that our role as parents is to pass on to our children the lessons we have learned, and not to expect too much in return. Not only did our kids not ask us to be born, let's face it—the world is a dif-ficult and challenging place. Sometimes, it may seem to them as if we haven't done them such a favor bringing them here.

Nevertheless, and despite our surface negativity, we Jewish mothers are optimists at heart. We do our best to instill in our children the values of education, justice, honesty and hard work, because we believe these values make the world a better place for them and their children. We kid about how often we think you should call your own mother, but the truth is that if you want your kids to be kind and caring adults to you when you get old, you had better be a kind and caring child to your parents. Otherwise, what else can you really expect? So be kind, to yourself and your families. And remember to say "I love you" before you hang up the phone.

Superstitions and the Clichés That Matter

Kaynahorah, pooh, pooh, spit.

Superstition in the Jewish Culture

Jewish people tend to be incredibly superstitious, even if they are not religious. They are forever "pooh-poohing," knocking wood, even if it happens to be Formica, and spitting. Aunt Cooky bites her tongue so often in the course of a single day that we wonder how she can swallow food. In Israel, Jews and Arabs alike wear the *hamsa*, a good-luck charm that looks like a hand with either an eye or a spiral drawn in the palm. What do all these superstitious behaviors purport to do? Keep away the dreaded evil eye. Many Jews can't even give someone a compliment without first parenthetically saying the Yiddish expression *kaynahorah* to ward off the evil eye.

For example, a typical Jewish mother might utter this to her friend: "My daughter just got engaged (*kaynahorah*, pooh, pooh, spit) to a nice Jewish doctor and they are going to buy a house, God willing, less than ten minutes away." This last bit requires at least another spit or two, in order to prevent the evil eye from swooping in to prevent such a miraculous stroke of good fortune.

Here is a typical exchange in our family:

AUNT COOKY: How is the weather there? I hear you may get snow.

LISA: Yeah, Aunt Cooky, it looks pretty nasty. I better be careful or else I could get stuck with a flat tire out in the freezing cold.

AUNT COOKY: Say "God forbid."

LISA: God forbid.

AUNT COOKY: Now bite your tongue three times. Three times. Did you bite it?

LISA: Yes.

AUNT COOKY: Okay, now say "God forbid" again.

The scary thing is that these superstitions are catching. We find ourselves passing down the biting-your-tongue and the spitting and the pooh-poohing thing to our husbands, friends, co-workers. It's a bit silly. But who are we to laugh at the evil eye?

By the way, we understand from our good Italian friends that Jews aren't the only ones with the superstitious behavior. Want a few more that we hadn't heard of? Money walks out the door if you put shoes on the table. You cannot have thirteen at a table, because the oldest one dies. If you have money in your wallet on New Year's Day you will have money all year long. Wear anything red to ward off evil, including underwear. Do not open an umbrella inside, it brings tears. We're sure there are good reasons for these superstitions—we just have no idea what they are. Apparently, superstitions are universal.

One could philosophize that the real lesson of this superstition is not to tempt fate, not to assume something will happen before it actually does. For example, traditional Jews do not throw baby showers before the baby is born. We do not celebrate an event before it happens. We also don't believe in furnishing baby rooms or bringing any gifts home before the joyful arrival. Is that superstition or wisdom? Is it because Jews do not want to tempt the evil eye to harm the baby, or is this a wise custom born of centuries of births that did not result in healthy babies? If, God forbid, the mother does not bring a baby home, then wouldn't it be cruel for her to enter a home with a newly furnished baby room? We think it is better to wait and see and pray for a healthy baby.

Do you want another reason for the Jewish predisposition to superstition? Superstitions constantly remind you not to be too arrogant or proud. In between the pronoun "my" and the phrase "son the nuclear physicist," if we insert a "*kaynahorah*" or two, or a "knock wood," what we are really doing is saying out loud to God, "Look, God, we'd like this to happen, but we're not counting on it. You shouldn't think we are too full of ourselves to believe that maybe it's not your plan for this to happen, and if, God forbid, it doesn't happen, then at least make sure that our family stays healthy and no one we know gets into a car accident today, God forbid again, pooh, pooh." You see what we mean?

✳ *Gloria's Superstition*

One of Jill's friends, who actually happens to be Jewish, wanted to throw a baby shower for Jill before Ally was born. When I found out, I asked her to rescind the invitations but she refused. I didn't go, and of course I told Lisa and Cooky not to go either. Jill, on the other hand, was happy to accept all the presents. Thank God Ally turned out okay. But I was upset about the whole thing—I still don't like the idea of baby showers. Better to wait until the baby comes home, and then you can throw as many parties as you want. ∎

Jill's Response

I did not really believe my own mother and sister wouldn't come to my party, but they didn't. I was devastated. I did learn a lesson, however. Even though I had a healthy baby, I swore never to tempt the evil eye again. I have repeated this story to Allyson over and over. If I have anything to say about it (although if history repeats itself, I may not), Allyson will never have a shower before her baby is born and home safely. God willing, she will have a healthy baby one day. ■

ask yourself

1. **Do you believe in or practice any superstitions?**

2. **If so, which ones?**

3. **Why do you believe in them—or are you afraid not to?**

4. **Do superstitions control your behavior in any way?**

Why did we include a section on superstitions? We're superstitious, that's why.

Clichés to Live By

We have repeated a few clichés so often to ourselves that we now believe either we invented them or our grandmothers did. Here are the ones we live by:

1. There is always another seat at the table.
   Even if there isn't, there is.

2. Always do the right thing.

You know what it is, even when it is difficult. The corollary to this is: Never be less than who you are.

3. Everyone wants to be right.

If you have a disagreement with someone, let the other person think he is right if you possibly can. Once he has "won," he will come off the offensive, and you can reason with each other.

4. Everything you learn in life you use.

Knowledge is never wasted.

5. You can have it all, but not at the same time.

There are times in life when taking care of your family is your first priority and takes up most of your time, and there are other times when your career takes center stage. If you are trying to do everything at full speed at the same time, you often end up believing you are not doing anything very well. We know the feeling. Go easy on yourself.

6. People do what they want to do, and they don't do what they don't want to do.

This is incredibly profound and takes time to sink into the psyche. But it explains so much of life.

7. There are no shortcuts in life.

You can cheat and think you are "getting away with it" in the short run. But in the long run, you never do.

8. If you want something in life badly enough, you will get it.

At some point your desires will manifest into action, and then you will be on your path. As Jill often says, "If you want to marry a tall man, then only date tall men."

9. Bring a gift.
Never go to someone's home without something in your hand, be it a plant, a box of chocolates or a nice candle. It truly is the thought that counts, so think ahead.

10. When you become an adult, the fact that you may not have had good parents as a kid is no longer an excuse for bad behavior.
Grown-ups need to accept responsibility for their actions.

11. We make plans, God laughs.
So we should not take ourselves too seriously to begin with.

12. The truth counts.
People like to pretend that the truth doesn't matter, and frankly they prefer not to hear it most of the time. But honesty matters in this world. If you are lucky enough to have people around you who do tell you the truth, treasure them. They are rare.

13. Everything in life is temporary.
People do not live forever; mend those fractured relationships while you still can. Recognize that just as the good times in life don't last forever, neither do the bad times.

14. If we don't laugh, we cry.
We prefer to laugh. It's better for the digestion.

15. Everything in life happens for a reason, even if we don't know what the reason is.
When things happen for a reason that we can see, we call that b'shert, meant to be. When we don't know why things happen, we throw our hands up and tell ourselves God has a plan for us, and there are lessons we must learn from everything we experience in life. Then we eat some chocolate, preferably with nuts.

In Conclusion

These particular adages are really the shorthand conclusions we've reached about so many of the lessons we have learned about relationships, values and finding meaning in life. Take them to heart. We certainly do. Both our superstitions and the above "clichés" accomplish the same thing, in a way. They keep us mindful of our actions, our words and our place in the universe. Also, they remind us to be grateful to the people who taught us these lessons, may they live to be 120, God willing.

Are You a Real Jewish Mother?

*Laugh at Ourselves,
and Love Each Other*

Now that you have learned our secrets, heard our stories, kvelled from our *nachas*, shared our *tsuris* and answered some tough questions about your own life, it is time to ask yourself one final question: "Are you a real Jewish mother?" Or for that matter, do you want to be?

After reading this book, we hope you have realized that you do not need to be Jewish to be a Jewish mother. Nor do you need to be a parent. Being a Jewish mother means carrying yourself with a certain attitude that is not necessarily confrontational, but always assertive. We Jewish mothers stand up for what we believe is right, for ourselves and our loved ones. We question authority. We enforce high standards. We demand the best from ourselves and try to elicit the best from those around us.

But our biggest secret, the one that has kept us together, is that we do two things well: We laugh at ourselves, and we love each other.

As we have said often, we judge our lives by the quality of our relationships. It has been a blessing for our family to write *Secrets of a Jewish Mother* and share our rules for living. Now that you have read our words, you are welcome to join our family. Let's face it; we could use more members of the tribe. But, before you can officially call yourself *mishpocheh*, turn the page to take our test. As Jewish mothers, we hope you pass with high marks. Remember, we are always watching your grades.

❑ 1. Do you ever give up, stop arguing or accept no for an answer?
   (*if so, please turn to page 1 and start rereading*)

❑ 2. Do you have to know every single thing about every single thing?

❑ 3. Do you have to know every single thing about every single person?

❑ 4. Are you always right? The corollary to this: Are you ever wrong?

❑ 5. Have you ever been asked to talk a little louder? (The correct answer for this would be no.) How about a little softer? (There we go.) Can your cell phone calls be heard in the next county?

❑ 6. Do you start your sentences by saying, "This is what you have to do"?

❑ 7. How early do you call your mother in the morning? (If not your mother, your daughter . . .)

❑ 8. How often do you remind your children that they always need to call their mother, and their grandmother?

❑ 9. Are you or have you produced a lawyer, doctor or investment banker?

❑ 10. No? Not yet? . . . What about a dentist or an accountant?

❑ 11. At what age did you decide which colleges your kids should attend? How about the top five options, in case you don't want to be too controlling?

❑ 12. Are you a natural, gifted matchmaker?

❏ 13. When it comes to your friends' events, are you an unpaid consultant on what to wear, what to give and whom to invite?

❏ 14. Do you read medical journals in your spare time? (WebMD counts.) If so, do you consider yourself a DWD, a Doctor Without a Diploma? And, if so, do your "patients" consist solely of family, or do they also include your wide circle of friends?

❏ 15. Can you recommend the best doctor in your area for every specialty, malady and infirmity known to mankind?

❏ 16. Do sports mean nothing to you?

❏ 17. Do you pepper your conversation with Yiddish words for emphasis or color?

❏ 18. Do you love your pets just a little more than your kids, parents and hubby? (You can admit it here; no one is looking.)

AND, most important:

❏ 19. Are you starting to sound like your Jewish mother? (Is that a *geshrai* I hear? If you are not married yet, watch it. . . .)

Have you answered most of these questions in accordance with the values of the Jewish mother we have explained in our book? If so, *mazel tov*. We welcome you to our club. Be sure to bring the *babka* and a picture of your handsome single son, brother, cousin or friend to the next meeting. We are always working on our next *mitzvah*.

A Coda from the Kinder

A NOTE FROM JONATHAN, ALLYSON AND JOANNA

We are the so-called lucky ones: those subject to the constant advice, love and criticism of our Jewish mothers. We are their children. The three of us—Jonathan, Allyson and Joanna—are the results of our mothers (and fathers), and we exemplify to the world whether or not our mothers were successful or utter failures. When we grow up, we too will be either Jewish mothers ourselves, or married to one, if our mothers have anything to say about it.

Our mothers are by no means perfect. They do not convey every point they think they do—in fact, we had not heard some of this advice until this book was written. We constantly bicker with our mothers and particularly with our Grandmother Gloria, but all give us many valuable lessons. Not everything that we have experienced as families is in this book; our parents would be lousy if they shared the intimate details of our lives with the world, especially during these sensitive teen years. But we honestly feel that the bulk of this book is reflective of our mothers.

We were happily able to recount stories to our mothers of incidents they forgot themselves. We have better memories than our often ADD mothers, after all. We were involved in the production of this book and had full approval about what was written about us. That shows a truly good mother, one who is not consumed by a "good" story and forgets the reasons for writing her stories in the first place.

We do not always say thank you or show appreciation for our

mothers. Most of the time we resent them for their advice and so-called wisdom. What makes them any better than any other mother to give advice? The truth is: absolutely nothing, but at least they are as good as anyone else. Our mothers have told you a lot of things in this book—ways to be a better friend, wife and mother. Well, we can speak only to the mothering aspect, and since that is the title of this book, we think it is pretty important.

If there is one thing our mothers have gotten across to us, other than "don't do drugs" and "marry a Jew," it is that they love us. We think that is the most important thing anyway. It makes up for take-out dinners and business trips because love is what we kids need the most. Every telephone conversation with our mothers and Grandma ends with "I love you, bye," or in Grandma's case "I love you—." She hangs up on us a lot.

Every gap of silence in conversations with our mothers and aunts is filled with "You know how much I love you, right?" The answer is always "duh" or "whatever." If we are in a good mood we may even reciprocate the phrase, but even though our moms don't always get the mutual response from us, they keep on saying it, a thousand times a day. This may seem trivial, but to us it is the most important thing in the world.

So even though we complain A LOT and we resent our mothers for their "sage" advice, much of it really does seep in. All of us are different and have very different personalities, yet we all are very close to our mothers, even Jon, who is by no means a mama's boy. Jonathan and Joanna have the same outspoken quality as the family members before us, whereas Ally is much quieter in her approach but just as effective. She has the quality of tact that the rest of our family lacks (and we have no clue where it comes from). Even though we fight, we know that our small family is all we have, and we could never imagine our lives without them. So, brace yourself, moms, a rare moment is about to come. We would like to say thank you and say that we really do love and appreciate you, and we will never let you grow old in a nursing home alone, especially without a dog.

Love always,
Jonathan, Allyson and Joanna

Addendum

When we finished this book, we thought we had written everything we knew on the subjects of parenting and friendship. As it turns out, we forgot to discuss two rather important issues: how to cope with criticism and how to deal with bullying.

W e had not realized the extent to which some viewers invested themselves in the plotlines of the *Housewives* show, particularly in the matter of Jill's breakup of her friendship with Bethenny, another cast member. At times, Jill was subjected to an onslaught of negative press and criticism from her fans. We discovered that there are people who have never met you who can take a personal hatred to you. It is scary stuff. But we are resilient people. We learn lessons, we bounce back, we move on, and we stick together.

There is a broad continuum of the ways in which humans treat and judge one another, from constructive criticism, to thoughtless and hurtful remarks, to intentional insults, to bullying, and finally to outright torment. We have all been the victims of most of these and, if we are being honest with ourselves, the perpetrator of many as well. Each of us responds to our feelings of hurt and frustration in a different way. For the three of us, many of our responses fall in the "woulda, coulda, shoulda" file. We certainly do not pretend to be experts on the subject and would not presume to substitute our experiences for yours. We decided, instead, to tell you our stories.

On Helping Your Child Deal with Criticism

Criticism, as distinct from bullying, is a normal part of life, whether the person giving it is well-meaning or not. Responding to legitimate criticism in as unemotional a way as possible is a marker of mature adulthood and an essential relationship skill. Of course, an unemotional Jewish woman is an oxymoron. We hate to be criticized. Don't you?

A good parent teaches her child that there are two kinds of criticism. One kind builds you up; the other puts you down. We say, consider the source. Constructive criticism from a mentor in business is essential to help you grow and improve in your profession. Kids should learn early on that not every negative comment justifies a war. Some criticisms are not only warranted, but deserved. Your job as a parent is to build a wall of self-esteem to help your child distinguish between an unkind comment whose intent is to make your child feel bad about himself, versus an instructive remark whose intent is to help your child grow. Maybe a change in behavior or an apology from your child is the right response. Parents cannot always save their kids, nor should they. Even though you may want to step out in front, most of the time it is far better to guide your child in how to fight his own battles.

If the criticism comes from a peer, then the best thing you can do is give your child the skill set to defend himself, to apologize, or to ignore it. Hard as this may be to do, ignoring the occasional put-down is usually the right response.

What if the source of the negativity is an adult? If the behavior is significant, and your kid is coming home crying or refusing to go to school, then you must act. Most people will apologize if they realize they were hurtful to a child. Apologies from adults to children are meaningful and powerful. But sending the message to your child that you will stand up against an unjust or unkind remark is much more important than whether you receive that apology.

Gloria's Take

My mother may have meant well, but she always knocked me. Maybe that's why I've been told my whole life, "Gloria, you can dish it out, but you can't take it." I guess it is true; I do take criticism very personally. But I know in my head that the right kind of criticism can be very helpful. And even if it isn't helpful, it is a part of life, so you need to get used to it. I always told my girls, "Every knock is a boost." What I meant by that was not to take criticism too seriously. Laughing it off takes out some of the sting. ■

Jill's View on Criticism

The *Housewives* show has been a tremendous opportunity for me in so many obvious ways: fame, some fortune, opportunities, brand exposure, and all the wonderful people I meet. But there is a downside: This type of show works only because of conflict and drama. I can handle a fight with my sister or even someone in business but not with women who are attacking my character just to make good television. When I cry on the show those are real tears. Some of the girls literally "turn on the faucet"; they recover as soon as the cameras are off, but not me. I am the real deal. I do take things personally. Though I always try to do the right thing, I can't control anyone but myself.

What happened to me during season three was like the perfect storm for reality television. I had no idea it was coming and I couldn't stop it when I realized things had gone too far. I really thought Bethenny and I were friends with a true emotional connection. We'd had a "wink wink" understanding going on in the past, in which we might spar on camera and then make up without taking it seriously in our off-camera lives. I didn't know she was leaving the *Housewives* show for good and that she did not want me on her new show. In hindsight, I see that she picked "the fight" but I finished it. Who got hurt? I did.

What I learned from being on this reality show is that we are judged based on how we are presented in front of the camera. You sign up for this experience, and good or bad, you have to live with the consequences. Some people take the show very seriously and live vicariously through the characters. Because of modern social media such as blogs, Facebook, and Twitter, people are empowered to say very hateful things without consequences. At the beginning, I took some of this personally and responded. Now I believe the best course of action is to ignore it.

I learned that you cannot let strangers judge you. You can't even allow yourself to be influenced by people in your life who know you but who do not care about you. The only criticism that counts is that which comes from those who you care about. ■

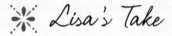

Lisa's Take

Whenever I was bothered about what someone had said about me, Ethel used to tell me to "pay it no mind." She understood that what most people think isn't important. What is important is what you honestly think of yourself. I really miss Ethel. ■

ask yourself

1. How well do you accept criticism? Be honest here; no one is looking.

2. Do you rush to defend your kid because he is your kid, or do you objectively evaluate the situation first? Blind loyalty does no one any favors.

3. Have you taught your child the difference between the kind of criticism that can really help in life and the kind that is meant to injure?

4. Under what circumstances do you, as a parent, intervene to deflect criticism of your child? What do you hope to accomplish?

On Bullying, in Real Life and in Cybertown

There will inevitably be incidents that fall into the "kids will be kids" category, instances of kids teasing other kids for a lousy haircut, or being a poor athlete, or having a bad pimple. Unfortunately, this is part of life—not a good part, but we wouldn't be in this life if everything was supposed to go our way. Part of growing up strong is dealing with unpleasant stuff when it comes your way. If the "sticks and stones" cliché sounds hollow even to you, quote Nietzsche to your kids: "That which does not kill us makes us stronger." Strong words, even harsh maybe, but when you say them out loud, sometimes they do make you feel better.

Bullying, however, is different from the occasional taunt or jibe. Bullying is relentless and frequently led by one person in particular. Bullying is always mean-spirited, and it usually has a specific goal in mind: to crush the victim either physically or emotionally, sometimes both. We all know bullying when we see it. Too often when we do see it, we look away. The three of us feel pretty strongly about bullying; we like to think we are not the kind to look away.

Bullying presents us with the classic dilemma: fight or flee? Is it wiser to ignore the behavior so as not to "feed the fire" or to take the bully on, crush him, and force him to retreat? If history is any indication, bullies do not go away by themselves; they need to be taken on and demolished. But looking again to history, those bullies were not destroyed by single individuals. It took armies to conquer Hitler, and there were many brave men and women who were killed for trying. So, what is the proper answer in the schoolyard?

In earlier generations, when it was usually just one bully taunting one victim on one playground, often parents and other adults did not need to become involved. Kids could and did fight their own battles, sometimes by ignoring the behavior, other times by duking it out. But nowadays, the playing field has changed. One anonymous bully can spread malicious gossip to thousands, even millions. Fragile egos of kids or teens can be utterly destroyed. Just because we were bullied in the past does not mean we should tolerate that kind of behavior now. Today, we think you need that army to fight the bully, but with the right kind of tactics and support.

Curriculums have been devised that have been proven to discourage bullying and intervene effectively when it occurs. We think that in an age when so many kids are being scarred by behavior outside the classroom, we need to make these curriculums a priority. In other words, even though you may be wise to ignore the bully, do not ignore the behavior. Get help.

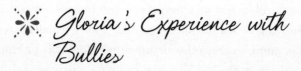

Gloria's Experience with Bullies

I was quite heavy when I was young and throughout my teen years. The kids in my apartment house would sing, "I don't want her, you can have her / She's too fat for me," which was a current popular song at the time. One day my "friends" decided to give each of us in the group a special name. At the end of giving themselves names such as "lovely figure" and "pretty face," they decided that since I had "no really good feature or quality" they would call me "the neck." I remember those exact words to this day—and they still sting with the same intensity. I am sure that I taught my children to stand up for other people because I never did stand up for myself when I was young. ■

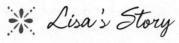

Lisa's Story

One summer I played tennis with the same girl every day because we were the only two girls of the same age and ability at our club. Every time I approached the net, she would hiss, "Bitch," just loud enough for me to hear it. Nobody had ever called me that, and it totally threw my game. She psyched me out again and again. I flubbed.

I choked. I couldn't win a set. I hated her and was really disappointed in myself. I wanted to wipe that smirk off her face. I tried to tune her out but that never worked. So I made up my mind to smile at her when she called me "bitch." I went to a happy place in my brain. It took me a long time, but by the end of the summer I had finally won a set. By the last day of summer, we were even. She could no longer beat me by calling me "bitch."

A therapist told me years later that you cannot change other people's behavior. The best you can do is change your *reactions* to other people's behavior and hope that by doing so, that other person will change their behavior. This girl got charged up by making me choke. She sadistically enjoyed baiting me. I was furious, but impotent. I was not going to beat her up or stoop to her level of name-calling. The only way I could think of to get back at her was by beating her at tennis. When I smiled at her remark, that threw *her* game. Ah, the irony of life. ■

 Jill's Story

Allyson was bullied in grade school. Why? Neither one of us knew. But she was depressed about it and I needed to help her. I had begged my parents to let me change schools when I was a kid because of bullies. My mother told me that whatever issues I had with friends would follow me to a new school. I didn't believe her and I always resented that she never transferred me to allow me to get a fresh start. I wasn't going to let Allyson live with bullies without trying to help her. I heard about a wonderful school that was very sensitive to students' emotional needs. Older students mentored and were "big brothers/sisters" to the little ones. It was the best move I ever made for Allyson. She was never bullied again and has since reconnected with some of those original "bullies."

Unfortunately, I have been revisited by bullying again as an adult. For those of you who are not familiar with the *Housewives* show, there was an episode during season three in which the other ladies had gotten together on the island of St. John. At that point, I was not in their good graces but decided to surprise them to mend fences. If you saw the episode, you will remember that I was turned away at the door.

This was the perfect example of what I learned from Ally's principal years ago about "packs" or "groups" of kids. Packs will do bad things as a group that they would not necessarily do as individuals. I believe that if I had been able to reach one of the women separately, the outcome would have been different; but as a group, they had decided to unite against me. I have to say, the hurt doesn't wound any less at age forty-six than it did at age six. ■

☀ *Gloria's Response*

Jill is right. I knew about the bullying then but thought the problem could not be solved simply by changing schools. I focused my energies and money on therapy that would help Jill, with the hope that in time she would make new and better friends. In retrospect, perhaps I erred. But 20/20 hindsight is so easy. Don't you know that whatever you do as a parent, you will still be wrong? If it happened today, knowing what I know now about how cruel kids are to one another, particularly on the Internet, I would act differently. ■

A problem that we didn't face as children was cyberbullying. "Cyberbullying" is the new word of our age; it refers to the relentless torment that one can do anonymously on the Internet or in text messages. In virtual life, bullies never have to face their victims. We all remember that horrid case of the parent who tormented a neighbor's child by using the identity of another child. Who would do such a thing? Unfortunately, too many people.

Our advice to parents grappling with the problem of cyberspace is to start with the recognition that the computer has migrated to the palm. Every handheld device contains the seeds of cyberbullying. The rules have changed. You need to eavesdrop on those social networking conversations. If your kid won't "friend" you on Facebook, then try closing down the Internet in the house for a week to see how fast he caves. At a minimum, you, the parent, must be able to screen the incoming and outgoing messages on your child's accounts. If you see language that is disturbing, speak up. And if you have spoken up and you are still being ignored, do not wait to seek professional help.

ask yourself

1. Have you ever been bullied? How did you handle it? Looking back, did you handle it effectively?

2. How did you feel when you were bullied? Who did you share the experience with? Were you ashamed?

3. Did you ever bully anyone else? Why?

4. Do you think you would know if your own kid was being bullied? Don't be so sure. If you found out, what would you do?

What Would Gloria Do?

Situation

You discover your child is being bullied by peers. The behavior is cruel, constant, and specific. Some incidents may be in the school hallway; others could be on Facebook. You know about this either from eavesdropping on your son, which we highly recommend, or from a friend who tells you about it. Your own kid has clammed up and refuses to talk about it. He tells you everything is fine but he is showing symptoms of emotional distress.

What would Gloria do?

A lot.

1. Report the situation. Go to school. Make an appointment with the principal and bring a lawyer with you if possible. Sit down with the principal and make very clear that if anything were to happen to your child during school or because of a classmate, the school would be held equally responsible. That should scare the hell out of them. Schools as well as parents share blame for allowing bullies to roam the halls and intimidate children.

2. Insist that the school bring in a special bullying mediator to address the situation without pointing fingers. These mediators work.

3. If you know the source, go to the parent and complain. You cannot expect the school to do all the work. You must be brave enough to confront the parent as well. We know this experi-

ence will not always end in an apology to you from a contrite parent, but you must try anyway. Give the parents of the bully a chance to do their job.

4. If any bullying is occurring online, close all those Facebook and social media accounts. Take away your kids' computers and cell phones. We lived without them for thousands of years; so can your kids. Do not allow your children to obsess about behaviors they cannot control.

5. Seek psychological guidance for you and your child from professionals. Let's face it: Your kid does not tell you everything, and most likely never will. But he needs to tell somebody.

6. Speak to other mothers in the school, especially the mothers of your child's friends. Alert your PTA. Let everyone know what is happening. Ask these parents to monitor their kids for signs of cyberbullying, whether as the receiver or perpetrator.

7. Enroll your child in a martial arts class, not to use violence but to bolster his confidence in his ability to defend himself.

8. If all else fails, then you must remove your child from this toxic environment. Transfer them to another public, parochial, or private school, or consider homeschooling—whatever is feasible. Just do it.

In Conclusion

Well, the old Carol Burnett theme is playing, and we are so glad we had this time together (and we certainly hope you've had a laugh or two). "Seems we just get started and before you know it / Comes the time we have to say, So long." Or, better yet, *geh gezindt.*

Yiddish Glossary

Peppered throughout this book are various Yiddish words. Yiddish is a language developed in Europe that originally began as a combination of German and Hebrew, using Hebrew letters. Many Yiddish words have been incorporated into everyday English usage—words such as *schmuck, shlep, mensch*. We have also included a few words and phrases in this glossary that aren't technically Yiddish but are used often throughout this book and have a particular meaning for our culture—see "affair," "High Holidays" and "appetizing."

Yiddish is incredibly expressive. Many Yiddish words include a syllable that is pronounced to sound like you are clearing your throat, from the back. In English, we spell it with a "ch," like Chanukah or *chutzpah*. If you know Hebrew, we are talking about the sound of the letter "chet." So when you read a word like *nachas*, don't think Mexican nachos with an "a." Think na-cccchhhhas, like you are about to make a spitball—only don't spit.

AFFAIRS: (noun) Maybe you were thinking illicit trysts in a motel in the middle of the afternoon? The Jewish wife was not. Jewish affairs are celebrations, such as Bar Mitzvahs and weddings.

APPETIZING: (noun) that which we eat together on Sunday mornings, consisting of bagels, nova (unsalted smoked salmon), cream cheese, kippered salmon, sable and, if we are really feeling rich, sturgeon.

AVLA: (noun) a grudge, something you remember about a person that you can't get over. Some people collect their *avlas* like fine wines, but like those wines that sit too long, they become bitter.

B'SHERT: (noun) meant to be. We use this for everything in life, as in "There are no coincidences, it was clearly *b'shert* that I should bump into you on the train, we should chat, and find out that we are both related to the same second cousin, and by the way, have figured out a way we can do business together." Also used for one's soul mate in life, one's *"b'shert,"* the person who you were meant to be with.

BUBKES: (noun) *See gornisht.* Nada, nothing, zilch. Could be a little more than *gornisht*, but it amounts to *gornisht*.

CHUTZPAH: (noun) nerve, as in, "Those gate-crashers had some *chutzpah* trying to sashay into a White House state dinner without an invitation."

FARKLEMPT: (adjective) speechless, which is why it appears nowhere else in this book.

GESHRAI: (noun) a yell!

GEZUNT: (noun) health—the most important thing in the world. *Gae gezunt*—go in health.

GORNISHT: (noun) nothing, nada, zilch.

HIGH HOLIDAYS: (noun) refers to the two holidays of Rosh Hashanah, the beginning of the Jewish New Year, and Yom Kippur, and the ten days in between, which are called the Ten Days of Penitence, in which one is supposed to pray to be sealed into the Book of Life for another year.

KINDER: (noun) the children.

KISHKES: (noun) the insides, the stuffing—as in "Teenagers take the *kishkes* out of their parents." Or "I don't have the *kishkes* to handle divorce cases." The best definition of *kishkes* is a synonym for guts, literally and metaphorically.

KNIPPLE: (noun) the stash of money a Jewish housewife keeps and spends however she wishes. The exact amount and whereabouts of the *knipple* are not usually disclosed to the husband, as it is really none of his business.

KVELL: (verb) exude pride in someone else's accomplishments; what you do when your daughter has just become a doctor.

KVETCH: (verb, noun) to whine, to complain. If you *kvetch* enough, you actually turn into a *kvetch*.

LE, THE SUFFIX: AS IN LISALE, OR KINDERLE: connotes affection; could also mean the "little one."

LEZEM GAYNE: (phrase) "Let them go. . . ." As in Mel Brook's famous shout in *Blazing Saddles*. Also as in "let it go," meaning, "forget about it."

MACHATUNIM: (noun) the parents of your kid's spouse. These are the people you need to go out of your way to be nice to, at least until after the wedding.

MACHER: (noun) an important person. Someone who has influence over something.

MAVEN: (noun) a person who knows everything about a particular subject. Mommy is a maven on cooking pot roast; Jill is a maven on social networking sites; Lisa is a maven on the schools in her neighborhood.

MAZEL TOV: (phrase) Congratulations! (Note: The literal Hebrew translation is "Good luck," but the phrase means "Congratulations.")

MEGILLAH: (noun) the whole thing, the entire situation. A huge thing is a *ganze megillah*; a small thing is a *kleine megillah*. For example, "She made such a *megillah* out of having to go through the airport baggage check. Couldn't she see that everyone else has to do that too?"

MESHUGAS, emphasis on the "gas": (noun or adjective) craziness. Come to our house when we are all together to observe the meaning of the term.

MESHUGANAH: (noun) crazy person, as in, "What is that protester doing carrying signs in the rain? Doesn't he know he can catch cold? A *meshuganah*." A *meshuganah* is someone who is not "normal," whatever that is. A person who does not conform to what the Jewish parent thinks is normal behavior is automatically a *meshuganah*.

MENSCH: (noun) a person with integrity, someone whose words and deeds can be relied on. Usually applied to a man. We have at least three *menschen* in our group, Sol, Bobby and Bill, and also Bill's dad, Jerry Wexler, and Jon Wexler, emerging as one, as well as Bobby's two sons, David and Jonathan.

MISHPOCHEH: (noun) family.

MITZVAH: (noun) Colloquially, it means a good deed, as in fixing up eligible single people. The literal translation is "commandment." There are 613 *mitzvot* (plural of *mitzvah*), or commandments, in the Torah.

NACHAS: (noun) the joy you experience for an achievement of which you are proud. This could be anything from watching your son become a Bar Mitzvah, to a daughter graduating college. It usually refers to the accomplishments of one's family.

NEBISH: (noun) an ordinary guy, on the *schlemel* side of life. Not the guy you want to show off to your parents.

NISHT TECFAYLACH: (phrase) not a big deal.

OY VEY: (interjection) a Jewish exhale. Also "*Oy gevalt*," "*Vey iz meer*" and the ever popular "*oy yoy yoy*." Loosely translated as "Now what?" "There's trouble," or "Just what I expected, but I didn't want to say I told you so."

RACHMONES: (noun) mercy, as in empathy and understanding for someone else's plight. You "show *rachmones*" to a person when you forgive him for doing something wrong because of a particular physical or mental condition he may have.

SCHMUCK: (noun) the *schlemiel* spills the soup. The *schlemazel* has the soup spilled on him. The *schmuck* pays the check for the meal.

SHANDA: (noun) a disgrace, as in what Bernie Madoff did to his victims. A *shanda* implies not just a disgrace on the individual, but a disgrace on others who are victims by association. Therefore, what Madoff did qualifies as a *shanda* because it also besmirched the names of honest Jews in business.

SHIDDOCH: (noun) a match. This is traditionally a match between a bride and groom, but can also be used to mean a match of two people with common interests who can help each other.

SHIVA: (noun) the seven-day period of mourning after a death. Think of it this way: Non-Jews observe the wake before the burial; Jews do the *shiva* after the burial, and for a longer time. Also, we never look at the body. Traditional Jews cover all mirrors in the home and sit on seats very low to the ground during this time.

SHLEP: (verb, noun) to carry, either oneself, or a thing. You wouldn't want to *shlep* to and from Jersey every day from Connecticut. The commute would be such a *shlep*. This can also mean a slob or sloppy person who moves without grace. When he gets worse, we call him a *shlub*.

SHUL: (noun) temple, synagogue.

SIMCHA: (noun) an event of happiness, celebration; someone's wedding, Bris or Bar Mitzvah.

TORAH: (noun) the first five books of the Old Testament, considered the most sacred text of the Jewish faith because they were "given" to Moses on Mount Sinai.

TSURIS: (noun) trouble, as in aggravation, as in most teenagers.

YOM KIPPUR: (noun) Day of Atonement, most solemn and holy religious day of the Jewish faith.

Acknowledgments

M any people were extraordinarily helpful to us in writing this book. We wish to thank them now, in no particular order, and to apologize in advance to the people we are forgetting to thank and will be sick about after we see the book in print. Please forgive us.

JILL'S ACKNOWLEDGMENTS

My sister, Lisa, and mom, Gloria, for writing this book together for our children and grandchildren. I never thought I would be an author, and without them, I would never have accomplished this dream.

My husband, Bobby, for letting me be me and encouraging me every step of the way. My daughter, Allyson, who is my first, my last and my everything. You have grown up to be a remarkable young lady who has made us very proud. I hope this book gives you a template for how to get through your life and helps you raise your family one day.

Steven Shapiro, Allyson's dad and my lifelong friend. My in-laws Leslie and Al Shapiro, who have never stopped being part of my life.

My stepchildren, David, Jill, Jennifer and Jonathan, who have welcomed me into their lives since day one. I am so happy to be an "O"ma to baby Micah and Lila.

I have a huge extended Zarin family. To Bobby's mother, Miriam, sisters Lenore and Zina and the entire Zarin clan, thank you for welcoming me to your family and making me part of it. Special thank-you to Jena and Julie, who always show up.

My assistant, Darren Bettencourt, who is my CMO and keeps me focused. I am so grateful to have you in my life.

Paul Schindler, my lawyer, who is always fighting for me with everyone! Amy Weiss, my manager and friend; Lisa Shotland, the first person in "the business" to really believe in me; Peter Jacobs; Lauren Hale; Andrea Ross; Ryan Tarpley and Alice Ann Wilson; and the rest of my agents from CAA. I hope I don't let you and your team down! To Michael Broussard, thank you for your enthusiasm, bright ideas and getting me on this road to start with.

Haylilie Salvador and Eyola Leydet take care of our family, including little Ginger, and I am so grateful to them.

My wonderful friends and mentors—Robert and Jill Kirschenberg, Patti Grabel, Elisa Rosen, Lisa Gastineau, Amelia Doggweiler, Jeff and Raelin Kantor, Monique Boshell, Iris Smith, Susan Haspel, Carole Crist, Judith Regan, Caryn Zucker, Sioux Saunders and Dean Norman.

I have a support team I want to thank—Anne Austin, Galina Shevchuk and the "two Laurens," Lauren Rae Levy and Lauren Solomon, who always make me look and feel good even when I don't want to!

Lauren Z, Francis Berwick, Andy Cohen, Christian Barcellos, Tory Brody and the entire Bravo team for giving me a platform to succeed in a way I never thought could happen.

Jennifer O'Connell, Barrie Bernstein, Keira Brings, Matt Elkind, Matt Anderson and the entire Shed Media team.

My fellow Housewives: Bethenny, Ramona, LuAnn, Kelly, and Alex. The original five. I am so grateful to all of you. Sonja and Jennifer . . . welcome to the club!

LISA'S ACKNOWLEDGMENTS

Jill, you are always in my corner. Thank you for helping me to achieve a dream I never even knew I had. Mom, thank you for only seeing the best in me. Thank you, Daddy, for being my example.

Bill Wexler, the love of my life. Thank you for being my anchor and pushing me to fly. Jon and Joanna, you have taught me more than I will ever teach you. If you ever forget my voice, open this book.

Joan and Jerry Wexler, for having always treated me like their own daughter, and my other two sisters, Laurie Stolowitz and Debby Dombrowski, for their unfailing kindness for the last twenty-eight years. "Aunt Marian," my adored nieces Anna and Erica Dombrowski and nephew Sam Stolowitz, and the entire Wexler, Josephson and Stolowitz clans. In memory as well of my two loving Wexler Jewish grandmothers, Etta "Toots" Wexler and the unforgettable Helen "Floogy" Flugelman.

This book would not have been organized and written without the invaluable assistance of these remarkable friends, who are my inspirations: Virginia DeCristoforo, Ellen Whitehurst, Simmy Indig, Carolina Fernandez, Sandy White Braem, Wendy White, Ellen L. F. Strauss, Marcia Harris, Joan Gmora, Carla Rea, Melissa and Brock Hotaling, Zehavit and Meir Laizerovich-Younes, Gail Sider, Dulce Maria (Luchy) Rodriguez, Cindy McCann, Jaimee and Brian Kelsey and Wendy Fitzgerald.

Thank you as well to Spencer Brown, David Landau, Rabbi Israel Stein, Yfat Gendell, Jerry Schnydman, Dr. J. Woodford Howard, Dr. Joseph Ho, Harry Reidler and Dr. Warren Steinberg for your wisdom and guidance. To Robin Faller, Bob Bayne, Greg Moceri, Kristen Okessun and Mike Raub, thank you for your faith in me.

Vicki Modell and Fred Modell, for allowing me into your lives.

Cara Gargano, reader and editor extraordinaire, how did I manage without you? Thank you for your enthusiasm, your focus and your wise observations.

GLORIA'S ACKNOWLEDGMENTS

In memory of my grandmother, Ida Miller, and my mother for telling me what and what *not* to do, my father for supporting me and Nat Baltor, who taught me how to teach. My baby sister Cooky for caring and being such a loving supporter of all of us. Dr. Bernie Zaontz, who was there for me when I was so sick those many years ago. Lisa and Jill, my left and right arms, who have given me new reasons to go buy clothes. Sol, who still makes me laugh. And Jonathan, Allyson and Joanna, so you remember where you came from.

FROM LISA AND JILL

Thank you to the Jewish mothers who came before us. This book is in honor and memory of you, Grandma Sylvia Levy and Grandma Helen Kamen, and their mothers, sisters and cousins, and also in memory of our wonderful grandfathers, Papa Jack Levy and Papa Benjamin Kamen.

Aunt Cooky and Aunt Gloria—what can we say? Have two nieces ever gotten luckier to have such wonderful aunts? You remember every birthday and anniversary. You call when we are sick, you worry about us and you always tell us you love us. You are model Jewish mothers, and our rays of sunshine. We love you with all our hearts. Thank you, too, Uncle Sy, for always being there for us.

Our first cousins Debby Hofmann, Sharon (and Larry) Caputo, David (and Marni) Zaret and Rebecca (and Mark) Sparberg. We love you like sisters and brothers. To their children—

whom we think of as our children—Michael Caputo, Alexa Hofmann and Noah and Sam Zaret.

Our agent David Vigliano and his staff.

Susan Haspel, my dearest friend who has always been there for us.

Fran Drescher, Patti Stanger, Taylor Dayne, LisaRaye McCoy and Molly Shannon—we so appreciate your early faith in this book.

Rita Cosby, Linda Fairstein, Anne Evans, Steve Cohen, Linda Gargano, Arlene Leiter, Dr. Bernard and Priscilla Zaontz, Dr. Frank Detterbeck, Ray Minella, Jane Rosen and Winnie White, for your contributions to this book and your influence on our lives.

Our superb publishing team at Dutton, including Brian Tart, Lily Kosner, Christine Ball and Monica Benalcazar. Carrie Thornton, our editor and cheerleader, for shaping this book with patience and love.

Our daddy, Sol Kamen, for answering the questions we asked and answering the questions we didn't know to ask. You have always made us feel so good about ourselves. We are so blessed to have you as our daddy.

Finally, thank you, Mommy. Without you, there was no book. Without you, there was surely no Lisa and Jill. As you have told us on more than one occasion, "Just remember. You're the copy. I'm the original." Indeed you are, Mom. A priceless original.

About the Authors

Jill Zarin is the breakout star of *The Real Housewives of New York City*, the hit Bravo series. The retail manager of her Zarin Fabrics, she lives with her husband and daughter in Manhattan.

www.jillzarin.com

Lisa Wexler runs her own law firm in Westport, Connecticut. Recently named the "Gold Coast Radio Personality of 2009," Lisa is also the host and executive producer of *The Lisa Wexler Show*.

www.livewithlisaradio.com

Gloria Kamen, mother to Jill Zarin and Lisa Wexler, was the surprise hit of the second season of *Real Housewives*. A former New York City public high school teacher, Gloria has been happily married for more than fifty years. She lives with her husband, Sol, in Boca Raton, Florida.

A portion of all proceeds from *Secrets of a Jewish Mother* is being donated to charity. To find out more visit www.secretsof ajewishmother.com.